Punkademics
The Basement Show in the Ivory Tower

Edited by Zack Furness

Minor Compositions 2012

Punkademics
Edited by Zack Furness
ISBN 978-1-57027-229-5

http://punkademics.com

Interior design by Margaret Killjoy
Cover design by Haduhi Szukis
Cover images by Rubén Ortiz-Torres & Haduhi Szukis

Released by Minor Compositions
Wivenhoe / Brooklyn / Port Watson
Minor Compositions is a series of interventions & provocations
drawing from autonomous politics, avant-garde aesthetics, and the
revolutions of everyday life.

Minor Compositions is an imprint of Autonomedia
www.minorcompositions.info | minorcompositions@gmail.com

Distributed by Autonomedia
PO Box 568 Williamsburgh Station
Brooklyn, NY 11211

www.autonomedia.org
info@autonomedia.org

CONTENTS

ZACK FURNESS

ATTEMPTED EDUCATION AND RIGHTEOUS ACCUSATIONS:
AN INTRODUCTION TO PUNKADEMICS

THE POSITION BEING TAKEN IS NOT TO BE MISTAKEN
FOR ATTEMPTED EDUCATION OR RIGHTEOUS
ACCUSATION.

-OPERATION IVY, "ROOM WITHOUT A WINDOW"

I THINK THE moment at which I realized I was actually turning into a college professor was not on the first day I taught a class in 1999, but when I
was listening to an old Operation Ivy tape about a year later and found myself wanting to sit the band's singer, Jesse Michaels, down to have a frank
discussion. Specifically, I wanted to ask him why, in a song written to both
illuminate the politics of ideology (*"walls made of opinions through which
we speak and never listen"*) and express the need for open-mindedness and
self-reflexivity, would he choose to intentionally denounce the educational
function of his lyrics from the outset? Not being a complete idiot nor unfamiliar with the band, I obviously realized that the song "Room Without
a Window" (quoted above) was penned by Michaels when he was in his
late teens, which is around the time when years of schooling and top-down
authority have unfortunately succeeded at the task of turning education
– or at least the compulsory, state-sanctioned version – into something

from which young people want to run; I imagine all the more so for the sizeable number of kids in the late '80s East Bay (California) punk scene whose parents, like Michaels's dad, were college professors. But whether the lyric intentionally gestures in this direction or is self-consciously ironic is hardly the issue. Indeed, even if the first line just sounded cool when he wrote it, the point here is that I wasn't singing along, tapping out the beat (as ex-drummers are annoyingly prone to do), or even just engaging in the kind of run-of-the-mill lyrical analysis that has been the bread and butter for both punk fanzine writers and music journalists for over three decades. Rather, it's that I was busy concocting some bizarre scenario in my head that, if allowed to play out in real life, would have undoubtedly translated into the world's most boring and pedantic conversation with one of my punk heroes.

As if it didn't feel weird enough to catch myself pursuing this rather strange line of hypothetical inquiry at the breakfast table one morning, the sensation was heightened when I also realized, perhaps for the first time, that my own internal monologue was now being structured around concepts and jargon from my graduate seminars. Since when, I thought to myself, did I start to throw around – let alone *think with* – phrases like "illuminate the politics of ideology"? Was I becoming the kind of person who ends up nonchalantly remarking upon the "narrative tensions" in a Jawbreaker song? Or using the word *oeuvre* to describe Bad Brains's discography? Was I heading down a path where I would eventually not even be able to go for a bike ride without theorizing it?[1] Just then, as if the universe wanted to accent the point in as cartoonish a manner as possible, I narrowly avoided stumbling over my cat while rising from the table, and I managed to spill half a mug of coffee onto the stack of student papers I had been grading. Muttering to one's self? Check. Coffee stained papers? Check. Analyzing one's music collection through the lenses of critical pedagogy and rhetorical theory? Check. Shabby outfit? Certainly. Disheveled hair and off kilter eyeglasses? Indeed. Exhibiting behaviors that one might objectively identify as 'wacky' or 'nutty'? Check.

It was official. All I needed now, I thought to myself, was the kind of jacket where the patches are sewn nicely onto the elbows instead of silk screened and stitched across the back with dental floss.

ELBOW PATCHES AND BACK PATCHES

Twelve years later I still don't have one of those professorial tweed jackets, though I did manage to attain the job, the eccentricities, and the shock of salt-and-pepper hair that would compliment one quite nicely.

And despite my initial anxieties over the prospects of compromising my then-entrenched punk ethics by turning into a stuffy academic, I actually ended up spending more time playing in bands and participating in various aspects of DIY punk culture as a graduate student and eventual professor than I did when I was younger. While far from seamless, I've often seen the relationship between these two 'worlds' as dialectical, though at first this mainly consisted of scrutinizing every new set of readings and concepts I learned in school through my own increasingly politicized worldview: a punk subjectivity that I fancied as something of a "bullshit detector." But fairly quickly, though, my immersion in critical theory, cultural studies, feminism and political theory started to help me hold up a mirror to sub-/countercultural politics and to generally unpack some of the bullshit that is often embedded within our own bullshit detectors, as it were. Part of what facilitated this process, aside from personal experience and the guidance of some older friends, was getting exposed to the broader gamut of political punk and hardcore and to the range of writers, teachers, artists and activists who, in publications like *Bad Subjects, Punk Planet, Maximumrocknroll (MRR), Clamor* and *Stay Free!*, not only connected many of the issues and concerns I'd previously encountered within different spheres, they also complicated and problematized (in the good way) a lot of my taken for granted assumptions about punk and the proliferation of ideas in general. It was through these channels – DIY punk and DIY publishing – as opposed to the classroom, that the relationships between politics, popular culture, education, and everyday life first started to make sense to me.

As crucial as the composition of these ingredients was to my own development and positionality as a teacher, writer and 'musician' (a term I use *very* loosely), I am hardly the first person to test out the recipe and I'm certainly not one of the best cooks. Indeed, my real interest in punk/academic border transgressions was not borne of my own maneuverings, but from learning about and meeting punk musicians who had dual careers as professional nerds (I use the term lovingly; it is my job description after all) and reading sophisticated work from writers who seemed as equally sure footed in zine columns and basement shows as they did in a theory heavy journal publications, political organizing committees, or in front of podiums lecturing to graduate students at prestigious research universities. In addition to being generally interested in what other people have done (or aspired to do) with the kinds of energies, knowledges and tensions generated through their involvement with, or their reflections upon, both punk music and culture, I had a personal interest in wanting to meet more of these folks and to pick their brain about their paths toward careers as nerdy rockers or punk professors (given that either one sounded ideal to me). I was also intensely curious about the ways in which people reconciled their interests and understood the dynamics between two very different 'scenes.' I wanted to hear what other people had to say about scholarship on punk, or their relationships to band mates and fans (if applicable). And broadly speaking, I wanted to know what kind of sense people made of their punk/academic situation; whether it was something they analyzed, disparaged, incorporated into their work, trumpeted, or simply took in stride. What kind of stories did they have? What kinds of insights about punk and teaching have they drawn from their experiences or analyses?

Unlike the prospects of time traveling to an Operation Ivy show in 1990, the possibilities for actually starting some conversations around these topics was quite real, and a few years ago I started the process with the aim of garnering essays for the book you are now reading. I asked people to contribute work that was either about punk specifically, or the intersections between punk and higher education, whether in the form of biographical pieces or chapters devoted to teaching and pedagogy. To keep things simple, I took the approach that punks of yore utilized when contacting bands they liked: sending letters. My interest was less in nostalgia (they were e-mails, after all) than in making contact with people whose work I admired and otherwise beginning what would become a long experiment. That is to say, part of my reason for doing the book was because, first and foremost, I wanted to see if it was possible. While I had long been attuned to the fact that there were some professors and many more graduate students who, like me (circa 2005, when I hatched the idea for this book), simultaneously played in bands while they taught classes and worked on their degrees, I often wondered about whether there are a lot of "us" out there. By "us" I mean *punkademics*, or the professors, graduate students, and other PhDs who, in some meaningful or substantive way, either once straddled or continue to bridge the worlds of punk and academia through their own personal experiences, their scholarship, or some combination thereof.

Part of the experiment was also to see if I could do the book without resorting to the preferred method that academics use to solicit contributions for an edited volume. This typically entails circulating an official 'Call for Papers' online, waiting for abstracts to trickle in, then sending out acceptance and rejection notices, and eventually waiting for the first drafts of essays to be submitted. Given the formalities and relative sterility of the whole process, it seemed much more organic (for lack of a less abused, greenwashed term) to try and find prospective contributors by simply asking my initial list of contacts for the names of friends, or other suggestions for people to look up. In addition to my desire to keep things on a personal level, it also dawned on me quite early in planning the book that there was simply no other way to do it. That is to say, I realized that any official announcement aimed at soliciting contributors would not only have to include the obligatory list of suggested topics or questions for authors to address (which I had ready to go), it would also have to delineate some sort of criteria for the authors themselves, given the core premise of the book. Well, establishing that someone is a professor or PhD student is fairly straightforward, but what exactly was I going to do, ask people to send me an abstract and a *punk résumé*? Aside from all the vexing questions it immediately raises about what punk *is*, what it means to *be* punk, what the objective qualities of 'punk-ness' might be, and so on, I couldn't imagine anything more obnoxious than the idea of asking people, even tacitly, to basically 'prove' that they were or are punks – let alone the awkwardness of someone having to actually write it up, or me having to read it. What the hell would that look like anyway? And more to the logistical point, how does one articulate that in a call for papers? Something like:

> Along with your abstract and an updated copy of your CV, please provide evidence of past or present punk affiliations. Acceptable forms of documentation may include, but are not limited to, any *one or more* of the following:
> - LP or 7-inch with legible recording credits on the insert (colored vinyl is a plus).
> - Copies of your *print* fanzine.
> - Notarized letter from a known punk who can vouch for your scene 'cred.'
> - Receipts for at least two previous years of annual subscriptions to *Maximumrockandroll, Punk Planet, HeartattaCk* or *Profane Existence* (PDF or low-res JPG files).
> - Photos of you doing punk things (i.e. dumpstering baked goods, swimming drunk in an urban river) or simply being punk (i.e. sporting a sleeveless Nausea t-shirt, a nasty dreadhawk, and a dog on a rope).[2]

While in hindsight this approach may have actually yielded some fairly spectacular results, I was fortunately able to avoid such potentially unforgivable transgressions with help from this book's authors and an ad hoc network of punkademics that, at times, I seemed to connect or expand through the very process of seeking it out. While I have no empirical data regarding the actual size and scope of this disparate population, I can confidently speak to one of my initial curiosities underlying this project by noting that there are, in fact, many punkademics out there: far more than I could ever hope to accommodate in a single book, even if given the opportunity to do so.

So what is one to make of this collection, its shamelessly punning section headings, and the punk-centric assortment of essays, people, and ideas in the pages that follow? Simply put, why *Punkademics*? Well, despite the admittedly experimental nature of this collection, there are in fact a number of carefully formulated reasons as to why this collection was assembled and, I can only hope, a few contributions it might make to the ways in which we understand the cultural, political and aesthetic dimensions of both punk music and culture, academia, and the apparently fertile ground in between. I want to walk through some of them here briefly, as a way to provide additional context for this project and to introduce some of the specific themes with which the book is engaged.

PUNK DISCOURSES

Punk is neither a homogenous 'thing' nor is it reducible to a specific time, location, sound or a select number of vinyl records and live performances. Its various meanings, as any self-respecting punk knows all too well, are subject to wild fluctuation and widespread debate.[3] One might say that it's because punk shapes – and is also shaped by – specific kinds of question askers, music makers, thought provokers, organizers, shit talkers, writers, artists, and teachers. At their best, the combinations of people, places, cultural practices, social relationships, art and ideas that co-constitute punk are rife with possibilities: creating new kinds of music or reveling in the ecstatic moments at the best shows; forging bonds of group solidarity and personal identity; carving out non-commercial spaces for free expression and the staking out of positions; and pushing people toward a participatory, 'bottom up' view of culture. Through the often conflicting accounts and histories of punk, one can identify the ebb and flow of countless scenes, interwoven subcultures, and a broader 'Do it Yourself' (DIY) counterculture in which people put ethical and political ideas into practice by using music and other modes of cultural production/expression to highlight both the frustrations and banalities of everyday life, as well as the ideas and institutions that need to be battled if there is any hope of living in a less oppressive world. And crucially, people have a lot of fun doing it. Those lucky enough to have experienced some of what I've just sketched out know what it feels like to sense that punk really can create something new in the shell of the old, to poach a phrase from the Wobblies.

At its worst, punk can be and has been a fashion show, a cultural ghetto, a minor league circuit for corporate entertainers, a merchandise peddling aggregate of aspiring capitalist hustlers, and a constellation of practices that perpetuate varying degrees of machismo, sexism, homophobia, white privilege, classism, hyper-individualism, anti-intellectualism, passive conformity, and at times, both conservative religious dogma and racist nationalism. And like the worst trends to emerge under the banner of cultural studies – the academic field in which I work – punk's incarnates have similarly been known to promote sloppy politics while championing 'resistance' in all of its self-styled affairs, regardless of whether such gestures (or fanciful arrangements of clothing, tattoos or words) bear a resemblance to anything like substantive political action, meaningful community engagement, or tangible social change. In this guise, 'resistance', 'rebellion', and of course, 'revolution', become just another set of buzzwords chirped in slogans, animated in bad songs and contrived writing, and emblazoned on t-shirts without a hint of Billy Bragg's sharp wit: "So join the struggle while you may, the revolution is just a t-shirt away."[4]

The various prospects and pitfalls associated with punk (I include hardcore in this designation throughout unless noted otherwise) are constant reminders that the stories we tell about it are always being folded into converging and often competing discourses about what punk *really* means, what it *does* or *doesn't* do, and why it *is* or *isn't* culturally significant, politically relevant, and so on. As both an academic and someone who spent roughly thirteen years drifting in and out of the punk scene (admittedly more 'out' in recent years), I'm invested in both the kinds of stories that get told about punk as well as the manner in they are put to work, as it were. Therefore, I think it is important to note from the outset that my interest in assembling *Punkademics* is neither to tell the grand story of punk (an impossibly arrogant and pointless task) nor to produce the scholarly cipher through which all of punk's secret meanings can be decrypted. Academics should not be seen as *the* authoritative voices capable of explaining punk to the masses, and I have no interest in presenting them as such. In fact, I have always been rather conflicted about how punk music and DIY punk culture get taken up by academics in the first place.

As a teacher, I tend to see punk – like all other cultural phenomena – as a messy but nonetheless fascinating cluster of things that can be analyzed, dissected and debated. Depending on the specific course, I've incorporated aspects of punk in my lesson plans to talk about everything from the underground press and the political economy of the media industry, to the role that punk music – like hip hop – plays in cultivating meaningful narratives about "the city" and the importance of space and place in everyday life.[5] And quite frequently, punk comes in handy when I need to give concrete examples to illustrate or clarify what certain social and cultural theorists mean when they throw around phrases like *cultural production, articulation, hegemony, resistance, commodification, cooptation,* and of course, *subculture.* In addition to being pedagogically useful, I also get a certain degree of satisfaction in knowing that members of the bands I discuss in class would be alternatively delighted or mortified by the idea.

However, my level of comfort with the melding of punk and academia decreases quite rapidly when punk becomes an object of study unto itself. As Roger Sabin notes in his introduction to *Punk Rock, So What?,* one of the main problems with scholarship on punk is the over-reliance on unquestioned assumptions about punk itself and, overall, the "narrowness of the frame of reference."[6] Along with what he describes as the "pressures to romanticize," Sabin suggests that the impulses and trends in punk scholarship foster the development of certain kind of "orthodoxy" that structures what it is possible to say, or most likely not say, about punk's history, its conjunctures with other ideas and artistic practices, and, I would add, its current formations, and its possible future(s).[7] Like many of the LP records that fit squarely and safely within the parameters of a punk's splintered subgenres, a number of the books and essays that fall under the umbrella of this 'orthodoxy' have their distinct merits.[8] Nevertheless, his point about the constrictive qualities of scholarship on punk is well taken and, broadly speaking, rather understated.[9] Because while there are plenty of exceptions (including excellent work published by this book's contributors), a significant amount of academic writing, conference presentations and the like are authored by people who – despite being fans of punk music and passionate about the topic – seem to have limited knowledge of punk music and DIY culture, and a level of engagement with punk scenes that is more akin to casual tourism than active participation. Nevertheless, this doesn't stop people from feeling entitled to make assumptions, lodge critiques, and draw conclusions based on what, more or less, amounts to an analysis of punk 'texts.' To be sure, there are a variety of things that broadcast this kind of work. Barring some notable exemptions, the telltale signs may include, but are certainly not limited to, any or all of the following features:

1. No interviews conducted with actual punks.

2. No ethnographic research done at any of the places where punks live, make music, work, play and see shows, hang out, ride bikes, get drunk, guzzle coffee, play kickball, raise a ruckus, stage protests, volunteer, cook food, and so on.

3. Little attention paid to punk scenes that fall outside the ostensibly holy quadrangle of New York – London – Los Angeles – Washington DC, despite the fact that in recent decades DIY punk and hardcore scenes have thrived in smaller, so-called second – or third-tier cities like Berkeley (CA), Asheville (NC), Portland (OR), Minneapolis (MN), Olympia (WA), Pittsburgh (PA), Bloomington (IN), Louisville (KY), Gainesville (FLA) and Richmond (VA), and this is just to name a few places in the US alone.[10]

4. Relatively little engagement with the vast amount of literature written by and about punks, whether in the form of zines, published essays, books, magazine columns, LP liner notes, blogs and so on.

5. The use of definite articles in places where they don't belong, as in "the Dillinger Four" instead of Dillinger Four, or "the Green Day band." Trivial? Absolutely. But it is the kind of mistake that a punk is not likely to make and thus suggests the likelihood of other mistakes, or a general lack of knowledge about the subject matter.[11] And moreover, it conveys an awkwardness on par with John McCain's reference to using "a Google," whilst ironically attempting to demonstrate his Internet savvy to US voters prior to the 2008 presidential election.

6. An almost obsessive fascination with the Sex Pistols and Malcolm McLaren.[12]

7. An obsessive fascination with the Sex Pistols and Malcolm McLaren.[13]

8. Any sustained, serious theoretical analysis of "moshing" or "slam dancing."[14]

9. Less space devoted to discussing what punks do, what they think, and why it matters, than the amount of space reserved for debating whether to call them a "subculture," a "post-subculture," a "youth culture," a "postmodern tribe," or a "neo-tribe." There are, in fact, many terms that are actively contested and discussed by punks: debates over what counts as 'punk', or what it means to *be* 'punk', are classic (if not exhausting) examples. But the merits of sociological/cultural studies nomenclature are

not part of the equation. To wit, the following exchange will
never take place:

> "Hey Zack, what are you doing this weekend?"
> "Well, I'm busy on Friday, but on Saturday
> night I'm going to participate in a vigorous rock
> and roll performance with members of my cultural
> neo-tribe."[15]

10. The conflation of punk with 100% pure authentic resistance to
    the culture industry/mainstream/system, or conversely, as 100%
    pure inauthentic commodified dissent in service of the culture
    industry/mainstream/system.

I recognize, of course, that this (partly tongue-in-cheek) assessment
may sound like the expression of someone who is too emotionally invested in his subject matter, or perhaps too ensnarled in punks' own preoccupations with boundary-making and authenticity ("no outsider could
ever know what it's *really* like," etc.) to make clear-headed judgments
about scholarship, let alone the researchers responsible for producing it.
It's certainly possible.

My position, however, is not based on some naïve desire to preserve
the sacredness of punk (*Hot Topic* put the final, pyramid-studded nail
in that coffin years ago), nor do I think that people who are totally immersed in their activities or communities are necessarily in the best position to speak thoughtfully about their endeavors, or to critically reflect
on the social or political significance of them; sometimes the exact opposite is true. Rather, my perspective is based upon what I see as a relatively uncontroversial point: whether due to shoddy research, distance
from the punk scene, or harmless excitement for a topic tackled earnestly
though wrong-headedly, the bottom line is that most academics simply
miss the mark when it comes to punk music and culture. It would seem
that I am good company on this point, even amongst fellow academics. John Charles Goshert, for example, argues that academic studies
"tend toward the uninformed, if not careless, homogenizing of styles,
personalities, and locales under the name 'punk.'"[16] David Muggleton
expresses similar anxieties over the academicization of punk when, in the
introduction to his own book, he describes his first encounter with Dick
Hebdige's *Subculture: The Meaning of Style:* "I fought my way through...
and was left feeling that it had absolutely nothing to say about my life as
I had once experienced it...The 'problem' lay not in myself and my failure

to recognize what had ostensibly been the reality of my situation, but in the way the book appropriated its subject matter."[17]

Here's the rub, though: appropriation is always a matter of perspective. As a case in point, when Muggleton organized the *No Future? Punk 2001* conference at the University of Wolverhampton ten years ago, it brought a wide range of academics and cultural critics together with some high profile punk speakers who weren't shy about airing their grievances when interviewed by the press. The ever-cantankerous writer/ artist/author, Stewart Home, stated, "I think punk is hyped up as an ongoing cultural force by people who are nostalgic for their youth."[18] Jordan (aka. Pamela Rooke), who was the former assistant at Vivienne Westwood's famed London SEX shop and one of the people who pioneered punk aesthetics/style, remarked that "the academic world reads more into punk than there probably was."[19] And most pointedly, Penny Rimbaud, a poet and the drummer for the now legendary anarcho-punk band, Crass, exclaimed: "It irritated me beyond belief...academics sitting round talking about something so anti-academic. It's as absurd as the Hayward Gallery putting on a show of dada art."[20]

Part of the reason I juxtapose these quotes and also call attention to the *No Future* conference is because at the same time I think academics should take criticism of their work seriously – particularly when its generated by human beings who unwittingly serve as their 'objects' of study – the notion of drawing a proverbial line in the sand between 'the punx' and 'the ivory tower' based on whether one's work is properly "academic" is somewhat amusing, especially if one has *ever* been privy to a conversation between collectors of obscure punk and hardcore records (musicology by other means, if there ever was such a thing), and even more so if one considers either Home's specific background as a historian of highly theoretical, avant-garde art movements or Rimbaud's own proclamation – leaving aside the militant seriousness with which Crass approached both politics as well as its aesthetic presentation of politics – that even his notion of *fun* has "always been more cerebral and intellectual."[21] There are, of course, completely legitimate reasons why punks should be radically skeptical about the ways their music, ideas and cultural practices are documented by representatives of institutions (colleges & universities) that are, by design, the antithesis of DIY. But in general, staking one's claim on the grounds that punk is inherently "anti-academic" isn't to state an uncontested fact; it is rhetorical move that, in part, allows punks to avoid dealing with thorny questions or critiques raised by outsiders (some of whom, it is true, may be utterly clueless), just as it simultaneously reinforces academics' tendencies to chalk up hostile critiques of their work (some lodged by people who may *also* be utterly clueless) to anti-intellectualism as opposed to taking them seriously. But more to the point, the perpetual debate over whether its acceptable to 'intellectualize' (the offense of academics) punk is a moot point: professors, music journalists and punks themselves have been doing it for well over thirty years.

While I have no doubt that the *No Future* conference, like any other event worthy of the designation, probably featured some obnoxious panel titles, a great many jargon-laced presentations, and more than a few cringe-worthy comments, the fact is that there were actually a number of people in attendance – including at least two of the contributors to this book – who had been playing in punk bands, living in punk squats, and being involved in local DIY music scenes years before they ever wore the unlikely moniker of Professor. Along with a few of their fellow "punkademics" – a term that, unbeknownst to me, was not only thrown around during the UK conference but also used by punk-turned-professor, Greta Snider (San Francisco State University), in a piece she wrote for *Maximumrocknroll* in 1995 – both Alastair "Gords" Gordon and Helen Reddington (aka. Helen McCookerybook) have used their unique insights to challenge existing academic work on punk while fostering a broader reassessment of punk history and culture that has relevance far beyond the porous borders of the university. Indeed, Reddington cuts to the core of some of the key issues at stake when it comes to research on punk. In an essay that previews the material she would later develop in the book, *The Lost Women of Rock Music: Female Musicians of the Punk Era*, she writes:

> "There is perhaps no better example of male hegemonic control over popular cultural history than the rewrite of punk to exclude the very large and productive presence of young women in the subculture from its very beginning [...] The collective memory of punk recalls young men as spitting, spiky yobs with the occasional nod in the direction of political commitment (until the obligatory signing ceremony with the major label), and young women as fishnet-clad dominatrixes [...] From the writings of academics to the reports of the tabloid press, there is a whole history missing from accounts of punk during this period in Britain."[22]

Whether it's the excising of women, people of color, and gay/queer-identified folks from punk history or, conversely, the way that punks have used film as a medium to re-write that history and re-think punk's dominant narratives, the process of documentation and analysis (not to mention debate) plays a discernable role in shaping how people understand what punk is, whom it is for, and why it is important.[23] Max Ward, a veteran hardcore musician as well as the founder/proprietor of *625 Thrashcore Records* and current Assistant Professor of History at Middlebury College, makes this point succinctly: "punk has a culture, and that culture is defined by how we try to remember our 'past.'"[24]

STORIES MATTER

Put simply, the stories we tell about punk matter. In the greater scheme of things, there is clearly much less at stake in the narration of punk than there is, for example, in the stories told about immigration, Indigenous land claims, prisons, or the philosophical and economic underpinnings of Neoliberalism. Nevertheless, they matter. Part of the reason why is because, like the stories told about other cultural practices and art forms, the relevant work on punk affects the ways we understand its specific histories, its present formations, and its possible future(s). Consequently, when the complexities and nuances of punk music, aesthetics and identities are ignored in lieu of sweeping claims and a reliance on problematic assumptions, this has a significant bearing on the ways in which people conceptualize, interpret and draw conclusions about the 'politics of punk', youth subcultures, and perhaps the social functions of art and music, as well. The concern here is thus not only the fidelity of the narratives – as in whether the accounts (of bands, scenes, events, etc.) are accurate and truthful – it is also a matter of *who gets to speak for whom:* whose stories are told and whose are silenced, and perhaps most importantly, who gets to shape public knowledge(s) that inform the ways in which we collectively remember people, events, institutions, ideas, cultural practices and cultural history. In addition, this body of knowledge is never *only* about punk in the first place: in academic research alone one finds discussions of punk situated within larger conversations about the music industry, the changing social status of 'youth' in the late 20th Century, the formation of identity, the nature of consumption, and the contentious dynamics of class, race, gender, sexuality and religion that are part of punks' everyday relationships and also addressed within their own songs, musings, dialogues and debates.

My point here is that the story and mythology of punk get reified over the years as much in academic writing as elsewhere. And it is not just dedicated books and peer-reviewed articles that do this kind of cultural work; it is also the hundreds of casual references that academics make to punk (for example in books on the 1970s or the Reagan Era) that simultaneously support the dominant narratives and constrain the possibilities of analyzing it without the compulsion to either validate its heroes or delineate its pure moment of inception.[25] Because what gets missed, for instance, in the habitual focus on punk's origins, its shining stars, its hottest locations, and its most obvious but nonetheless vital contributions – such as punks' amplification (with all that the term implies) of independent music and art – are the *everyday practices, processes, struggles, ruptures* and *people* that make it so interesting in the first place.

Like the work produced from music journalists, cultural critics, and punks themselves, academic scholarship plays a distinct role in both the cultivation and reproduction of knowledge about punk. While some of this work is admittedly fraught with problems, academics – or, rather, punkademics – have also done some of the best work at rethinking punk history, re-conceptualizing its present dynamics, taking issue with dominant scholarly readings of punk politics and punk scenes, and also expanding the parameters of research itself. While much of this research remains cloistered in academic journals and restricted access university libraries, a number of these stories – as well as the storytellers themselves – are widely read and have had an impact on both the ways in which punk is interpreted and the ways that punks see themselves. Notably, this has taken place both from within and outside of The Scene by people who have poked and prodded at the social significance of punk and DIY culture through a variety of different print and digital formats (sometimes concurrently). While by no means comprehensive, this book is a contribution to that broader effort.

UP THE NERDS!

One of my primary goals with *Punkademics* is to encourage a marked shift away from the punk-as-style paradigm that has become so commonplace in the wake of Dick Hebdige's *Subculture: The Meaning of Style* but also from a number of the binary oppositions scholars have used to reduce 'punk' into a static, singular thing that can be mapped along an axis of success vs. failure, resistance vs. recuperation, authenticity vs. inauthenticity, and so on. Instead of producing another series of instrumental readings of punk that are strictly concerned with what it ultimately *does* or *does not* do, or what it definitively *means* or *doesn't mean* at one specific moment, or within the confines of one specific scene or musical recording, I'm more inclined to think about what possibilities emerge within and through it. Scholarship on punk has sometimes pointed in this direction, though it's typically focused on which kinds of musical and stylistic hybrids become imaginable or possible through the production of punk music and culture, or somewhat differently, which aesthetic and artistic trends are rendered most visible in punk's history or that of its precursors. While I am interested in these linkages and the kind of work that, for example, contributors to the book *Punk Rock, So What?* take pains to highlight, I have always been much more curious about the kinds of *subjectivities, people* and *communities* that become imaginable or possible – or perhaps even probable – through DIY punk, i.e. the "vectors of punk that strive to escape models of production and consumption otherwise omnipresent in the entertainment industry."[26]

A fruitful way to approach these interrelationships, as I've tried to demonstrate with this very book, is to consider some of the ways that punk maps onto or even organizes certain constellations of cultural practice, artistic expression, ethics, and notions of community. But crucially, I think this begins by reframing punk as an object of study and asking some rather different questions about peoples' relationship to it. Through a combination of essays, interviews, biographical sketches, and artwork, one of the aims of this collection is to do this by way of example as opposed to merely stacking critique on top of critique. While not without its own limitations, *Punkademics* tries to offer more nuanced perspectives on various aspects of punk and hardcore – and in particular DIY punk music and culture – that stem from contributors' academic backgrounds as well as their collective participation within and experience of punk scenes.

But of equal importance is the attention focused in the opposite direction, which is back at the university, the classroom, and both the norms and ethics that get embedded into higher education. Given the fact that little research has been done about where punks end up or what their career paths and adventures (as well as struggles and failures) might tell us about punk or why it matters, this book offers some tangible examples that speak to these concerns, inasmuch as colleges and universities function as some of the places where people with 'punk' values can ostensibly thrive, or more accurately, where they can potentially put their ethics and ideas into practice; though not without great effort, considerable friction, and at times, complete train wrecks.[27] The idea behind *Punkademics* is thus not only to offer some different perspectives on punk, broadly speaking, but to also tell some entirely distinct stories about academics and punks themselves, and how their priorities and passions get reconfigured by and through their experiences as theorists, artists, activists, educators and misfits working amidst the often tumultuous landscape of the modern university/edufactory.

1, 2, 3, 4, Go!

NOTES

1   See Zack Furness, *One Less Car: Bicycling and the Politics of Automobility* (Temple University Press, 2010).

2   Credit for the last line goes to the esteemed Willie Stein. (Sorry to disappoint you, Willie).

3   Any terms used to label specific assemblages of punks and/or punk practices are necessarily inadequate and bound to raise more issues than they resolve. Consequently, I use the terms 'punk culture', 'DIY punk culture', and 'DIY punk scene' interchangeably not out of laziness but because they are simply different ways of talking about the same clusters of non-corporate practices, independent institutions, and politicized people, however resistant to classification some of them might be. My primary reliance on 'culture' instead of 'subculture' is, however, deliberate because I don't think the term 'subculture' can encompass both the punk practices as well as entire "way of life" that is sometimes cultivated around and through punk. Like the term 'counterculture', which I specifically use to designate self-consciously political/politicized cultural formations, I used the term subculture where it's appropriate. Longtime zine writer and punk drummer Aaron Cometbus makes a nice point about the inaccuracy of labels as a point of pride: "I like that about punk and fanzines—that it's a community that's very ill-defined. As much as 90% of what we talk about is defining it, and still it's very ill-defined." In "Interview with Aaron Cometbus," *Maximumrocknroll*, no. 200 (2000). For more on defining and naming punks and/or punk practices, see: Alan O'Connor, *Punk Record Labels and the Struggle for Autonomy: The Emergence of Diy* (Lanham: Lexington Books, 2008), p. 3; Alan O'Connor "Local Scenes and Dangerous Crossroads: Punk and Theories of Cultural Hybridity," *Popular Music*, Vol. 21, No. 2 (2002): 226.

4   Billy Bragg, "Waiting for the Great Leap Forward," *Workers Playtime* (Elektra, 1988), LP.

5   On the relationships between urban space and punk, see my discussion of 'DIY Bike Culture' in *One Less Car*, Chapter 6. On the dialectical spatialities of hip-hop, see Rashad Shabazz, "Hip-hop and the Black Geographical Imagination," a talk delivered at Marlboro College, October 13, 2009. Online at http://youtu.be/AJ4Ne-wbxDw

6 Roger Sabin, "Introduction," *Punk Rock: So What?*, p. 2.

7 Ibid.

8 For example, a book like *Subculture: The Meaning of Style* is often read against, if not held causally responsible for, the tidal wave of shoddy style-as-resistance themed critiques that followed its publication in 1979, and consequently, some of the more complex relationships that Hebdige actually does acknowledge between socioeconomic class, music, ideology and, yes, *style* receive the short shrift. His argument is problematic in a variety of ways, but certainly not on par with much of the work that reduces his analysis to a close reading of people's outfits; all the more so when one carefully reads his discussion of the twinned process of ideological and commodity 'recuperation' —a concept best defined by the Clash, or perhaps Crass (who used the slogan to critique the Clash), as "turning rebellion into money"—on pages 92-99, under the section heading "Two forms of incorporation."

9 In fact, one of the ironies regarding Sabin's book—aside from leading off with an essay on the Sex Pistols just pages after asking rhetorically, in his introduction, "*how many more times must we hear the Sex Pistols story?*"— is that despite the quality of the essays and the authors' successful effort to demonstrate that "punk was not an isolated, bounded phenomenon, but had an extensive impact on a variety of cultural and political fields," the book is simultaneously a reminder of some additional trappings that one could also attribute to the 'orthodoxy' structuring analyses of punk, such as methodological approaches based almost exclusively on textual analysis (no ethnographies, for example) and a perpetual overemphasis on both British punk and the years 1976-1979.

10 For an excellent corrective to this trend, see George Hurchalla, *Going Underground: American Punk 1979-1992* (Stuart, FL: Zuo Press, 2005).

11 Neil Nehring, "The Situationist International in American Hardcore Punk, 1982–2002," *Popular Music and Society*, Vol. 29, No. 5 (2006): 524; Lisa M. Chuang & John P. Hart, "Suburban American Punks and the Musical Rhetoric of Green Day's ''Jesus of Suburbia','" *Communication Studies*, Vol. 59, No. 3, (2008): 183–201. Aside from the triviality of calling the band "the Dillinger Four," Nehring suggests that their sound "fairly distinctively crosses classic punk with sub-genres such as speedcore." First, 'speedcore' is a genre of electronic music (not punk) and, second, no punks have ever used this term to describe punk music, unless it was a joking reference to an all-tweaker (meth addict) rock-n-roll band haunting some dive bar on the outskirts of Portland, OR. These are among the smallest errors in an essay that largely misunderstands punk as well as its connections to situationist politics. Finally, I also found it

somewhat odd that in Nehring's attempt to find evidence of D4's situa-
tionist-inspired political and/or artistic critiques, he fails to mention the
fact that Paddy – who is shirtless if not naked at *every* D4 show and in
most pictures of the band – has the phrase HOW MUCH ART CAN
YOU TAKE? tattooed across his entire chest. It doesn't get much clearer
than that.

12   There are many examples from which to choose, including the following: Ruth Adams, "The Englishness of English Punk: Sex Pistols,
Subcultures, and Nostalgia," *Popular Music & Society*, Vol. 31, No. 4
(2008): 469-488; Sean Albiez, "*Know History!: John Lydon, Cultural
Capital and the Prog/Punk Dialectic*," Popular Music, Vol. 22, No. 3
(2003): 357-374; Pete Lentini, "Punk's Origins: Anglo-American
Syncretism," *Journal of Intercultural Studies*, Vol. 24, No. 2 (2003):
153-174; Geoffrey Sirc, "Never Mind the Tagmemics, Where's the
Sex Pistols?" *College Composition and Communication*, Vol. 48, No.
1 (1997): 9-29; Karen Pinkus, "Self-Representation in Futurism and
Punk," *South Central Review*, Vol. 13, No. 2/3 (1996): 180-193; Neil
Nehring, "Revolt into Style: Graham Greene Meets the Sex Pistols,"
PMLA, Vol. 106, No. 2 (1991): 222-237.

13   Greil Marcus, *Lipstick Traces: A Secret History of the Twentieth Century*
(Cambridge: Harvard University Press, 1989). Also see Jon Savage, *The
England's Dreaming Tapes* (Minneapolis: University of Minnesota Press,
2010), and especially Jon Savage, *England's Dreaming: Anarchy, Sex Pistols, Punk Rock, and Beyond* (New York, Macmillan, 2001).

14   For example, see William Tsitsos, "Rules of Rebellion: Slamdancing,
Moshing, and the American Alternative Scene, *Popular Music*, Vol. 18,
No. 3 (Oct., 1999): 397-414; Bradford Scott Simon, "Entering the Pit:
Slam-Dancing and Modernity," *The Journal of Popular Culture*, Vol. 31,
No. 1 (1997): 149–176; Leslie Roman, "Intimacy, Labor, and Class: Ide-
ologies of Feminine Sexuality in the Punk Slam Dance," in (eds.) Linda
K. Christian-Smith and Leslie Roman, *Becoming Feminine: The Politics of
Popular Culture*, (New York and Philadelphia: The Falmer Press, 1988),
pp. 143–84. With all due and sincere respect to punkademics who have
jumped, or rather *moshed*, their way into this analytic fray (particularly
Prof. Tsitsos, who plays in bands and runs a DIY label), I would argue
first and foremost for a thorough re-assessment of the problematic. Indeed, the set of kinetic practices under question (moshing, slam-dancing)
are not physical performances as much as enigmatic expressions of latent
potentialities/possibilities that simply transcend the boundaries of theory's utility. The 'wall of death', for example, is admittedly a fascinating
spatio-corporeal phenomenon, if not an elegant, ludic/haptic realization

of what Henri Lefebve calls a *moment*: "the attempt to achieve the total realization of a possibility"(*Critique of Everyday Life, Vol I*, p. 348). But it is nonetheless an eruption of such primal force that, when bounded by the homoerotically charged protocols governing 'the pit', becomes wholly resistant to classification and can thus only empty the words used in such vain explanatory efforts from the very meanings which they are employed to signify. Only in its more practical applications elsewhere – for example, when the wall of death is deployed against "the system," as a tactical/militant adjunct to the anarchist goals of achieving a society based on mutual aid, self-rule, non-hierarchical social relations, and the proliferation of fake meats – could one even begin to effectively grapple with its theoretical implications. See, R.A.M.B.O., *Wall of Death the System* (625 Thrashcore Records, 2001), LP. For more on the cultural/ political logics of the moshing ("Fuck your individualist mosh / No neoliberals in the pit") as well as the potential uses of the wall of death against Christian anti-abortion protestors, see Crucial Unit "Thrashaholics Unanimous," and "Wall of Death the Chain of Life," *Crucial Unit/ Municipal Waste, Split LP* (Six Weeks Records, 2002).

15   I have seen no clear evidence that subcultural researchers have ever asked – or even thought to ask – what their research "subjects" actually *do* call themselves, or what they would like to be called, or why it matters. Punks are creative and quirky; perhaps they would prefer to be known, in peer-reviewed journals, as a "pack," or a "gaggle," or even a "murder." For an exhaustive/exhausting treatment of the politics of subcultural research terminology, see most essays from Andy Bennett and practically every monograph or edited collection published in the last fifteen years with variations of words "subculture," "post-subculture" and also "youth culture" and "club culture" in the title.

16   John Goshert, p. 87. While I think his definition is insufficient, Goshert offers a notable description of punk (in contrast to singular phenomenon) as "a set of only loosely assimilable vectors and forms of expression."

17   David Muggleton, *Inside Subculture*, p. 2. Also see, Andy Medhurst, "What Did I Get? Punk, Memory and Autobiography," in (ed) Roger Sabin, *Punk Rock: So What?*, pp. 219-231.

18   Lucy O'Brien, "Academia in the UK," *The Guardian*, September 27, 2001.

19   Ibid.

20   Ibid.

21   Andy Capper, "Anarchy and Peace, Litigated," *Vice Magazine*, Vol. 17, No. 8 (2010), p. 99.   Online at http://www.vice.com/read/ anarchy-and-peace-litigated-490-v17n8

22   Helen Reddington, "'Lady' Punks in Bands: A Subculturette?" in (eds.) David Muggleton and Rupert Weinzierl, *The Post-Subcultures Reader* (Oxford and New York: Berg, 2003), p. 239.

23   These documentaries include Scott Treleaven, *Queercore: A Punk-U-Mentary* (Toronto: V-Tape, 1997), VHS; Martin Sorrondeguy *Beyond The Screams/Más Allá de los Gritos: A U.S. Latino Hardcore Punk Documentary* (Self-released, 1999), VHS; James Spooner, *Afro-Punk* (Los Angeles: Afro-Punk, 2003), DVD; and most recently, Amy Oden's film about women in the DIY punk scene, called *From the Back of the Room* (Self-released, 2011), Film.

24   Quoted in reference to the compilation, *Possessed to Skate Vol. II* (625 Productions, 2002), LP. Ward also suggests that the recurring theme of punks recycling 'old school' styles similarly relies upon a tenuous relationship to punk history: "Trends come and go…and it seems that every now and then the punk scene harks back to the 'good old days' for inspiration, which of course is good in some respects. It never is an exact copy of what was […] because what is being copied is only what we construct from a few record covers, a couple myths, or for those of us old enough, a few fuzzy memories that aren't based in reality." See Scholastic Deth, "Lyrics and Explanations." Online at http://www.geocities.ws/scholastic-deth/lyrics.html

25   For examples of such references, see Bradford D. Martin, *The Other Eighties: A Secret History of America in the Age of Reagan* (New York: Macmillan, 2011), pp. 95-118; Bruce Schulman, *The Seventies: The Great Shift In American Culture, Society, and Politics* (Cambridge, MA: De Capo, 2002), p. 153.

26   Goshert, p. 88.

27   It is possible that punkademics could be mapped onto what Linda Andes refers to as the "stages of punk." Linda Andes, "Growing Up Punk: Meaning and Commitment Careers in a Contemporary Youth Subculture," in ed. J.S. Epstein, *Youth Culture: Identity in a Postmodern World* (Oxford: Blackwell, 1998), pp. 212-231. Andy Bennett has written one of the only pieces about 'old' punks, but it focuses rather narrowly on fans attending a concert. See "Punk's Not Dead: The Continuing Significance of Punk Rock for an Older Generation of Fans," *Sociology*, Vol. 40 No. 2 (2006): 219-235.

'CAUSE I WANNA BE... PHD?

DYLAN MINER AND ESTRELLA TORREZ

TURNING POINT:
CLAIMING THE UNIVERSITY AS A PUNK SPACE[1]

PUNK AND ACADEMIA are queer bedfellows.[2] The very nature of this collection presupposes the antagonistic relationship between the autonomy of punk and the structured nature of the university. Any hardcore kid who has spent time in a university classroom will recognize the inherent contradiction between her/his anarchic (and activist) desires to create an alternative and equitable society and the university's ability to restrict all counter-hegemonic voices within it. As professors, we deal with this on a daily basis. We feel this contradiction in our classrooms, in our syllabi, in our research, how we relate with students, and even how we interact with our colleagues. How do we, as *punkademics*, continue to resist the process of institutionalization, while working within an institution? Moreover, how do we do so when, in the eyes of many students, we represent the power and legitimacy of the university?

Thankfully, we are not alone in our quotidian struggles against the hegemony of dominant institutions. In fact, this everyday struggle is one with roots in the modernist, as well as anticapitalist, tactic to resist the ongoing power of the state and its multiple institutionalized apparatuses. From this position, artists, intellectuals, and activists have frequently been at the forefront of these confrontations. In his discussion of the anarchist-oriented avant-garde, Situationist International (SI), Berlin-based critic Gene Ray comments on the way that modernist artists, whom he places in dialectic tension with the avant-garde, aimed their critiques at institutions, while the anarchist-oriented practices of SI challenged the very legitimacy of institutions by intentionally choosing to not participate in these institutions. According to Ray,

The SI was a group founded on the principle of autonomy – an autonomy not restricted as privilege or specialization, but one that is radicalized through a revolutionary process openly aiming to extend autonomy to all. The SI did not recognize any Party or other absolute authority on questions pertaining to the aims and forms of revolutionary social struggle. Their autonomy was critically to study reality and the theories that would explain it, draw their own conclusions and act accordingly. In its own group process, the SI accepted nothing less than a continuous demonstration of autonomy by its members, who were expected to contribute as full participants in a collective practice.[3]

Since Guy Debord, a key situationist and author of *The Society of the Spectacle*, is common reading in most anarchist and political punk scenes, Ray's characterization about SI has direct implications on our discussion of claiming the university as a punk space. In fact, Debord and the SI begin to challenge the legitimacy of institutions like the university, the site where punkademics work. Like mainstream arts institutions, the university, as an institution, frequently inhibits one's autonomy at the very point when an individual begins to participate in its everyday workings.

As punkademics, which seems to be a fitting title for who we both are, we feel that this intimately fraught relationship between punks and the university is a contest we must individually and collectively confront. In many ways, punk intellectuals, both inside and outside the academy, may turn to the history of Chicana/o or Mexican-American activism as a model of how to compel the institution to work for the people, not only those in power. According to the *Plan de Santa Barbara*, a 155-page manifesto collectively written by the Chicano Coordinating Council on Higher Education in 1969, "we do not come to work for the university, but to demand that the university work for our people.'"[4] As insider-outsiders, and as punks and people of color within the university, we are adamant that the university be accountable to "our people," as the Plan de Santa Barbara so significantly articulates. So while we both understand the tactical decision to disavow dominant institutions, such as the university, we have nonetheless chosen different tactics: to insert ourselves, and our intellectual and cultural labor into the confines of the university in hopes of changing the very nature of the institution.

Conservative pundits, such as David Horowitz, portray the university as an autonomous sphere where old Left intellectuals train and inform new generations of anticapitalist activists. Inversely, we have come to see the university as a space that allows only a minimal degree of dissent before discarding those rebellious and anti-authoritarian voices which, at one point, may have been *allowed* to speak. We both have witnessed hostile attacks on friends and colleagues whose ideas were viewed as too confrontational, too challenging, or just too radical for the university. The high stakes examples of tenure dismissal and tenure denial for Indigenous activist-intellectuals Ward Churchill and Andrea Smith are only two examples of times when our allies were denied a space within the university.

Another example is that of Norman Finkelstein, a political scientist writing on the Israel-Palestine conflict. Finkelstein was denied tenure at DePaul University in 2007. For university officials, his critical views on Israeli foreign policy and professional demeanor were deemed against the university's "Vincentian values." The Illinois Conference of the American Association of University Professors (AAUP) criticized DePaul's decision because it felt that the verdict was based on the misconception that Finkelstein's research "might hurt [the] college's reputation."[5] I wonder how Indigenous inhabitants feel about the 'Vincentian values' that precipitated missionaries who "came to America to work especially for the salvation of the poor Indians," as Bishop Joseph Rosati wrote in the nineteenth-century?[6]

In fall 2010, DePaul was once again in the news following the tenure denial of two women of color, an all too frequent event in a labor force which does not formally recognize the unique labor performed by women and faculty of color. One of the women, Namita Goswami, a philosopher of race and postcoloniality was, according to media accounts, denied tenure because her work was "insufficiently philosophical."[7] While neither of us know the specifics of these preceding cases, they are each indicative of a system which speaks of institutional "diversity," yet is unwilling to re-evaluate the institution's relationship to counter-hegemonic or challenging forms of knowledge.

In this same way, most institutions of higher education could care less about the things punks care about. Our own identities as punks are intimately intertwined with radical feminism, anticapitalist self-organization, Third and Fourth World liberation, veganism and food justice, and DIY, not even mentioning the most fundamental desire to produce new and liberated societies "within the shell of the old."[8] In *The Philosophy of Punk*, Craig O'Hara discusses the humanizing efforts of punk in a never-ending capitalist world of alienation. He writes that

> Punks question conformity not only by looking and sounding different (which has debatable importance), but by

questioning the prevailing modes of thought. Questions
about things that others take for granted related to work,
race, sex, and our own selves...By acting as anti-authoritarian nonconformists, Punks are not usually treated very well
by those people whose commands to conform are rejected.[9]

While the university may have the façade of radicalism, it is all too
frequently a "free-trade area" where the capitalist model of "intellectual
entrepreneurship" supersedes any organic means of knowledge dissemination. With recent budget cuts, faculty have been asked to "tighten
our belts" and be "entrepreneurial" by seeking extramural funding for
research, the very basis for how the university credits its faculty.

Stuart Hall, the Marxist founder of the Birmingham School who began his career teaching night school to British workers, recognizes the
immense authority of capitalism to suck the life from oppositional movements, an idea that Slovenian critic Slavoj Žižek has developed to its
logical end. For Hall, the conciliatory power of capitalism facilitates the
cooptation of any and all oppositional projects into the capitalist model.
Hall asserts, "that in order to maintain its global position, capital has
had to negotiate, has had to incorporate and partly reflect the differences
it was trying to overcome."[10] So punkademics, those of us struggling
against capitalist globalization and the university's disavowal of our specialized knowledge, must be doubly cautious about cooptation. Using
the language we all understand, punkademics must never sell-out.

Most recently, the university has become a space that proposes the development of an "engaged global citizenry," while ignoring the most fundamental issues of inequality. While punk ontology is founded in, using
the language of the anarcho-indigenist Zapatistas of southern Mexico,
realizing that *otro mundo es possible* (another world is possible), dominant
institutions are embedded in maintaining existing worlds. As individuals
who pride ourselves on being part of a self-constructed and prefigurative
society within the shell of the old, punk alternatives do not easily map
onto the notions of global citizenship that are being laid out within the
entrepreneurial and colonial desires of the university.

It is clear, however, that by documenting these structural changes to
the university, we are not naively reminiscing on some ideal past in which
the university successfully met the needs of community. Inversely, it appears to us that the university may be more open now than it ever has
been, particularly in relation to subaltern knowledges and the position of
ethnic studies: programs which are being cut indiscriminately across institutions. Even so, Linda Tuhiwai Smith, a Māori scholar from Aoteoroa

(New Zealand), positions the development of Western knowledge as one that systematically marginalizes Indigenous knowledge and is active in colonizing global populations. She writes,

> The globalization of knowledge and Western culture constantly reaffirms the West's view of itself as the centre of legitimate knowledge, the arbiter of what counts as knowledge, and the source of the "civilized" knowledge. This form of global knowledge is generally referred to as "universal" knowledge, available to all and not 'owned' by anyone, that is, until non-Western scholars make claims to it.[11]

While many punks come from privileged sectors of dominant society, to identify as a punk is a maneuver to intentionally position one's self in solidarity with oppressed and colonized people, both locally and globally. A trip to San Cristobal de las Casas, a highland municipality in Chiapas (Mexico) and one of the four cities overtaken by Zapatistas on January 1, 1994, will reveal the high level of crusty punks who have descended on the city. While this may have some negative implications on local community, with Anglo-American and European punks not fully understanding Mayan *indigeneity*, it nevertheless demonstrates a profound admiration and solidarity with Indigenous struggles. These are movements toward autonomy and ones directly confronting capitalism. In this way, these punks are helping to build another possible world.

Even while institutions attempt to create "global citizens," the way this commonly transpires disregards the basic pedagogical tools needed to truly open discussions of who this sort of individual may be, why this move is important, and how (as North Americans) we may actually become "engaged global citizens." One aspect of being a global citizen is commonly interpreted into a crass form of *volunteerism*. Therefore, each year, thousands of students enter "volunteering obligations" (what was once known as service-learning and then became recognized as civic engagement) without understanding the very systems that necessitate them partaking in such practices. Volunteers enter soup kitchens, homeless shelters, suicide hotline centers and the like spending a few hours (enough to report back to their professor in the form of a power point presentation or final paper) without the rudimentary knowledge that would enable them to critique the capitalist origins of their need to volunteer. Of course, this does not mean that all universities practice these in a naïve or impractical fashion. At the moment, we both teach these types of courses, educating students about how to engage in solidarity work with Latino and Native communities in the Great Lakes. To date, they seem to be developing quite successfully.

Instead of evoking a commitment to active social transformation, the university has become a space where corporate colonization impedes and inhibits the (presumably) public space of the university, the inverse of how punk autonomy seeks to ascertain parallel institutions. Although dialogue is at the core of any revolutionary education, the dominant pedagogical (teaching) mode used within the university classroom remains alienated from any real or authentic learning. This is not to say that the university (and those of us operating within its grasp) does not foster the vision of a new and better world. In many ways, as life-long students and intellectual workers, we wholeheartedly believe that the university can become one of the spaces where we may help to create an alternative universe, one which challenges the dominance of capitalism. This is the reason, we suppose, that there are punks and anarchists operating within the university's framework, both as students and professors. But all too frequently, this specter haunting academia is simply the veneer of potential democratic engagement.

In turn the university has become adept at pretending to allow resistant practices to exist *within* its structure. These dissenting voices may be politically motivated, such as those identified as anarchist, punk, Marxist, council communist, or anti-authoritarian, or their very presence in the university may challenge the status quo (particularly when they are Chicana/o and Latina/o, Black, American Indian, immigrant, working-class, or women and feminists). As many critical pedagogues have correctly argued, including but not limited to Paolo Freire, Antonia Darder, Paul Willis, and Joel Spring, public education has historically been the location where students learn (and accept as natural) their marginal place in the existing social order. From this perspective, schooling is a system of dominance, one that maintains the existing order. This makes us wonder where punks and hardcore kids have learned to accept their/our role on the margins of society?

Although neither of us believe that punk should be mainstreamed and therefore lose its oppositional nature and liberatory potential, we are nonetheless of the opinion that by infiltrating the academy, the presence of punk knowledge systems (we could call these *punk epistemologies*) will likewise begin to penetrate capitalist infrastructures. Moreover, by alienating certain sectors of society from the university system (or those of us that negate our privilege by choosing not to attend university), we simply begin to accept our own place on the margins of contemporary society. Although we advocate for the creation of parallel institutions, such as free schools and open universities, we also believe that punk intellectuals and other radicals must never consent to being denied a place within the university. In this fashion, we must claim the university as a site where knowledge is recognized and will, in fact, help transform contemporary society.

Unfortunately as punks, we continue to self-marginalize ourselves, our views of the world, and the potential role we could play in building a new world. At times, we both minimize our "punkness" so as not to isolate the other significant perspectives we may bring to the table. We have each had many conversations over the years with friends, acquaintances, comrades, and fellow punks whose base-level knowledge and lived experiences were deemed insufficient against those of the university. Forced out by biased and un-accepting professors, many of these punk kids decided to leave academia, rather than stay and (re)claim the academy as their own. So at this moment, we stand firm. We demand that the time is now when we begin to declare the university as a punk space.

The tenants of hardcore, as expressed in Craig O'Hara's *The Philosophy of Punk*, are based on our collective response to the shared experiences of capitalist alienation, in many the same alienation that all workers of the world share. If we have any hope to circumvent capitalism and the affiliated processes of corporate globalization, we must begin to use pedagogy (both within and without dominant systems) as a means toward liberation. Although we may begin to create alternative infrastructure, which we believe must be amplified, the reclamation of the university must also occur. A two-tiered tactic must include claiming the university work for us, as happened with university students throughout the world in 1968.

Unfortunately, a pessimistic punk orientation only highlights one vantage point of the oppressive nature of schooling. Inversely, education also has the propensity to democratize civil society, a notion that all too many nation-states have used to their benefit. This concept was discussed in-depth by John Dewey, a seminal figure in educational theory. Propaghandi, the prominent vegan, anarchist, pro-queer, peace-punk band from Manitoba, posits an alternate relationship between knowledge, equity, and the education system. Accordingly, Propaghandi maintains it in their typical tongue-in-cheek fashion:

> At some turning point in history
> Some fuck-face recognized
> That knowledge tends to democratize…

We cannot help but comment on how beautifully written (and simultaneously crass) these lyrics are.

Although the educational system commonly marginalizes and oppresses certain segments of the population – often times the majority – it may also be used to counter these practices. Education, in the eyes of Paulo Freire and his revolutionary text *Pedagogy of the Oppressed*, is at the core of any radical social change. It is here, in the emancipatory annals of education, where cultural workers choose to either actively work to politicize or depoliticize those that enter the space. As punkademics, we situate ourselves here.

If we, as punk teachers and professors, are truly intent on creating a democratic and equitable society, we must 1) begin to open up what we consider "knowledge" to include *punk epistemologies*, as well as; 2) begin to infiltrate the university, both as students and faculty, in a way that opens up the university to our knowledge; 3) engage in discussions centered on topics concerning power and privilege; 4) directly confront those notions embedded within a hidden curriculum meant to perpetuate a neoliberal agenda; 5) recognize ourselves as agents of change; and 6) enter each social situation as a potential revolutionary act.

By doing so, we amplify what is presently being done both in punk and in some spaces at the university. By doing so, we must prevent the negative progression of the industrial university that produces depoliticized (and all-too-frequently precarious) workers. This is not to say that faculty and students who are actively creating radical spaces within the academy do not exist; in fact we do. However we have not fully claimed the university in any critical manner or centralized within one locale. Once punk academics establish intellectual communities that support critical thinking, encourage activist work, and develop alternative futures, the capitalist tide within the academy will begin to change. This book is but the first move in that direction.

NOTES

1   An earlier and abridged version of this article was previously published in the "Teacher's Column" of *Give Me Back* #5. The author's would like to thank Fil at *GMB*, as well as all of the hardcore kids who continue to read zines.

2   While punk is generally queer, only certain sectors of academia operate to queer normative binaries of straightness.

3   Gene Ray, "Toward a Critical Art Theory," in eds. Gerald Raunig and Gene Ray, *Art and Contemporary Critical Practice: Reinventing Institutional Critique* (MayFly Books, 2009), pp. 84-85.

4   According to the document, this statement is attributed to José Vasconcelos, a problematic and anti-Indigenous bureaucrat during the

early-to-mid twentieth century. While we do not deny this attribution, we believe that situating within the radical activism of the Chicano movement makes more sense for the sake of articulating a punk argument.

5   Sierra Millman, "Students Will Begin Hunger Strike in Support of DePaul Professors Denied Tenure," *Chronicle of Higher Education*, June 25, 2007. http://chronicle.com/article/Students-Will-Begin-Hunger/39107

6   Joseph Rosati to Nicola Rosati, December 19, 1820, from Barrens, cited in working papers of Frederick Easterly in preparation for his The Life of Rt. Rev. Joseph Rosati, CM (Washington, D.C., 1942) original notes in Mary Immaculate Seminary, Northampton, Pennsylvania.

7   Rachel Cromidas, "DePaul Faculty Members Call for Tenure Probe." *Chicago News Cooperative*, December 7, 2010. http://www.chicagonews-coop.org/depaul-faculty-members-call-for-tenure-probe.

8   The concept of building a new world within the shell of the old is one created by the Industrial Workers of the World (IWW), a pre-punk and anarcho-syndicalist labor union formed in 1905. The IWW or Wobblies, as they are commonly known, have been influential on prefigurative punk politics and aesthetics. Miner, a long-time Wobbly whose dues are presently unpaid, made a series of relief prints for the 2005 commemoration of the 100th anniversary of the union. These images, some of which were included in *Wobblies!: A Graphic History of the IWW* (New York: Verso, 2005), traveled to union halls, anarchist bookstores, and alternative spaces throughout North America, Europe, Australia, and South Africa.

9   Craig O'Hara, *The Philosophy of Punk: More Than Noise!* (Oakland: AK Press, 1999), pp. 27-28.

10   Stuart Hall, "The Local and the Global," in eds. Anne McClintock, Aamir Mufti, and Ella Shohat, *Dangerous Liaisons: Gender, Nation, and Postcolonial Perspectives* (Minneapolis: University of Minnesota, 1997), p. 182.

11   Linda Tuhiwai Smith, *Decolonizing Methodologies: Research and Indigenous Peoples* (Zed Books, 1999), p. 63.

ROSS HAENFLER

PUNK ETHICS AND THE MEGA-UNIVERSITY

INTRODUCTION

ONE SEMESTER IN my Sociology 101 course I noticed a visibly upset student, Christie, sitting in her customary spot near the front of the room. On a typical day she was generous with her contributions to our class discussions, but that day she was quiet and looked to be on the verge of tears. As I wondered what I could have said that so offended her I recalled that she had missed the previous two sessions. I decided to catch up with Christie after class, but before I could ask her to stay she approached me with a folded sheet of paper in her hand. Still holding back tears, she handed me the paper, which I immediately recognized as a *funeral program*. A picture of a young man stared back at me along with the order of service and directions to the cemetery where he was to be laid to rest. Christie explained that she had missed class to attend her little brother's funeral and to grieve with her family. Before I could offer my condolences, Christie began *apologizing* for missing class, pleading that I not count her absences against her. As I looked at her with an expression of sympathy mixed with astonishment, I reminded her that I *never* penalized people for missing class due to an illness or, especially, a family crisis. Somewhat relieved, Christie told me with a touch of bitterness that several of her professors had required that she produce the funeral program to "prove" she wasn't lying about her brother's death.

As Christie left I thought *What the hell kind of system have we created that a student feels compelled to apologize for attending a funeral!?!?* Christie's story is one of many I've heard during my years in higher education that reflects the dehumanization running rampant across many large college campuses.

Long before I became a "punkademic" I was simply a punk. It seemed like every interesting person in my high school – the artists, activists, skaters, musicians, and other outsiders – were connected in some way with the punk scene. More than torn up clothes and abrasive music, punk *ideas* lured me in, especially the *question everything* mentality. Hearing Nausea call upon us to "Smash Racism" or Downcast rail against white/straight/male advantage in "Privilege" was revolutionary. Listening to Minor Threat sing about the virtues of being "Out of Step" with the world showed me there was more to being young than the booze culture that measured manhood by alcohol content and sexual conquest. Seeing feminist bands like Spitboy and Tribe 8 helped me question patriarchy and homophobia. The punk scene was *transformative* for me. The opportunity to continually ask questions, pursue the answers, and examine my own life, made me fall in love with punk and, later, university life. In other words, the same yearning that brought me to punk rock helped me find a home in academia. But just as I was naïve about the revolutionary potential of punk so too was I naïve about life in the academy.

This chapter follows a punk-themed critique of the modern mega-university and the academic profession based upon the punk values of anti-authoritarianism, nonconformity, creativity/originality, anti-hierarchy, social change, and the do-it-yourself (DIY) ethic. Based on over ten years of experience as an academic, I discuss how the bureaucratic *system* creates alienation in the primary academic activities of teaching and research. Along the way, I offer possibilities for resistance that punkademics and others might exploit.

PUNK GOES TO COLLEGE:
MEGA-UNIVERSITIES AND PUNK ETHICS

The idyllic image of sagely professor and eager students engaged in Socratic dialogue beneath an ancient oak tree in the midst of majestic stone buildings has on many campuses been supplanted by cavernous, cement lecture halls filled with texting undergraduates and a professor droning into a microphone. Modern "mega-universities" are enormous, mostly state-sponsored research schools that grew exponentially in the post-World War II era, often known as much for their big-time sports teams as for their academic programs. Mega-universities typically have tens of thousands of students (several have over 50,000), huge, complex bureaucracies, large class sizes, research oriented professors, and sprawling campuses. I have taught, briefly, at a small liberal arts college and while such places certainly have their own peccadilloes and elitisms they seem to me to serve their students and faculty relatively well in comparison.

Never doubt there are wonderful people doing amazing work at mega-universities. However, the *system* of the mega-university is at best seriously flawed and at worst designed to make education efficient and cost effective, alienating students and teachers in the process. Thus, for example, faculty committed to being wonderful teachers on mega-campuses are often working *against* a system that pays little more than lip-service to working with undergraduates.

Just as universities have grown, so too has punk, changing from a mostly underground and marginalized scene to an industry where "punk" bands win Grammy Awards. Yet for every Green Day, Blink 182, and Sum 41 that makes it big there are a dozen bands playing in basements and garages to forty kids, seeking to keep alive punk's countercultural, anti-consumerist roots. Hot Topic, MySpace, and MTV2 might change punk, but they can't kill its spirit in the underground. Just as punk continually reinvents itself so too can we re-enchant the enlightening spirit lacking in too many the mega-universities.

Critiques of higher education are nothing new. In 1918, Thorstein Veblen described universities of his time as "impersonal," "mechanistic," and "dispassionate," with researchers worshipping value free science just as men of previous eras worshipped mythological gods.[1] In 1922, Upton Sinclair criticized the plutocratic control of universities by business elites, claiming schools created conformist students ready to take their place in the capitalist machine.[2] Sociologist C. Wright Mills, believing education was inherently political, took academics to task for conducting and teaching supposedly "value free" social science that in actuality reinforced the oppressive establishment.[3] Similarly, historian Howard Zinn critiqued the "rules" of academia, including "disinterested scholarship," calling on scholars to "become the critics of the culture, rather than its apologists and perpetrators" and to "work on modes of change instead of merely describing the world that is."[4] Numerous feminist scholars revealed the academy's sexist biases and marginalization and exclusion of women and people of color. Page Smith chastised professors for being in "full flight from teaching" and universities for celebrating an "academic fundamentalism" that produces a "poverty of spirit" in its pursuit of unsentimental science.[5] Finally, cultural critic and author bell hooks laments an education system that squashes children's natural predisposition for critical thinking by educating them for "conformity and obedience only."[6] My critique shares much in common with these great works but also emerges from my education in punk rock, where my teachers were the Bad Brains, Dead Kennedys, Born Against, Crass, Fugazi, Bikini Kill, and more. Their lessons for me included questioning hierarchies, elitisms, and injustices while committing to originality, creativity, and nonconformity.

RESEARCH

When I mentor undergraduate or MA students about pursuing a PhD I often extol the virtues of an academic life, claiming, "What could be better? You get to choose a topic that completely fascinates you, learn everything there is to know about it, make your own contribution to that knowledge, and hang out with students, sharing what you've learned. And you get paid!" Of course the research enterprise, and more specifically *publishing* research, is rarely so picturesque. Too often, rather than creating space for groundbreaking, creative, transformative research, the mega-university system pushes faculty towards simply filling arcane academic journals with articles.

Every assistant professor at a mega-university feels the anxious pressure dictated by the maxim "publish or perish," that is, publish your research in respectable peer-reviewed outlets or we will deny you the holy grail of tenure and send you packing. For some young scholars, the publish-or-perish imperative leads to an obsession with *quantity* rather than *quality*. "How many "pubs" do you have?" becomes operating directive, regardless of a piece of scholarship's particular significance or usefulness. "What have you got in the pipeline?" suggests that article production is an assembly-line-like process, that churning out one piece after another is just part of that process, and that professors are workers fulfilling a monotonous task. One of my past chairs even suggested (in a well-meaning way) that I not aim too highly, just publish in some lower-tier academic journals to fill my tenure "quota." Yet even meeting some imagined quota of publications might not satisfy, as the next concern becomes *where* the articles appear: how prestigious the journal or press? Sometimes the mega-university doesn't even bother masking the crass commercialism expected of new faculty, judging them not only on their publications but also on their ability to bring in big grants.

Tenure-terror results too often in jargon-laden, esoteric articles disconnected from reality that only a handful of people in the world can comprehend and even fewer will read. The entire process is stressful, competitive, and alienating. And crossing the tenure finish line hardly ends the status games now firmly entrenched in the young scholar, as one's professional and self-worth continue to be measured by lines on a curriculum vita.

Even more bizarre are the tenure requirements for "professional engagement" which are satisfied by, among other things, presenting work at professional conferences. At their best, such meetings provide a space for colleagues to form new friendships, exchange ideas, be inspired by new research, and wrestle with the current debates in their chosen field. At their worst, they are a train wreck of ill-prepared and poorly-delivered PowerPoint presentations with speakers talking way too fast and yet still managing to not finish in their allotted time. Of course such presentations produce another line on your vita, even if you gave your paper to five people, one of whom left halfway through.

The original punks disdained conventional, commercialized, cookie-cutter music, art, and fashion fed to the "mainstream," taking a stand for creativity, originality, and innovation. Punk musicians were long skeptical of signing to major labels, fearing that record executives – driven by the profit imperative – would push artists to compromise their creative vision. Likewise, young scholars may feel pressure to research something "marketable," a topic that won't ruffle too many feathers or be perceived as too "political." Again, given the ominous threat of a tenure review, the many years of schooling, and the difficulty of landing a faculty position, you can hardly blame people for hedging their bets and "cranking out" articles and conference presentations. Still, many of us could remind ourselves that all the effort leading up to landing a job is worthless if we're not pursuing what thrills us rather than tailoring our work to some academic convention.

Here academics might also take a lesson from punk's anti-elitist roots. One of punk's early inclinations was to make music and art for everyday people, not for critics or curators and certainly not for rich, high-culture snobs. In academia, sometimes the more jargon-filled and convoluted the writing the higher praise a work receives, as if being obtuse were a virtue designed to deny the plebes some sacred, forbidden knowledge. A certain degree of complicated language and specialized concepts may be necessary to communicate complex ideas, but any honest scholar will admit that academic writing is rife with posturing, due in part, perhaps, to the fear of not appearing smart enough. Why not make our writing less pretentious and more accessible? And why not occasionally write for non-academic audiences – a blog, newspaper editorial, or popular-press book – just as DIY punks spread their work via 'zines?

Punk taught me to be very critical of social hierarchies, hierarchies often reproduced, rather than challenged, by higher education. Consumed by the practical considerations of earning a degree (i.e. the cost), I didn't even consider – didn't even have the *notion* to consider – the prestige of one school vs. another. After a successful undergraduate career, I knew I wanted to leap directly into graduate school, but I somehow missed the memo that *where* you do your graduate work can be just as (or more) important than *what* you do; prestige of school/department impacts future job opportunities. During a professionalization seminar in my first year of grad school, I recall the department chair explaining that schools typically hired new scholars from one "tier" below their own prestige and therefore we should give up any notion of teaching at major research universities, regardless of our talent or productivity. Put another way, the "top" schools hire almost exclusively from each other. Even my own field, Sociology, known especially for analyzing (and often critiquing) hierarchies and unearned privilege, perpetually recreates social stratification by fetishizing "prestige degrees," that is, giving hiring preference or graduate program slots to people from top-ranked schools. As the punkademic generation assumes the mantle of department and university leadership, will we continue to aggrandize diplomas adorned with the name of a fancy school?

Another punk ideal is a basic commitment to becoming more than a cog in a machine. Yet the modern mega-university is precisely such a machine that manufactures cynicism and dehumanizes its members. Imagine, for a moment, denying someone tenure because they published in the 11th ranked journal rather than one of the top five. Or, spending years researching a topic because it is "hot" or "publishable" as opposed to what truly interests you. If punk teaches us anything it's that we are too often governed by social rules imposed by a conformist society that cares for little aside from creating more workers and selling more products. It's ironic that academics have more autonomy than many, free to create the lives we want to live, and yet we build and maintain our own prison of status hierarchies and self-imposed competition. Punkademics can hold out for something better.

TEACHING

My first semester of graduate school I was a teaching assistant for a Sociology 101 course servicing 500 students. While the professor was organized, fairly interesting, and even kind, there was simply no way he could reach out to every student. In the modern mega-university, big classes, standardized textbooks, and multiple-choice exams are the norm. As state appropriations for higher ed decline, campuses raise tuition and let in more students to make up the shortfall. The entire enterprise is geared towards efficiency – serve the most students possible with the least amount of expenditure. It's no secret that smaller classes improve learning outcomes, but it's also no secret that paying one professor and a few TAs to teach 500 students is cheaper than paying ten professors to teach classes of 50. Some universities are going a step further and replacing flesh and blood teachers with computers by expanding their online education programs (less classroom space to build and maintain). The logical extension of the efficiency/profit model is the for-profit 'universities' such as University of Phoenix that make little effort to hide the fact that education is, primarily, a business. In short, at the mega-university transformative teaching is sacrificed at the altar of efficiency; students too often feel like a number, a face in a crowd, a customer, rather than a valued member of a learning community.

As the previous section suggests, on most mega-campuses, teaching undergraduates takes a far back seat to research (or more specifically, publishing). Some faculty members speak of teaching "loads" as if dealing with undergrads were a burden rather than a privilege. Others purposefully schedule their office hours at inopportune times to avoid being bothered by students. Still others secure grants to help them "buy out" of teaching, freeing them to pursue their (presumably more important) "work," while turning over teaching responsibilities to temporary adjuncts and instructors. Exams, especially multiple-choice exams, save hours of grading time but often evaluate rather than educate, driving students to be grade- rather than learning-oriented. I am not suggesting there are no professors who care about teaching; some clearly do care a great deal for their students. Still, the system of rewards – particularly tenure, but also status and raises – favor research production over teaching, leading even many well-intended teachers to sacrifice teaching and pursue publishing. The combination of larger class sizes and pressures to publish leaves little time for individual students and little opportunity to forge meaningful mentorship relationships with undergraduates.

Caught up in the same commercialized, McDonaldized system, professors and students war with one another rather than uniting to pursue their common interests. Each "side" views the other with increasing distrust, disinterest, and disdain. Teachers see many students as lazy, apolitical, looking for shortcuts, often-privileged, and lacking in creativity and any sort of attention span – and sometimes the teachers are right. Students would rather watch reality television or send text messages than read literature or listen to NPR. Students, on the other hand, view teachers as uncaring, boring, rigid know-it-alls who make little effort to connect their teachings to students' lived experiences and interests – and sometimes the students are right. Yet the classroom remains one of the most important arenas in which to challenge the shortcomings of the mega-university.

First, and most simply, teachers need to share their passion and excitement with students. One of punk and hardcore's special contributions to the broader music world is the intense, frenetic live show that leaves both performer and audience exhilarated and exhausted. While I have never been in a band, I've often considered what it would be like if I *taught* as if I was fronting a hardcore band. I don't mean running back and forth at the front of a lecture hall, screaming at students and stage diving into the first few rows. Rather, what would happen if I brought the same level of intensity and communicated the same level of passion I received from a Fugazi show? How would students respond if I taught like the Dead Kennedys played? Granted, such feeling is easier with a receptive, energetic audience. But I was always inspired by a story of Henry Rollins playing with Black Flag. The band had arrived to play a show in some small, midwestern town to find that only a few kids had turned out. Disappointed, Rollins gave a lackluster performance and was later chastised by bandmates who insisted that those few fans deserved the same intense performance Rollins might give to a crowd of hundreds. Rollins took the criticism to heart and committed to playing his guts out for whomever showed up, one person or a thousand. The lesson: even if there is only one eager student in the classroom (and there nearly always is) then that student deserves everything we have.

Inside and outside the classroom, professors have tremendous opportunities to build relationships with and among students in defiance of the inhuman, bureaucratic mega-university. Virtually any punk can compare and contrast "concerts" and "shows"; a concert is big, relatively anonymous, and features professional, godlike musicians performing for mere mortals (a.k.a. fans), while a show involves an intimacy between performer and audience: a symbiotic, energetic relationship between equals. Concerts feature barriers and security guards between the band and the crowd; shows allow performer and audience to become one as the singer passes the mic to kids while others dive into the audience from the stage. The distinction is significant. Sometimes we have literal barriers between us and our students: podiums, tables, and empty spaces at the front of a lecture hall. More often we have symbolic barriers: credentials, status, and "expertness." Overcoming these barriers is crucial to transforming the hierarchical teacher-student relationship. There are many possibilities. Using reusable nametags throughout the semester can help everyone, teacher and students, get to know one another. Having everyone introduce themselves and shake hands on the first day begins the process of connection. Creating a challenging, but validating, space that welcomes student conversation and participation builds rapport and encourages students to find their voice; imagine a classroom where everyone thinks of her/himself as both student *and* teacher. Allowing and encouraging students, whenever possible, to pursue *their own* interests, rather than completing prefab assignments, fosters imagination and ownership over their work. Above all, bringing originality, humor, and, especially, creativity to the classroom sparks student engagement while humanizing what is too often a very sterile, predictable academic atmosphere.

Finally, the classroom can be a place to imagine a more just and sustainable world: a place where professors can, as bell hooks suggests, teach to transgress. While early punks were often extremely cynical, espousing a "no future" attitude that reflected their often dismal and hopeless surroundings, many punks have since committed to social change in one form or another. Cultural critics and former punks have been tolling punk's demise since 1979. But perhaps, as Dylan Clark suggests, "The threatening pose has been replaced with the actual threat."[7] My education in social justice really began with punk rock. At my high school, punks dominated Amnesty International, the student environmental group, and the opposition to the Gulf War. They were anti-racist, pro-feminist, and often vegetarian or vegan. More recently, bands like Good Riddance supported animal rights and radical politics; NOFX's Fat Mike rallied youth to vote against George W. Bush in 2004; and Rise Against championed environmental and animal rights causes.

At its core, punk is about anti-conformity and countering hegemony. Punkademics are especially situated to help students question *everything*. But being a nonconformist simply for the sake of being different is a shallow form of resistance. Instead we can find inspiration in Martin Luther King, Jr.'s call that we be "transformed nonconformists," radically challenging the status quo – militarism, sectarianism, racism, and poverty – in meaningful ways.[8] In the humanities and social sciences we can reveal the inequalities of race/class/gender/sexuality and debate alternatives. In anthropology and international studies courses we can challenge students' ethnocentrism and nationalism. In economics classes we can question the excess, exploitation, and inequalities of capitalism but also move beyond knee-jerk anticapitalist rants. In political science we can teach students to decode politicians' and pundits' lies, while in math courses students could study how leaders use statistics to persuade and mislead. In chemistry and biology courses we might critically consider the role of biotech and genetically engineered food in our future. English courses can explore marginalized writers and encourage students to find their own voice. The opportunities to educate for critical thinking and personal transformation are limitless. Students will remember the *feeling* of the course along with the *facts*, and, like a great punk show, no one will remember a few missed notes.

STUDENTS

Much of this chapter has focused on the role that faculty and the university structure play in creating the dehumanizing mega-university experience; after all, individual students come and go, faculty, administrators, and university agendas persist. Nevertheless, students are not powerless puppets or mindless zombies; they will play an especially crucial part in any potential resistance or reforms. They must take a DIY approach to their education, actively creating a meaningful experience in spite of the mega-university. If you are a student, you might try these ideas:

- Get to know a few of your professors, early on! Visit them during their office hours, and not only when you have a problem or a complaint about a grade.
- Think like a student, not a robotic consumer. Yes, a degree will serve you well in your future career, but education is more than grades and credentials.
- Pour your energy into the classroom! Pay attention, answer questions, debate. Students outnumber the teacher; your energy impacts everyone's experience.
- Find out about the stellar teachers on your campus; take their classes; and nominate them for teaching awards.
- Question your beliefs. Approach your classes with "beginner's mind," letting go of your preconceptions while thinking critically about course material.
- Be creative! Take risks! Approach your professors with your own ideas for projects or independent study.
- Put down your smart phone. Just for a bit. Not every class session will blow your mind, but it would be tragic if you missed a transformative discussion because you were updating your Facebook page.
- Seek an intentional community. Mega-universities can make us feel anonymous and insignificant, but there are always small

pockets of interesting, engaged people. Many schools have residential colleges, an Honors program, a music scene, and of course, numerous student organizations and clubs.

- Agitate! Work for progressive change on your campus, in your community, and for the world.

CONCLUSION

A wise mentor and award-winning mega-university teacher once told me that universities were full of people creating suffering for each other. Whether it's the professor proclaiming with pride on the first day that half the class will fail the course, or the student who plagiarizes a paper or gives a prof undeserved poor reviews, there is plenty of antagonism to go around. The mega-university is a creature of our own making: a monster that has escaped the control of its makers. But we can take it back.

I believe punk is to some degree about recognizing and reconnecting with our humanity and the humanity of others. Punk calls us to resist the dehumanizing systems that crush not just our individuality and creativity but also our compassion and ability to connect with people. Downcast tore apart the American Dream in "System," suggesting "Society must dig to the root of the problem: separation – again rearing its ugly head." 7 Seconds asked that we learn to "walk together," honoring our differences while realizing our connections. Too often in contemporary life, people become tools, obstacles, annoyances, and cartoonish caricatures to be used, degraded, or simply ignored entirely. A good punk show is more than strange hairdos, obnoxious music, and circle pits: it's an indescribable feeling, an emotional experience made meaningful because it is shared. More than superficial individualism, punk is a way of fighting not only our own alienation but also our separation from our fellow human beings. While a university may never duplicate such feelings, it offers its own arena in which to build community.

Perhaps a truly punk rock response to the mega-university would be more revolutionary than some of the reforms I have proposed here. My aims are fairly modest because I have witnessed both the resistance to change and the transformative potential of universities firsthand. I believe that punk, despite its many shortcomings, has provided many of us a space to grow into the people we hope to be, rather than becoming just what society expects of us. And I believe that universities can do the same. Inspired by underground punk, we can rekindle the habit of undermining hierarchy, questioning authority, and defying convention. And we must *do it ourselves*.

NOTES

1   Thorstein Veblen, *The Higher Learning In America: A Memorandum On the Conduct of Universities By Business Men* (New York: B.W. Huesbsch, 1918), p. 5.

2   Upton Sinclair, *The Goose Step: A Study of American Education* (Pasadena: Self-published, 1922).

3   C. Wright Mills, *The Sociological Imagination* (Oxford: Oxford University Press, 1959), pp. 50-75.

4   Howard Zinn, "The Uses of Scholarship," in *The Zinn Reader: Writings on Disobedience and Democracy* (Seven Stories Press, 1997), p. 541.

5   Page Smith, *Killing the Spirit: Higher Education in America* (New York: Viking, 1990), pp. 5-7.

6   bell hooks, *Teaching Critical Thinking* (New York: Routledge, 2010), p. 8.

7   Dylan Clark, "The Death and Life of Punk, the Last Subculture," in eds. David Muggleton and Rupert Weinzierl, *The Post-Subcultures Reader*, (New York: Berg, 2003), p. 234.

8   Martin Luther King, Jr., "Transformed Nonconformist," *Strength To Love* (New York: Harper and Row, 1963), pp. 8-15.

ZACK FURNESS AND MILO J. AUKERMAN

MILO WENT TO COLLEGE:

AN INTERVIEW WITH A DESCENDENT

DON'T WORRY ABOUT AN IMAGE
DON'T GOT NO ATTITUDE
I KNOW I WON'T GET LAID
IF I WON'T BE LIKE YOU
DON'T GOT NO BICEPS
DON'T GOT NO PECS
BUT I'LL READ YOU UNDER THE TABLE
WITH MY THICK SPECS!

–DESCENDENTS, "MASS NERDER"

FOR ANY PUNK who came of age in the 1980s or 1990s, Milo Auker-man hardly needs an introduction. As the singer and front man for the influential U.S. punk band, the Descendents, Aukerman's clever wit and catchy vocals helped the band carve out a musical niche that lay some-where between the aggressive hardcore musicianship of Black Flag, the toilet humor of a moody 15-year old Ramones fan, and the pop sensi-bilities of 60s rock bands that long permeated the Southern California beach town culture from which the band emerged. It is the unique inter-pretation of such elements that, in hindsight, has arguably most defined the Descendents legacy as hundreds of bands routinely cite their ang-sty, love-scorned, caffeine-fueled melodies as part of the bedrock upon which the genre of 'pop punk' was built. However, of equal significance is Milo himself, whose unpretentious demeanor and heart-on-the-sleeve lyrical forays became part of a persona that was as equally defined by his notoriously bookish looks. Yet unlike the self-consciously 'outsider' image cultivated by imitators of Elvis Costello and DEVO, one could tell early on that Milo's tussled hair and thick black glasses were not part of 'a look,' rather, it was simply how he looked. It is for this very reason – i.e. the most honest expression of not giving a shit – that Milo almost singlehandedly, if not unintentionally, forged the "geek chic" mold for punk rockers years before Rivers Cuomo (Weezer) and droves of thick-rimmed hipsters learned to wear their inner nerd like a badge of honor. One could argue that too much has been made of Milo's role as the "gangly bespectacled" front man, or for being, as one interviewer boldly put it, the "nerd king of punk rock."[1] Then again, not every punk band documents their singer's scholastic pursuits in the title of their first LP (*Milo Goes to College*) or actively promotes a cartoon image of his likeness – replete with boxy spectacles, a dress shirt and tie – as their enduring visual icon. And most certainly, not every punk vocalist spends his time between records and touring – over a 30-year span, no less – in pursuit of a Microbiology PhD and, eventually, a career as a research scientist.

As a torchbearer for nerdy rockers and a pioneer of the PhD/punk juggling act that few musicians in the scene have attempted to pull off, Dr. Milo J. Aukerman is the godfather of punkademics. Indeed, when I first kicked around the idea for this book some years ago, it was partly as a response to the fact that I was singing in a band, working on my PhD, and would periodically find myself in conversations – typically outside of shows – where small talk about my job inevitably lead to someone making a Milo reference. On one occasion, I remember a guy introducing me to his friend as the "PhD punk" who was "doing the Milo thing." Recently, I got the chance to ask Milo some questions about how his 'thing' is done.[2]

ZACK FURNESS: *As I was reading through some of the interviews you've given over the last 10-15 years, I noticed a trend whereby the interviewer asks you a token question about your PhD, but he or she never wants to get into the nitty-gritty of it all. This always bothered me because science and education are obviously big parts of your life, and they have also defined the persona of the Descendents, to some extent. In addition, I'm a nerd and am largely fascinated by the endeavors of other nerds, especially when the person in question happens to front a legendary punk band. So I guess the best place to start is by asking: what kind of work do you do as a biochemist, and how did you first get interested in the field?*

MILO AUKERMAN: I work on plant genes, trying to identify genes that help plants be more tolerant to drought or nutrient deficiency. On a day-to-day basis, I work a lot with DNA (plant or bacterial), which suits me just fine…that's how I got interested in this area. I was doing an oral report in high school and chose to talk about DNA, and got hooked on the subject. In fact, that was right about when I was getting into punk rock, so the two passions of my life competed with each other from the very beginning!

ZF: *Who are your scientific heroes?*

MA: My scientific heroes are Francis Crick, the co-discoverer of DNA, and Sydney Brenner, the co-discoverer of the genetic code.

ZF: *It seems like you were the first well-known punk to earn a PhD. To your knowledge, were there others who blazed the punkademic trail before you? And were there also punks that gave you shit for it?*

MA: The closest thing to a predecessor I can think of is DEVO, who I liked (not ashamed to admit it…this was before I discovered Black Flag and the Germs). Although they were not academics per se, DEVO were clearly nerds and even mentioned DNA in a song or two, so that was good enough for me! I can't say they inspired me to get an education, but they made it okay to be a nerd and like new wave/punk rock. I never got any shit for the school thing, probably because it seemed like such a natural transition for me…Bill (Stevenson, the drummer) pretty much knew all along I was going to do college, for example.

ZF: *It's obvious that you were very interested in science classes when you were in college, but what were some of the other courses or writers that you really enjoyed?*

MA: I took a poetry class where I formulated some of my most embarrassing and bombastic lyrics ("Impressions," for example). I also minored in music literature, and got exposed to classical and experimental music. I actually failed a course on Wagner; I couldn't relate to him as a human being. Berg, on the other hand, I loved, especially *Wozzeck*. I also remember reading Herbert Marcuse's *Aesthetic Dimension* and relating to the idea that true art by necessity transcends politics.

ZF: *You've written a number of songs about struggling with growing up, and in reading the lyrics to a song like "Schizophrenia," it's pretty clear that you've* *also had some past difficulty reconciling your passions for music and science. What made you finally decide to pursue the latter on a full-time basis (aside from the obvious fact that punk doesn't exactly pay the bills)?*

MA: It was the "long look" – what could I see myself doing in my 50s, 60s, etc. Not very punk, I know. The reality was, I got just as excited about biology as I did about punk rock, but only one of those two you could actually make a career out of, at least in 1982, anyway. What I didn't realize is that the music addiction is hard to shake; I tried hard to leave it behind but always found myself coming back to it.

ZF: *Are you happy with the choices you've made?*

MA: Considering the on-again-off-again nature of my approach to music, I'm surprised it worked out as well as it did. I sometimes regret not having chosen music as a full-time career (after all, the Basemaster General states we should always try to achieve ALL in whatever we do). But I've always thought that as long as I'm doing something creative, it doesn't matter whether it's music or science, or both. So I'm OK with how it all turned out.

ZF: *Most of the punks I've met who were/are grad students or professors are in the humanities or social sciences, though I've also worked outside of a research university for the last four years. Have you met many other punk scientists?*

MA: Greg Graffin (Bad Religion) is a professor of Biology at UCLA. Dexter Holland (Offspring) is another punk scientist, although he never finished his PhD. He got a Masters from USC, and once told me if he ever wanted to go back and get the PhD, he'd just go give the school a huge chunk of money!

ZF: *How do most scientists respond when they find out about your 'other' career, or listen to your band? For example, has anyone ever brandished a Descendents tattoo in front of you at a conference, or have you ever been propositioned to be in an all-scientist punk band?*

MA: When I interviewed for my science job, two funny things happened. First, I had to give a seminar, and afterwards a few employees who were Descendents fans came up to get an autograph, which made me look really good to the hiring committee! Second, I let it slip that I was going to jump on stage with ALL that same night, and so a few members of the hiring committee actually came to the show. It was like "Part Two" of the job interview! So I feel blessed to be associated with some scientists who have an open mind, and like to rock out. Now, playing with scientists in a band is another matter. The temptation would be to write a magnum opus to DNA, and that is something to be avoided…I mean there's nerd, and then there's SUPERnerd, and I can't go there.

ZF: *Have you ever wanted to be a professor?*

MA: That's what I went to grad school for, but I found myself in the position to take an industry job, and I went for it. It was totally the right decision for me, and now academia doesn't sound so appealing. I have no tenure battles, no grants, no teaching to do, only research. In exchange, a loss of some autonomy, but a fair trade in my estimation.

ZF: *I've met a lot of really smart people in the punk scene throughout the last 15 years and, on the whole, I tend to think of punks as being more well read and politically aware than their peers, particularly when it comes to young people. At the same, punk hasn't exactly been considered an "intellectual" affair throughout its history, and there are numerous examples of punk bands that take a certain degree of pride in being anti-intellectual. Have you noticed any changes over the years? Has punk become nerdier?*

MA: Lyrically, the Descendents are probably more anti-intellectual than a lot of other bands; I mean we have multiple songs about farting. Then there's the Germs, who were one of the more intellectual bands lyrics-wise, but this intelligence was overshadowed by Darby's excesses. It does seem like lyric matter has become more high-minded of late, especially the political-leaning bands. But as for nerdiness, I think it's always been a part of punk, not from the cerebral point of view, but more viscerally. When I celebrate the nerd in punk rock, it's as much for the spastic, outcast nature of a nerd as it is for the intellectual connotations. There's a danger of thinking too much, when what we really need is to spazz out.

ZF: *While the general public isn't all that conversant on the subject of plant biochemistry, there is an increasing level of controversy (particularly outside the U.S.) regarding the implications of bioengineering crops…I'm thinking of debates over the development and use of GMO crops, and the patenting of particular forms of plant life. Does your specific work on plant genetics force you to stake out positions on these issues, or ones like them? Is there a particular set of ethics or politics that inform your research?*

MA: I don't work directly on a crop plant, but a weed called Arabidopsis. I view my research as more basic in nature, i.e. acquiring knowledge about the organism. Nonetheless, there is an applied angle to everything I do, and this definitely leaves me open to criticism from anti-GMO people. As you implied, GMO plants are currently accepted by a good portion of the American public; does this mean they're OK? All I can say is that breeders have been creating "recombinant plants" for many decades without controversy, using traditional genetics; we are not doing anything radically different from that. And there are definitely checks and balances against creating so-called "monster" plants; the USDA makes sure of that. My feeling is, technological advances in agriculture will be essential in order to boost crop production enough to feed an ever-growing world. No risk means no boost in production and more starving people, and that is a much worse fate.

ZF: *Can biochemistry help us to achieve ALL?*

MA: MUGMUGMUG…of course! Having said that, I'm a firm believer in moderation. Do what you need to get that edge, but don't go over the edge. Too much, and you're only achieving ALL in your head, but not in reality.

ZF: *I assume that the Descendents and Bad Religion have shared the stage more than a few times, and I'm curious about your encounters with fellow punkademic, Greg Graffin. Have the two of you had the opportunity to properly geek out together? Because I have an image in my head of the two of you frenetically discussing the nuances of animal & plant biology on a tattered couch in the backstage of a shitty club, while surrounded by tattooed drunk punks who are either confused, intrigued, or both. Has this scene ever played itself out?*

MA: It's odd, but I don't think I've ever met Greg. He's a great singer and lyricist (I loved *Suffer*), but actually we inhabit two separate biological spheres, so I don't know if we'd be able to geek out too much. I would be interested in hearing how he handled post-PhD life in academia, i.e. whether it met his expectations (I can say for me, it didn't).

ZF: *Can you name the chemical composition of caffeine off the top of your head?*

MA: I remember making a point of knowing this when I was an undergrad. One night, after too many bonus cups [of coffee] mixed with beers,

I tried to draw out the chemical reaction of caffeine with ethanol (poor man's speedball?)…I think I ended up with putrescine as an end product. Ah, college days.

ZF: *If punk could be isolated as a chemical compound, what would it look like?*

MA: My rendition of the ultimate punk protein is below; I call it the FTW protein. The "zinc finger" is an actual structure found in certain regulatory proteins, and there also exists a related protein structure called a "zinc knuckle." The FTW protein consists of four zinc knuckles and one zinc finger, in a tandem array. The placement of the zinc finger in the middle position is crucial for its function…and, of course, its function is self-explanatory.

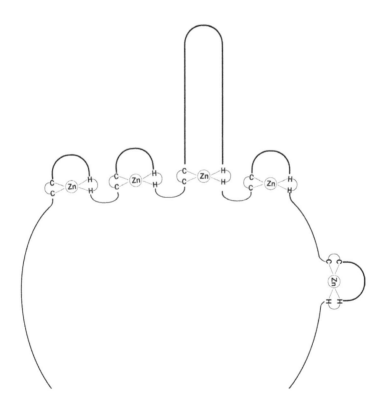

NOTES

1   Rick Reger, "Descendents Still Playing By Own Rules," *Chicago Tribune*, December 2, 1996; Mike Powsner, "Milo Aukerman: The Nerd King of Punk Rock," *Yo Beat* #8 (Summer, 1998). Online at http://www.yobeat. com/aukerman.htm.

2   Thanks to Andy Cornell for contributing ideas for questions.

RYAN MOORE

ON BECOMING A PUNK
ROCK SOCIOLOGIST

I WAS BORN in Long Beach, CA and raised in the adjacent city of San Pedro, graduating from San Pedro High School in 1988. I'd like to be able to tell you all about how I was influenced by our hometown heroes, the Minutemen, or Black Flag, or the Descendents, or any of the other hardcore bands that emerged from the nearby cities of Los Angeles' South Bay at this time. I can imagine a really good story about how the radical politics and do-it-yourself ethic of the local hardcore scene would inspire me to become the Marxist sociologist I am today. However, that story would be a lie, because the truth is that my paths to both punk rock and radical sociology were never that direct or linear. And, I'm just not that cool.

In high school I was a devout partisan of thrash metal bands like Slayer, Metallica, Anthrax and a couple dozen others with a more limited following. By the second half of the 1980s the California hardcore scene had fizzled out. There was this one punk dude who had "Minor Threat" written on the jacket he wore to school every day, but I didn't know anything about them because the only people I hung out with were other longhairs and stoners. Still, there was a lot of punk influence in thrash metal, which was less about devils and dragons and more about indicting real world authorities, creating a local scene with indie record labels, and maintaining a veneer of authenticity that mocked the posturing and pomposity usually associated with heavy metal

My headbanging roots notwithstanding, I almost voted for George Bush in the first election I was old enough to vote in, until my mother talked me out of it at the last minute. Like many other metal heads, I was personally rebellious but my half-baked political views amounted to nothing more than simple, knee-jerk libertarianism. I was entranced by power, enthralled by violence, and envious of wealth, and I also hated people I thought were weak or dependent, so it probably isn't surprising that I almost voted for Bush.

I had begun college during that fall of 1988, as my parents were eager for me to leave my troublemaking metal friends behind and move north to attend San Jose State University. It wasn't long before I found myself in classes taught by veterans of the New Left. One of them was Professor Douglas Dowd, who had been part of the *Monthly Review* editorial team with Paul Baran and Paul Sweezy and cofounded the National Mobilization to End the War in Vietnam. Dowd would typically begin his classes in Microeconomics with some thoughts about Marx or Ricardo before launching into a series of tirades that indiscriminately covered everything from the wastefulness of capitalism to the insanity of war and nationalism to the cruelty of child labor. This 70-plus year-old man would yell and point and curse and then stop suddenly, look out the window, and silently shake his head while muttering something about the insanity of our world. Many of the students in class were horrified and stopped attending after the first two weeks, but I was captivated. One day Dowd recited the lyrics to John Lennon's "Imagine" and asked the class if that sounded like the kind of world any of us would want to live in, and I was the only student to raise my hand. "Then you're a God-damn Communist!" he shouted at me.

O.K., so I guess I'm a Communist now. This was admittedly a major political about-face, but to this day I think my metal roots and cultural rebelliousness prepared me to embrace this stigmatized, marginalized political identity. I had grown up in a working-class seaport with a vague sense that the world wasn't right, and now I was engrossed in my education to try and understand why. I was listening to the Bay Area's progressive radio station KPFA and reading everything I could get my hands on, especially Howard Zinn's *A People's History of the United States*. My identity and style morphed from headbanger to something like a retro countercultural radical as I became absorbed in Todd Gitlin's *The Sixties: Years of Hope, Days of Rage* and anything else I could read or watch about the Sixites, Students for a Democratic Society, and the counterculture.

I enrolled in a social theory class the following semester, and it was there that I read Marx for the first time and met my friend Mike Roberts, who today is also a Sociology professor at San Diego State. Mike and I started a left campus organization and worked on publishing a newspaper that was unfortunately sabotaged by some other students just before it was about to be printed. Our social theory professor, Talmadge Wright, had also started a group called the Student Homeless Alliance in which we became involved. This was late 1990, and the United States was gearing up for our first war with Iraq, so Mike and I began working with other campus activists to create an anti-war coalition and organize an anti-war demonstration. I experienced my first 15 seconds of fame when my speech commencing the demonstration was sound-bitten for the local TV news.

At this time I knew a lot of people who were into punk rock, but my tastes hadn't progressed that far yet. Some of my friends regularly made trips up to Berkeley to go to the Gilman Street club, but I never went. They played Dag Nasty, Green Day, and Big Drill Car for me but I absolutely hated all that melody. I thought it was cool that Bad Religion could reference Noam Chomsky and the like, but to this day their singer's voice drives me crazy. One of my roommates was really into Fugazi, and although they've since become one of my favorite bands they just didn't compute to me at that time. What my metal years had prepared me for was grunge and the whole Sub Pop/Seattle scene, so of course I took to Mudhoney and Soundgarden almost instantly. And then more locally there was Primus, Mr. Bungle, Psychefunkapus, the Limbomaniacs, and a bunch of other bands that formed a metal-funk-punk scene in the Bay Area.

By now my career goals had changed such that I wanted to go to graduate school and hopefully grow up to be a tenured radical like my professors. UC Santa Cruz was known to have a lot of Marxist and radical faculty members, especially in the Sociology department, and so I transferred there in the fall of 1991. I did an internship with *Capitalism, Nature, Socialism*, the journal of Marxist ecology founded by James O'Connor, and worked with the Bay Area activist Frank Bardacke on a project about farm workers. Other than that, however, there were a lot of people who talked radical politics at UC Santa Cruz but there wasn't a lot of action – a possible result of the campus's relatively isolated location in the mountains of central California. I joked with friends: if a bunch of students demonstrate in the forest and there is no TV crew there to film them, do they make a sound? My only brush with revolution was accidentally getting hit in the side of the head with some sort of firecracker on the night of the Rodney King riots as the Santa Cruz students marched into town and trashed the local police department headquarters.

Nirvana's *Nevermind* came out during my first semester at Santa Cruz. I remember that for weeks I would walk around the dorms and count how many rooms were blaring "Smells Like Teen Spirit" or some other song from the album. I knew it was a really big deal when the dreadlocked hippie kids who spent all day playing hacky sack and, as far

I knew, listened to nothing but reggae and the Grateful Dead were suddenly talking about how much they wanted to see Nirvana when they came to San Francisco. The next two years or so would represent the pinnacle of the alternative rock/Lollapalooza era. Then the questions began: Did Nirvana sell out? Is alternative the new mainstream? Did I really just see a runway model wearing Doc Marten's? Does anyone know anyone who likes to be called "Generation X"? Did that douchebag on the TV really just tell me that the new Subaru Impreza is just like punk rock?

At Santa Cruz I took a great class in the history of U.S. imperialism in Central America, read the Frankfurt School for the first time, and wrote research papers about the Black Panthers, American foreign policy, and the Wobblies. But by this time I had also been introduced to cultural studies, both in my courses on mass media and popular culture and in my conversations with activists who were influenced by identity politics and postmodernism. My relationship to cultural studies, as I discuss in more detail below, has always been deeply ambivalent. In the context of all these questions about alternative culture and Generation X, I could see that the issues raised by cultural studies about youth subcultures, hegemony, and resistance were still very pertinent and could not be ignored. I was especially taken with Lawrence Grossberg's *We Gotta Get Outta This Place*, which as any reader of the book knows, is loaded with pomo jargon but still raises what I thought were prescient questions about postmodern society, the ironic cynicism of youth culture, and the role that these phenomena had somehow played in maintaining the hegemony of conservatism.

I wrote a senior thesis under the direction of Professor Herman Gray about the media coverage of the movement against the Gulf War and graduated from UC Santa Cruz in the spring of 1993. I was on my way to graduate school and chose to enroll in the Sociology program at UC San Diego because it advertised itself as having a strong emphasis in culture, which had quickly become my main field of interest. My first two years of graduate school were a rude awakening. I had chosen to study sociology because as an undergraduate it seemed so interdisciplinary and open-ended, like it was the best of all possible homes for my combination of interests in critical theory, radical politics, social history, and cultural studies. But as a graduate student I quickly discovered that professional sociology was a different animal altogether.

In time I learned that the Sociology department at UC San Diego had indeed specialized in culture at one point in its history, but in recent years there had been a major shift toward historical-comparative sociology, and those faculty always seemed to be repeating the mantra that they were trying to make the program more "professional," "competitive," and "rigorous." Yuk. Moreover, what the department did offer in terms of culture was mainly rooted in the apolitical traditions of microsociology like symbolic interactionism and ethnomethodology. Double yuk. Fortunately, critical theory and cultural studies had made strong inroads in UCSD's departments of communication and literature, and in ethnic studies I discovered Professor George Lipsitz, who would serve as a de facto mentor in my study of neo-Marxist theories of culture.

San Diego was home to a bustling alternative music scene centered at a club called the Casbah, and I began going to shows there on a regular basis. After the success of Nirvana and other grunge bands, the major labels had gone scouting for new alternative rock acts to sign, and San Diego was one of a number of cities that was pegged as a potential "next Seattle." Seven San Diego bands had signed with major labels during this time, and everyone from *Rolling Stone* to *Details* to the *E! Television Network* had done feature stories about the local scene. Beyond the hype, I discovered that there was indeed an exciting and musically diverse scene, and I instantly became a fan of the spastic noise of Trumans Water, Drive Like Jehu, and Heavy Vegetable, the retro punk of Rocket From the Crypt, and the cyborg prog rock of Three Mile Pilot.

I was beginning to envision a dissertation project that brought together the cultural studies focus on music and subcultures with the sociological methods of ethnography and the neo-Marxist inquiry into the place of culture in post-Fordist capitalism. How all those pieces of the puzzle actually fit together would be something I would have to figure out along the way. Unfortunately, most of my sociology professors were vocally unsupportive of this idea. I had impressed many of them with my self-motivated interest in social theory, but for them music was a frivolous concern without any real sociological import. When I told the professor in my field methods seminar what I planned to do, he replied with a snarky tone, "It sounds like you're just going to hang out with your friends." Another one begged me to do something else – anything else, really – because I was "too close" to my project, and he eventually removed himself from my committee when I refused.

In actuality, I didn't have any friends inside the scene, and rather than being "too close" I constantly felt like an outsider because not only was I not a musician, I was this geeky grad student who had all these esoteric theoretical and political questions about music and the scene. Lots of people told me that my project sounded like "fun," and it was fun to go shows and hear live music in what I thought was a great scene, but it was nerve-wracking as hell to approach these people in a club and awkwardly ask them if we could arrange an interview. Let's just say I found myself drinking a lot of "liquid courage" during those years.

Getting into the local scene enhanced my political consciousness, not because the bands themselves were concerned with political issues (most of them weren't), but because I could see how they had formed a community based on creative work and participation. It wasn't a dogmatic scene of the sort advocated in the pages of *Maximumrocknroll*, and therefore a great variety of musical styles and influences could be thrown together without apology. And so I began to see the form of democratic cultural production as more significant than the content of any particular political protest or "message." This understanding of "punk" as a method of production rather than a specific style or sound opened up whole vistas of possibility and informed my belated musical education. Maybe I can explain it this way: Drive Like Jehu led me back to Fugazi and then even further back to Wire and then forward to the Minutemen and Hüsker Dü and then back again to the Gang of Four and Television. See, I told you my path to punk was ass-backwards.

While the Casbah and other local nightclubs were becoming a second home for me, I was still suffering from quite a bit of intellectual homelessness on campus. I was getting a lot more out of the graduate courses I was taking in other departments, so I stopped enrolling in sociology seminars after completing my minimum amount of required coursework and came very close to dropping out of the program. I took a position as a teaching assistant in an interdisciplinary freshman-level writing course, where the levels of overwork were legendary. Before long I had become heavily involved with the effort to unionize the academic student employees at the University of California and would be elected to serve on the strike committee as we planned a number of strategies for work stoppage. This took me further out of the bounds of the Sociology department, as my social circle was now mainly composed of humanities students who were involved with me in organizing the T.A. union. Intellectually, however, I never embraced the kind of cultural studies that is practiced in the humanities, where meaning is mainly located in the "text" and acts of resistance are conceived as symbolic matters of reading and style. I was still fundamentally concerned with social process, and the Marxist in me still sought to link culture back to social structure. My experiences in the music scene redoubled these convictions: resistance was a matter of how people organized their community and engaged in creative work, not what people wore, how they cut their hair, or what they sang about in their lyrics.

My intellectual homelessness was glaringly evident and became a huge liability when I went on the job market for the first time in the fall of 1999. It seems that what transpired in my graduate program was something like a microcosm of what was happening in American sociology in general. There has been a great expansion of interest and research in culture among American sociologists since the 1980s, but these cultural sociologists have taken great pains to distinguish and insulate themselves from the broader field of cultural studies. The studies of popular culture and media, much less popular music, are very few and far between. American cultural sociology is significantly more conventional, eager to be accepted within the mainstream of the discipline, and rarely engaged with questions of power and resistance. Don't take my word for it, listen to what one of the leading proponents has to say in its favor: "American cultural sociology is conservative rather than revolutionary in its academic program, unlike the British cultural studies model which has attempted to transgress disciplinary boundaries and create a completely new academic and discursive field."[1]

No matter what kind of theoretical and methodological spin I try to put on it, my work reeks of cultural studies simply because it is has the word punk attached to it. I sent out over 100 job applications during my first 3 years on the market without landing a single on-campus interview. I nearly gave up on the idea of an academic career on several occasions, but a lack of other marketable skills and job experience made me feel trapped, and I still had a deep intellectual passion, not necessarily for sociology but for understanding social processes and contributing to social change. Fortunately I was able to hang on as an adjunct instructor of sociology at UC San Diego, as my courses on popular culture and youth attracted very high student enrollments; I taught a total of nearly 1,000 students during my final year there in 2001-02.

As my contract with UC San Diego and a long-term romantic relationship both came to an end at virtually the same time, I found myself living with my mother and collecting unemployment in late 2002. I was ready to give up on academia once and for all when I miraculously got a temporary position at the University of Kansas that began in the Spring 2003 semester and lasted through the 2003-04 school year. I sent out another heap of job applications but still couldn't land a satisfactory tenure-track position, so I accepted another temporary appointment at Colgate University for 2004-05.

In 2005 I finally landed a tenure-track position at Florida Atlantic University. It's not a prestigious school by any means, but it's a good place for a punk like me: lots of older, "non-traditional" and working-class students, many of whom have roots in the Caribbean. Securing a permanent academic home has afforded me the time to finally finish turning my dissertation into a book titled *Sells Like Teen Spirit: Music, Youth Culture, and Social Crisis* which was published by New York University Press in 2009. Meanwhile, American sociology continues to aspire to the status of a science along the lines of economics and political science while attempting to avoid the stigma of the humanities conferred by cultural studies, and so there is no reason to expect that the study of punk or any other form of music will be moving into the center of the discipline any time soon. But somehow this feels like the appropriate place for a punk rock sociologist: screaming from the margins, denouncing the mainstream, and maybe – just maybe – developing the new ideas that are destined to shake up the establishment.

NOTES

1   Phillip Smith, *The New American Cultural Sociology* (Cambridge: Cambridge University Press, 1998), p. 9.

FINDING BALANCE IN THE ACADEMY

FINISHING MY PHD in 2004 took me to Brooklyn College/CUNY where I took what they call a Substitute Line, which is a full time position, but without the institutional security of a tenure-track job. You are basically hired on a semester-by-semester basis. Your standing is probationary. I did not transition into professor life very well. Living a few blocks from campus, I remained (and still do) a hardcore punk rock skateboarder, but without any strategic room for adaptability. I was still suffering demoralization from having a social movement I helped start in Southern New Mexico infiltrated and destroyed.[1] I was never really accepted by the majority of faculty as legitimate or serious – I was too resistant to accept university culture. However, my classes were outstanding at Brooklyn College, which has left me a legacy there. I was also active in the union where I worked with students doing punk rock street theatre protesting contract disputes.

After leaving Brooklyn College as a result of being pushed out, I went to D'Youville College in Buffalo, New York where I learned to find balance and develop the ability to focus, intensely, on developing my critical pedagogy through becoming a better writer/researcher/scholar and critical educator.[2] For me, this has included, among other things, learning to identify where power resides, understanding how it operates, and then devising methods of challenging if for a more democratic, less-oppressive future through the development of a community of activist scholars. In short, revitalizing my social movement background in the context of academia. Enduring the cold winters in Buffalo, NY in a small studio apartment, in an old downtown building, with no car, and living on a low wage working at a very humble institution with very little money, taught me humility. Outside of Buffalo, very few academics have ever even heard of D'youville College. That does not necessarily make one feel special or important in the world of academia. Raised in the competitive fervor of U.S. dominant society, it is most difficult not to succumb to its pressures. That is, while punk rock strives to reject and live outside of dominant society, it is difficult not to be influenced by its hierarchical values of prestige. At the same time, however, I know that it is good for critical pedagogy to have critical pedagogues at well-respected universities. If leading critical intellectuals did not hold important positions at the most well-respected institutions, it would be much easier to discredit the Left.

Despite these contradictory motivations, my epistemological and ontological punk rock desire to stay out of reach of cooptation has led me to become a very effective, and very critical classroom teacher and activist scholar. When I am teaching or observing student teachers I no longer wear my punk uniform; I traded it in for a more intense and *critical* pedagogy and content. This has made me more acceptable, on an institutional level, and more effective at the student level. By no means do I intend this to be taken as a prescription. It is working for me, a white male from working class southern Ohio, but that does not mean it is the answer for others. It was not the answer for me five years ago and it may not be the answer for me five or ten years down the road. Currently, I am working at West Chester University as an Assistant Professor and am making great personal gains in honing more practice and skill. To make these determinations and have this consciousness, however, I must stay open to the late critical pedagogue Joe L. Kincheloe's insight that:

> "In their search for ways to produce democratic and evocative knowledges, critical constructivists become detectives of new ways of seeing and constructing the world."[3]

NOTES

1   See Curry Malott, *Policy and Research in Education: A Critical Pedagogy for Educational Leadership* (New York: Peter Lang, 2010).

2   Curry Malott, "Schooling in an Era of Corporate Dominance: Marxism Against Burning Tires," *Journal for Critical Education Policy Studies,* Vol. 4, No.1 (2006).

3   Joe Kincheloe, *Critical Constructivism Primer*, (New York: Peter Lang, 2005), p. 4.

WALEED RASHIDI

PUNK ROCK DOCS:
A QUALITATIVE STUDY[1]

"WOULD YOU STOP WORRYING ABOUT THE PUNKS?
THEY'RE JUST A BUNCH OF KIDS WITH GROWING
PAINS. THEY'LL PROBABLY BE DOCTORS AND LAWYERS
SOMEDAY."

- FROM THE TELEVISION PROGRAM CHIPS

OVERVIEW

THIS RESEARCH INVESTIGATES a group of punk rock musicians with
doctoral-level education via a series of in-depth interviews. The study
aims to develop a stronger understanding of punk rock musicians' motivations, justifications, philosophies and conclusions regarding the
way they balance a punk rock lifestyle and persona with careers in academic and/or highly intellectual professions (e.g. medical, legal, scientific). Though such highly educated punk musicians are a minor subset
of the punk genre's total population, this segment contradicts many
of the negative perceptions about punk rock as well as the messages
relayed by mainstream media and culture that have often stereotyped
punk rockers as uneducated, antisocial, delinquent, or violent.[2] Such
balancing acts and contradictions serve as the study's point of entry.

EXCLUSIONARY/INCLUSIONARY
FACTORS

The primary criteria for the study's participants include being musicians in the punk rock music scene and having been students in a doctoral

program. Musicians may be self-described as punk rock, or may hail from an ancillary scene that is related to punk rock (e.g., emo, hardcore). The selected participants must have performed in a touring band in the American punk scene for a minimum of two years and have at least one domestically distributed, commercially-available album recording to their credit. These minimum requirements formed a participant population that had strong insight into the commercial operations and background of the U.S. punk rock scene. Participants must also have doctoral degrees, though an experienced punk rock musician whose status is A.B.D. (all but dissertation) also qualified as a participant for this study.

RESULTS

A number of in-depth interviews were conducted in the winter and spring of 2008. The responses from the participant population were transcribed and analyzed. Each response was then parsed into sections that were subsequently coded into categories that included: *Upbringing, Current Occupation, Education, Punk Ideology/Philosophy, Recurring Words, Time Management, Negotiation of Identity, Personality,* and *Intellectualism in Punk Rock.* Coded responses in each category were then further subcategorized into 'aspects' that are meant to offer more exacting detail about what constitutes the broader categories themselves. Interview excerpts are presented here for a more transparent understanding of the data that led to the formulation of each category.

The first category, *Upbringing,* includes the aspects *parents' education, motivation, socio-economic status,* and *punk attraction.* In regard to *parents' education,* most participants hailed from a background that included at least one parent with an advanced degree and had been (or currently is) employed in a highly regarded profession, such as university professor, attorney, and engineer. One participant detailed his parents' background, "Both of my parents were college professors. My mom taught at Michigan State University and my dad taught at University of Michigan. Both taught sociology and both were PhDs." Another participant, a psychologist who specializes in adolescents, also noted his parents' educational credentials, including the fact that he and his mother have similar educational backgrounds: "My mom has her master's degree in child psychology, ironically enough, and my dad has his doctorate in chemical engineering."

In the next aspect, *motivation,* it was found that participants were either self-motivated to pursue higher education and advanced degrees, or that they were encouraged by parents or other authority figures. With respect to self-motivation, one participant, who had entered a history graduate program stated, "So when I went back to [graduate school], you know, I was like, 'Well, I had done the English thing, I had done the philosophy thing, I don't know nearly enough about history.' And in part it was because I started reading history on my own shortly after I graduated, when I moved to San Francisco with the band." Two participants said that career paths and educational pursuits were established at a very young age. One stated, "I always had aspirations to do something professional. I was going to become a doctor since I was seven years old. That's kind of been my whole push." Another provided a similar answer, even in reference to the timeframe, "I always knew I wanted to be a lawyer, like from the time I was five or six. I just always knew. It just, my brain was wired that way. You know, a lot of kids, they want to be this, they want to be that, but I pretty much knew." Other responses suggest the role of outside influences in participants' decisions to pursue professions that required advanced degrees. One notes, "It was always expected that I would go to college, even though I started [music] when I was 15." Another participant said, "In the area that I was raised, college was like 13th grade. It's just [...] what you did." Furthermore, one participant had not actually thought about completing his undergraduate education until motivated by a guidance counselor:

> I was walking through the halls of community college, and I was a straight 'A' student there. And the guidance counselor, who I didn't really know, sort of saw me in the hall and he said, 'Hey, you know, what are you going to do when you're done this spring?' And I hadn't given it any thought, so I talked to him a little bit about it just informally in the hall, and he said, 'Well, you know, these colleges have some great scholarship programs.'

In discussing the *socio-economic status* aspect of the participants' upbringings, almost all had stated that they were from middle-to-upper class households. Class was mentioned in a few interviews, including one participant, who stated, "You know [...] I went to high school in an upper middle-class suburban community. You know, one of those high schools that's allegedly, you know, one of the top few in the state, blah blah blah." Another participant said, "And I don't come from a very wealthy family at all, you know, probably very solidly middle-class family." Other ways of determining socio-economic status could be ascertained from the occupations of the respondents' parents, including a particularly revealing statement from this participant, "This is weird because this is going to sound like, and I don't mean this in, like, a bragging way, but just because I know you're looking for these common denominators or not in background – they were very high up, especially my father, in state government."

Punk attraction is also a particularly noteworthy aspect to the participants' upbringing, in that many were attracted to punk rock music and the punk lifestyle at an early age – mostly before they enrolled in college – and some found that it helped shape their decision-making at later junctures in life. As adolescents, some noted that alienation was cause for their gravitation towards the punk aesthetic. One participant first discovered punk rock around the ages of 15-16, using a metaphor to explain his attraction, "Well, I was alienated. And, you know, it was like all of a sudden, it was like I was wandering around in another country where I didn't speak the language, and then I met somebody who spoke my language. And fell in love." Such alienation, he continues, stems from the lack of interest in athletics, a particularly powerful determinant in adolescent male social circles:

> If you're a man in this society, and you suck at sports [...] ages 7 to 14 are [a] pretty outright hostile [...] period in which to live...Your 'malehood,' if there's such a word, is defined essentially by, you know, if not excellence in sports, at least competence. Sort of not having that was a pretty terrifying experience for me...I think that's an extreme experience with alienation. And then like, to learn about politics and the, you know, Reagan government and the, you know, the Cold War and McCarthyism and all that shit. In the town I lived in, I was just like, 'God. This place is a nightmare'...So, I was pissed and alienated and like, punk just spoke to it so directly and in such a visceral way. My first show was *Reagan Youth* and, you know, it was exactly about everything I was pissed about.

Others echoed such sentiment, particularly in the formation of an identity:

> I was a teenager and wanted to create an identity, and the punk scene was in its infancy here in L.A., so it was a very exciting time to be an L.A. punk...as a teenager, you don't really understand what you're doing. You just feel good, when you feel like you're a part of something. It's a social

connection, it's something, and if that social group can be a
unique group, you can tell you're different from others. That
gave me even greater satisfaction, knowing that it was something unique. And by unique, I realize that we didn't invent
anything. But you sure feel unique when you're a minority
in and amongst the kind of culture that it was back then.

Lastly, responses also included the fact that punk rock was decidedly
easier to play than other rock music derivations – particularly during
the time period of many of the participants' introduction to the genre,
and that such simplistic empowerment was crucial in the development
of their musical careers. According to one participant, "Punk was the
antithesis of progressive rock. You didn't have to be classically trained to
play punk. And I think that was very attractive, that we could actually be
in the band." Another stated, "It was like, you listen to the *Ramones'* first
record, like 'Beat On The Brat' […] and even as an 11- or 12-year-old,
you're listening to this, going, […] 'Wow, I could do that too. That seems
like something I could do.'"

The second category, *Current Occupation,* yielded the aspects *authority, self-employment/autonomy, punk-professional interrelations,* and *punk
values in occupation.* The first aspect, *authority,* suggested that nearly all
of the participants were employed in influential positions within their
respective fields, whether over others in their occupation, or in the case
of professors, an influence in the classroom with students and colleagues.
One participant, who holds a rank in the U.K. academic system equivalent to a U.S. Assistant Professor, is also charged with running his own
academic research group, and is thus an authority on two levels:

So, yeah, my basic job is to write grants, get money and
then hire people. And right now I've got about eight people
working for me. So I've got three post-doctoral fellows, a
couple Ph.D. students and an M.Sc. student, a master's
student, and a technician and visiting scientists, so that's
kind of […] how it works…mainly doing research and then
you do some teaching.

Another participant, a physician, is deputized with overseeing his immediate hospital staff as well as other aspects of emergency care, "I'm
actually not only an emergency physician there, but I'm also the EMS
medical director, so I'm in charge of the medical direction for the emergency medical systems, which includes the paramedics and pre-hospital

care that goes out to the patients. It's four different providers out there picking up the patients."

Some participants found their *autonomous* occupational positions to be not only conducive to their schedules – especially for those who are currently performing and touring musicians – but also a reflection of their punk rock philosophy, i.e. being independent from outside constraints. In regard to a prevailing do-it-yourself culture at his current occupation, one participant noted, "I think it was easy for me to embrace this kind of research lifestyle, because of the fact that I always felt like, when we were doing our music, that we had to put in all this effort to make it happen. We had to organize our T-shirts, we had to organize our [merchandise] and our music, and write the songs, and you wore a lot of different hats. And I feel like that same sort of spirit is also in my research career, so I think that aspect of it does translate over." Another participant, a psychologist with his own private practice, stated that his choice for *self-employment* was, in itself, punk rock, "Yeah, being self-employed is very punk, and it's something that I always kind of fantasized about when I was younger."

Within their present occupations, there was a distinct divide between whether the participants accepted an infusion of their pre-established *punk values and/or background* into their professional settings, or whether they purposefully tried to sever these ties once they entered their respective professions. Some had elected to keep aspects of their musical careers out of the workplace, as evidenced by this participant's response, "You know, in a lot of ways, I keep my band life very separate from my [professional] career life, which is just a boundary that I'm comfortable with." Another participant, who is employed as a science lecturer at a university, added, "No, I'm actually very careful not to infuse values into science. It's really important. And it's not a soapbox up there." To the contrary, other participants spoke of how their punk background and history had merged with their professional pursuits, including another university science professor, "I kind of got that training, that life training, if you will, from being in these sorts of bands, you know, to think creatively, to solve problems that are kind of outside the box sort of thinking, if you will [...]"

Another aspect, *punk values in occupation,* emerged after participants acknowledged that their interpretation of the punk value system had indeed been incorporated within their professional careers. One of these values includes the idea of bucking stereotypes, as detailed by this participant:

> It's a matter of you standing for...I mean, hell, I'm a 6-foot-5 black guy with dreadlocks who's a physician. People have

to make assumptions when they see you. I'm like bucking
their assumptions right there. When I walk right into the
room, it's like, 'You don't look like a doctor.' My first words
out of my mouth are, 'What does a doctor look like?' I
mean, right there, it's affronting their whole belief system
and showing them that there's another way to be.

Another participant, an adolescent psychologist, spoke of a similar
way in which punk values affect his work, "It informs my career in that
I want to challenge, especially with boys…I want to offer an alternative
construction of masculinity."

The third category presented, *Education,* includes the aspects *school
selection* and *success compulsion.* In regard to *school selection,* many sought
undergraduate and graduate programs that were fitting for their majors
and eventual career goals, while others just had a generally positive overall feeling about the school. Most notably, some participants used proximity to punk scenes and bandmates as factors in choosing schools and
respective programs. One participant noted, "I was like, 'fuck it, I'll go to
U of I.' My best friend was going there, you know, I was super involved
[at] that point in the [city, state] punk rock scene." Another stated, "I
ultimately went to […] Washington University at St. Louis, which is
also very strong in biology and biomedical sciences, too. Part of my decision again there, was proximity to Lafayette. Obviously St. Louis is only
about a four or five hour drive from Lafayette, versus being on the West
Coast. But I could still kind of do music a bit, as much as I could with
the guys and that sort of thing." One participant, however, selected his
graduate program due to the fact that his school had rebelled against
another program with which it was once associated, "It also had a very
kind of 'punk' tradition that I found appealing."

The second aspect of the *Education* category is *success compulsion.* This
refers to the way participants felt challenged or compelled to succeed in
both their musical and academic endeavors. One participant explained,
"It's one of those things where you think of a manifest destiny, where
you go, 'Hey, I'm thinking of this, I want to do this. I am going to do it.'
It's like that book *The Secret,* or whatever. It is just a matter of something
I wanted to do. And it's what always interested me. And I attained that
goal." Some participants noted the influence of other punk rockers that
attained doctorates, even referencing them by name during the course
of our interviews. For example, the participant quoted above also stated,
"When I heard about the guy from [punk band name] or when you hear
about [other punk rocker with doctorate], and you go, 'Those are the

guys that I idolize and they're doing something,' it's like, 'Whoa, what the hell? I could do that too.' That's why I had a kinship with this stuff."

Another category that had surfaced is *Punk Ideology/Philosophy*. This is a core category due to the fact that it is considered to be very personal, highly subjective and interpretive, given that punk rock itself does not have clearly demarcated boundaries of what it is considered 'acceptable' for the genre, either musically or philosophically. However, after interviewing the participants, I discovered that nearly all responses could be categorized and coded into one of three aspects: *questioning, ethical foundations,* and *community.* *Questioning* was mentioned in the context of challenging the status quo and/or being intellectually provocative. Some of the viewpoints shared around *questioning* included one from this participant:

> The whole punk rock thing is questioning authority…you're told one thing, and you're like, 'What the hell, that doesn't make any sense.' And you investigate and you go, 'Really. It doesn't make any sense!' And that's something that I think is a punk rock sentiment…you question things that are actually told to you…And that, in my opinion, might be one of the reasons why you find a lot of academics that come out of punk rock because of a questioning attitude…and thirst to gain more knowledge about a topic.

Another participant said, "Being punk, I think, means always questioning and never settling. Always moving and always progressing. It means challenging the status quo, whether it's in the world at large or within the punk scene." This participant offered his views on *questioning* as it relates to both his punk rock philosophy and his academic study of philosophy, "I like to think at some level, the notion of questioning the world around me, and accepting the fact that you don't have to take things as they're given to you, you don't have to accept the standard order of things, I think that's partially what I was looking for in philosophy, too." Furthermore, one participant was able to relay the idea of *questioning* as a punk rock philosophy within his occupation as a scientist/academic: "It basically means that you're provocative, but not in a violent way. You make people ask questions. You make them wonder… The only way to search, the only way science really works is if you can completely dismantle the framework of science by asking the questions that haven't been asked before. And the only way you can do that is by provoking people who are content with the way that this framework is already erected."

Other punk rock musicians described an *ethical foundation* on which they based their punk philosophy, which was partly tied to ethical business practices. One participant noted, "I think it has a lot to do with how you conduct your business in terms of touring and being fair to other bands, and uh, being fair all around." Another participant stated, "I definitely define it as a community and an ethic and an approach, [but] an approach to what is still, essentially, in some ways, a business. As opposed to a certain music scene." In addition to these responses, some participants also expressed resistance towards mass marketing of the punk sound and likeness. The *ethical foundation* of punk rock also extended into aspects of *community* and the social organization of punk. One participant noted:

> I don't even know if it's a punk ideal anymore, but when it got
> started punk was very tolerant; very much about accepting
> people for who they were. It quickly became a fashion culture,
> so there's a lot of judgment of who wore certain clothes, versus
> other clothes. That didn't interest me at all, that part of it. The
> part I liked is that if you were a misfit, you were welcomed in
> the club. You were welcomed to come and be a part of this
> community. And that was very attractive to me.

In understanding how the participants have been able to parse the time between their professional obligations and their musical activities, I found it necessary to include a category labeled *Time Management*. The aspects of *Time Management* include *time balance (between schooling/ bands)*, *current time negotiation*, and *difficulties in time management*. The *balance* of performing in a punk band and being engaged in academia was discussed throughout the interviews, with several taking time off of school for their punk band-related activities (mainly touring and recording), as noted by this participant, "I moved home to Jersey, moved in with my folks, got like a social work job and started looking into grad school and started a band. And then I did that for two years before I went back to school. And my doctorate was a five-year program, but I took a year off in the middle of it to tour."

Two other participants recounted their decisions to put school on hold for their musical endeavors. One stated:

> Just at that moment, the first [participant's band] record
> was doing really well. We had broken up after the first tour
> in '90 and basically, it was a choice of, 'Do I stay in New

York and continue in academia, or do I do the band thing?'
I decided, 'I'm going to do the band, because I could always
come back to school.' And so that was always in the back of
my mind. And so, eventually, when the band broke up in
'96, I started going back.

Another said, "We decided to [...] try to do it full-time for a while.
And that's kind of when the whole [participant's band] 'thing' happened
for us. So we took a break there from the academic thing for a few years,
and then ultimately, after two years, decided to eventually get back to it."
However, others performed in bands while concurrently enrolled in their
academic programs, whether during vacations or throughout the school
year. One participant, who was touring in her band while simultaneously
attending law school, recalled her experience:

> First semester of law school, [participant's band] was still a
> growing concern and you know, we did like a week-and-a-
> half tour with [another band], which happened to be their
> last tour. But I had class every day. So we would literally,
> like, drive to Columbus, play a show with them, drive back
> overnight so [participant's name] can go to class. Drive back
> to Cleveland. We were doing a tour, but making it back to
> Chicago every day in between and that sucked.

Another participant recalls his experience with his band while attending medical school, and how his prioritization ultimately led to the
demise of his band:

> Well, things had to be neglected. But things that were never
> neglected were school. That was the priority. That was the
> thing. That was one of the reasons why the band broke up,
> initially, because I had to start residency during one of our
> last tours. So, [the] tour was going to go on, but I had to
> start residency, so I was like, 'Guys, I've gotta go. That's
> it.' I had to leave in the middle of a tour because I had to
> start residency. What was I going to do? Tell the residency
> program, 'Hey, you know what, one of your residents isn't
> going to be there, because I'm in a band right now tour-
> ing, and I can't make it in. Can you guys just have my calls
> covered?' No, it wasn't going to go that way. My priority
> number one was being a physician.

Current time negotiation relates to the principles of maintaining a schedule that is both conducive to performing in a punk band and working as a professional. This aspect includes employment scheduling, and the consideration of family members and spouses. Since many participants are in positions of seniority at their respective workplaces, some found it easy to create and maintain time schedules that would allow for recording, touring, and band-related engagements. One participant is employed in academia as a lecturer at a university during specific quarters; his schedule is such that he is able to take time off from academia to tour and record. In fact, he said that his band is where he generates a majority of his income, which is not the case for nearly all the other participants in this study, who have to generate their primary income from their non punk-related occupations. However, there are times – particularly in rehearsals for upcoming events or during recording sessions – where an overlap of functions is possible for this particular participant, as explained here:

> The days start early, and they end late. But, you know, [...]
> we'll spend our days here on campus, meeting with students
> and lecturing. And then I head out of here by 4 or 5 p.m.,
> and for instance, tonight, we'll be at the rehearsal studio
> at 7:30 until probably 11:30. And some years – like last
> year – after lecture, I'd zoom into Hollywood and we would
> be recording a new album. I was there from 6 p.m. until
> midnight every day.

Another participant, a private practitioner, explained that his balance between his professional occupation and musical endeavors is manageable because he is self-employed, and can therefore work as little or as much as he chooses. This participant said that he works four days a week, and is easily able to perform a string of Friday-Saturday-Sunday shows. He often does not work mornings and therefore has time to make it home by the start of a Monday workday:

> Like most people have to come in after school or after work,
> so I'm generally seeing people between 1 in the afternoon
> and 10 at night. So [...] all the kinds of mechanics of being
> in a band are much more doable. I can go to practice until
> midnight, I can go to rehearsal until midnight, and then
> sleep in. I can play Baltimore, D.C. and Richmond in the
> same weekend, and still not miss any work. And I could,

you know, unlike the average working American, I can take
six weeks off a year, as long as it's spread out, to tour.

Because all of the participants interviewed were older than 30, many
had spouses and children to factor into their time scheduling. This sometimes created additional complexity and *difficulty*, as explained by this
participant:

> "I mean, sometimes no thought goes into it at all, and
> sometimes I'm extremely stressed out. It's mostly because
> I'm married, and I don't want my wife to be abandoned. I
> don't want her to be a music widow. And I'm real sensitive
> to, you know, being available for her, and I'm [...] often
> anxious about whether I'm pushing the limits a little bit, in
> terms of how much time I'm away. So it's not so much tak-
> ing the time and making the time, it's anxiety about making
> the time. That's what actually wears on me. I don't want
> to jeopardize my relationship, nor do I want to make her
> unhappy. So, that's the hardest part."

Another participant mentioned that he had to receive his spouse's bless-
ing: "In my situation, where I'm married and I have a baby, you have to
have a very supportive spouse." Another participant echoed a similar sentiment, "I have a very supportive family that allows me to do these sorts of
things...that makes it easy." In addition to spouses and family considerations, one participant also spoke of the changes in financial responsibility
that were linked to his participation in a punk band: "It's different when
you're in your 20s, you're 21, 22, and you live in a house with a bunch
of other guys, and you know, maybe you pay a $100 or $150 a month
in rent...[but] I'm 35, and I'm married and I have a daughter, and three
dogs, and a mortgage and a business and everything like that, it just makes
it more difficult to leave for significant periods of time."

Negotiating Identity is a category that relates to how the participants
view themselves in a punk rock context, how they believe they are perceived by others for their punk rock and educational backgrounds, and
which stereotypes and assumptions are made about them because of their
backgrounds. The category also discusses how the participants believe
their lives have been affected because they are punk rock musicians who
have climbed the ranks of higher academia and are now in professional
employment positions. A number of aspects emerged from this particular category, including *fan perception, professional colleague perception,*

lifestyle, prestige, stereotypes and assumptions, and *punk musician.* Regarding *fan perception,* the participants often spoke about what they believed their fans and supporters of their musical endeavors thought of their educational and professional pursuits, either from information they received directly from fans, or based on inferences. For the most part, participants felt that their fans were largely accepting of the fact they had advanced degrees and worked in professional settings. One mentioned that a fan had actually been inspired to pursue higher academics based on the fact that he had done so:

> Some girl told me once, she emailed me, and said, she
> went into medicine because of me, which is kind of cool."
> Another participant also had "direct evidence" about
> inspiring fans to engage in such professional pursuits based
> on his profession, "A lot of fans write to me, and say, 'I
> wouldn't have gone to college if it wasn't for [participant's
> band name]' and 'I'm becoming a biologist because of your
> lyrics.' So I mean, I have some pretty direct evidence that
> some students are affected by it.

However, another participant felt that although she was accepted by her fans, she wasn't always completely in step with her fellow punk rock musicians because of her professional background, "But I definitely think other musicians-promoters were always cool with it, and writers were always very into it – but you know, I felt sometimes like it set me apart from other musicians. Like I didn't totally fit in because there was this other side of me, always."

The aspect *professional colleague perception* compartmentalized reactions that the participants received from their colleagues in their professional settings, when their punk rock background and history is revealed. Many stated that their co-workers were often apathetic about the participants' punk backgrounds, as this professor noted: "Well, academics, as you know, are pretty much out of touch. So they don't really care. They think it's interesting, you know, and they're happy that somebody can have another career other than academia. They don't really take it very seriously." However, some stated that their dual-career became noteworthy amongst their peers. Two participants specifically mentioned their co-workers discovering YouTube videos of their musical endeavors and sharing them in their workplace: "I think that most find it amusing. You know, I mean [...] I haven't heard anything negative there, I think most people just think it's kind of cool that I did that sort of thing." Another added, "My firm, for the most part, they know my story, they know where I come from […] they probably seek that out in me more than I want to show them. Like there are partners who love it, and everybody they introduce me to, they're like, 'This is [participant's name]. She was in a band.' And I'm like, 'Okay, I'm a lawyer. Can we just drop it?'" And for one participant, mentioning his punk background actually triggered like-minded responses from his colleagues who were also interested in punk music, "Somebody will then start mentioning their little forays into punk rock. 'I used to listen to such and such' and 'Yeah man, oh, you like the *New York Dolls?*'"

Prestige is another aspect of identity negotiation, and most participants seemed to enjoy the placement in society that their current occupation has afforded them. However, one participant is uncomfortable with the punk scene's identification of his doctoral status, "…That's kind of annoying, but like, I really think it creates an artificial distance. I'm not actually that comfortable with it, but I'm not going to yell at people for calling me that either." The same participant suggested that punk rockers attaining these positions and degrees allows for the genre to be given more credence in society: "I think some people are like, 'Wow…okay.' I think it maybe helps some people take punk a little more seriously […] and music a little more seriously…maybe it shows people the possibility of what you can do with your life. That you could have a grown-up, straight job and still, like, yell about the government, jump in the pit and write protest songs and still be furious and have your eyes open."

A key aspect of *identity negotiation* is *stereotypes and assumptions* that are made about both punk rockers and those who engage in higher academia. As stated earlier, one participant – a physician – shatters people's assumptions about what a physician should look like. Furthermore, he adds, "And so, a part of me wearing dreadlocks, and walking around is kind of a total 'fuck you' to a person's mindset, to say, 'Hey, you know what, you're looking at me, and you don't even know anything about me.'" Some have chosen to neither buck nor embrace the stereotypes on either end of the spectrum, and still other participants felt like they were not entirely accepted within either 'realm,' as noted by this participant, "I feel like I'm a perpetual seventh grader, in that, like, I maybe will never feel like I fully fit in anywhere. I was kind of freaking out a few months ago, and I was like, 'Oh my god, you're 31, you could not be doing this.'" Another participant expressed a similar view, "I think, to some degree, that I've always kind of felt, not like an outsider, but I just don't feel like I'm the standard of either one […] a little too academic for your standard punk, and probably a little too punk rock for your standard academic."

The last aspect of *identity negotiation* is that of the *punk musician*. While for some participants, playing punk rock music was just a hobby (and for some it was their former career/former second career), other participants identified punk rock as a secondary career. And for one participant, performing punk rock was a current, main source of income, even though he concurrently held a professional position in higher academia.

The merging of *Intellectualism in Punk Rock* is a category that emerged with a number of wide-ranging responses from the participant population. Aspects of this category include *the art form, articulated ideals and ethics, subgroup dependency,* and *punk rock in academia*. Viewed as *the art form,* some believed that punk rock was inherently intellectual, as stated by this participant, "Well, punk is an art form, and […] art is an intellectual movement, so yes, absolutely." Another participant concurred, though from a slightly different position, "I would have to say from the standpoint of it being an intellectual art form […] it's an acquired taste. Maybe it's for the person that has an eclectic set of values to [interpret] things, versus, 'Feed it to me on a big spoon because it's sugary sweet and I like it, and I don't care who actually is behind it, it's all good for me.' That's the general masses." Many participants noted that punk rock's intellect was best displayed in musicians' ability to *articulate ideals and ethics*. One participant offered this reasoning: "If it's protest music, it should be a place for intelligent discourse [about] what you're protesting, and why. I think the idea that punk is somehow anti-intellectual is also in some ways antithetical to its core tenets. You know what I mean? It's like, how do you do critique if you're not coming from, like, an intellectual perspective?" An additional position was highlighted by a participant who found punk rock's intellectual foundations to be more substantive than those evident in the standard rock genre, "I think that there is more room in punk rock to be intellectual, because I think, to some degree, it's very accepted within the genre to be, to have, political views; to have kind of deep thoughts on things, which maybe, in your standard rock environment, wouldn't be as appreciated."

Despite these shared perspectives, the responses of some participants reveal a certain level of *subgroup dependency* which, in this scenario, means that intellectual discourse within punk rock was not universal and that only particular subgroups – perhaps divided by region or by individual factions – were thought to maintain an intellectual climate. For instance, one participant noted, "At this point, punk rock encompasses a broad spectrum of music styles and different bands and different people. And you know, just like society itself, there's a subgroup of that section that's not going to be intellectual, and there's a subgroup that will be.

And you know, you just gotta find the people you want to talk to." A supporting example is offered by a different participant:

> I think it so depends on the scene, and the town, and the bands. I think there are people in punk rock that are immensely intellectual. And those are probably the people I've gravitated towards over the years in the sense that they're part of the punk rock community; there is an ethic or ideal behind it. There is this philosophy that's not accidental, that's very thought through and articulated in their heads. And there are tons of [other] people who are just like, 'It's rebellion! Fuck this and fuck [that].'

Furthermore, some participants noted that the anarchist tradition in punk rock – a subgroup in itself – had an intellectual bend, as articulated by one response, "The *[Sex] Pistols* use of anarchy was just like, posturing. But *Crass* and the anarchists […] everything that grew out of that, it was very intellectual. It was connected to the intellectual tradition of anarchism and situationism and I think those are pretty intellectual movements."

The final aspect of this category, *punk rock in academia,* sought to develop answers from participants based on their thoughts of whether they could see punk rock merging with academia in any way. One participant stated that an over-analysis of punk rock at an academic level could "sterilize" it:

> I'd hate to see it, like, too overly subjected to analysis, because I hate the idea of people who have no first-hand knowledge of it, like bandying about terms in […] a teacher's lounge somewhere in a university. I mean, I guess they can if they want. But I don't know how much meaning it has if they haven't lived it some way. But I guess it's the same way that an anthropologist looks at the !Kung in the Kalahari, you know…intellectual inquiry is distancing in a lot of ways. Just like, you know, intellectualization as a defense mechanism distances us from our emotions and other people, I think that an over-application of intellectual inquiry, or of intellectual methodology, to the punk subculture can kind of sterilize it.

The infusion of punk's ideology into academia, on the other hand, was found to be acceptable and feasible to most participants, notably as a vehicle to expand critical thinking and its inherent appeal to college-aged students. Still, one participant expressed concern with punk's ability to merge with academia by stating, "I think there's not enough organization in punk rock. You know, it's just too disorganized."

REVIEWING THE DATA

The data presented several key findings. First, the idea that punk rockers are not only attracted to higher academia, but actually enter and succeed in this domain, is in line with the shift in stereotype of the traditional academic. The now-cliché image of "ivory towers" being solely occupied by "bookworms" is belied by the presence of an increasingly more diverse population of graduate students, professors, researchers, and the like. This includes the group of punk musicians interviewed for this study, whose backgrounds are unlike most career academicians. Though not all the participants were employed in academia after attending graduate school, the fact that they were engaged in higher academia as students contributes to the changing profile of both punk rock and academia itself. Findings also reflected a general acceptance of punk rockers as intellectuals, from both fans and colleagues alike, which helps to support this assertion. The disappearing stereotype of the uneducated, unruly punk rocker is partly a function of punks' involvement in higher academia and a variety of professional endeavors.

Second, because many of the participants retained their punk philosophies, particularly via grassroots/DIY ethics and an independent outlook, most of the participants were doubly motivated to succeed, not just in academia but also in their musical careers. The participants were also found to primarily hail from middle- and upper middle-class families, and their academic and professional success was driven by parents who had encouraged their children to succeed and/or instilled this idea at a young age, pointing to the significant role that socioeconomics play in providing a solid foundation for the upbringing and personal development of a highly-educated punk rock musician.

Third, the present study's findings further advance the notion that current punk rock norms and expectations are anywhere from slightly to vastly different than those prevalent in the genre's initial phases, over 30 years ago. The acceptability of higher education and a professional lifestyle in the punk scene appears to be much greater now than it did during punk's infancy. This insight not only updates sociological research on punk rock from prior decades, it reflects the idea that punk rock is a dynamic and constantly evolving musical genre.[3]

Fourth, the findings demonstrate that, although many in the participant population have followed similar educational and musical paths, their current engagement in the punk scene, as performers, is highly varied. This latitude of engagement ranges from zero participation to performing punk music as one's main profession and source of income.

In general, the participants spent less time as punk musicians while involved in their professional pursuits (particularly when compared to their younger punk counterparts) than before entering their professional careers. This was mainly due to additional work, family, and financial obligations, much of which increased with age. The influence of participants' punk rock backgrounds is particularly noteworthy. Punk rock influenced such specific aspects as school choices, overall academic success, degree goals, creative occupational tactics, and relations in the workplace. Though such influence sometimes extended into participants' professional settings, their colleagues were often indifferent, if not outwardly accepting, of the participants' prior musical endeavors. Though some participants felt the initial need to divorce themselves from their punk 'heritage,' many acknowledged that learning to negotiate a presentation of self was often sufficient to ensure success in both punk and professional roles.

Lastly, similarities of both punk rock and academic realms were discussed. Several parallels were presented, including one participant's argument that since punk rock is a bona fide art movement, it is creative and therefore requires a degree of intellect for mastery, much like an academic discipline. Punk rock's advocacy for criticism, social commentary, self-awareness, and questioning of ideas also bear a strong similarity to the practices espoused in academia.

Implications of these findings include a reassessment of the punk rock scene generally, and more specifically, a better understanding of an increasingly popular music genre that has changed (in some ways, drastically) since its inception and has, at times, been misrepresented in mass media. Although some punk rock songs may feature incendiary lyrics and aggressive performances, it is also a genre formulated on critical thinking and therefore able to be tethered to intellectual pursuits including higher academia. The findings also suggest that punk rock musicians can be ambitious, goal-driven, productive, responsible, academically elite, and still seamlessly integrate into mainstream society, all without having to shed the values cultivated by and through their involvement in punk music and culture. Other implications include the idea that these multifaceted professionals can be accepted on either end of the balance, and can also be highly valued in two seemingly disparate realms.

CONCLUSION

Though moldy and used in boundless contexts, the time worn adage, "You can't judge a book by its cover" once again rings true with punk rock musicians, particularly with the subset of highly educated musicians investigated in this study. Though some perform with hurried tempos, inciting mosh pits at concerts, while others pen deeply moving, mature, emotional, and profound punk anthems, in the end, these musicians are simply part of a blanket musical movement that has inspired them to create, investigate, and independently shape the course of their lives. For the study's participants, they – as well as the remainder of the limited, qualified population of those unable to participate or be located – are an enigma or anomaly to some, a special population to others, and just an educator, doctor, attorney, researcher, vocalist, drummer, guitarist, or bassist to the rest of the world. They have beaten odds, shattered assumptions, jumped through the rigorous hoops of academia, been bestowed with the highest educational credentials and, in the end, might still somehow relate to the kid on the street corner with a spiked hairdo and black leather jacket. Joey Ramone, vocalist of punk rock pioneers, the *Ramones,* once sang the line, "Gonna get my PhD" in the band's 1977 song, "Teenage Lobotomy." Ramone never did attain such level of education before his passing in 2001. But at least his ambitions – like those of our participant population – were definitely couched in the right place.

NOTES

1   "Punk Rock Docs" is excerpted from a Masters thesis completed in Summer 2008, based in grounded theory methodology.

2   Craig O'Hara, *The Philosophy of Punk: More Than Noise* (Edinburgh: AK Press, 1999), p. 42; Steven Blush, *American Hardcore: A Tribal History* (Los Angeles: Feral House, 2001), pp. 114, 165, 330-334; Kevin Mattson, "Did Punk Matter?: Analyzing the Practices of a Youth Subculture During the 1980s," *American Studies*, Vol. 42, No. 1 (2001): 70; Sharon M. Hannon, *Punks: A Guide to an American Subculture* (ABC-CLIO, 2010), pp. 71-84.

3   For examples of older sociological research on punk, see Philip Lamy and Jack Levin, "Punk and Middle-Class Values: A Content Analysis," *Youth & Society*, Vol. 17, No. 2 (1985): 157-170; Kathryn Joan Fox, "Real Punks and Pretenders: The Social Organization of a Counterculture," *Journal of Contemporary Ethnography*, Vol. 16, No. 3 (1987): 344-370.

HELEN REDDINGTON

La Lectrice Gourmande

PUNK THEORY MIX TAPE, SIDE A

MICHAEL SICILIANO AND ALAN O'CONNOR

MAXIMUMSOCIALSCIENCE:
AN INTERVIEW/CONVERSATION WITH ALAN O'CONNOR

EDITOR'S INTRODUCTION

I'M NOT SURE where I first encountered Alan O'Connor's writing on punk, but I remember being immediately impressed by the way he balances complex ideas, clear prose, and methodological rigor in nuanced analyses of both punk music and culture, as well as the social structures in which they emerge and exist. Unlike most scholars who venture into the fray, O'Connor is extremely knowledgeable about all facets of punk and his respect for his subject matter is evident in his systematic engagement with the bands, music, literature, ideas, ethics, performances, and institutions (record labels, non-profit spaces) that co-constitute what he describes as the "field of punk." In addition to being an active participant within this field, his research on it stems from extensive fieldwork and expansive interviews that provide the basis from which he probes the social, political, and artistic dimensions of punk throughout the whole of North America.

At the same time that I was debating how to best incorporate O'Connor's work into this collection (he was gracious enough to give me options), I had the pleasure of reading a really smart MA thesis from Michael Siciliano, a graduate student at the University of Chicago whom I knew not from academia, but from our shared experience of spending years immersed in the same punk scene back in Pittsburgh, PA. Given the nature of Siciliano's recent work on independent record labels, his astute attention to the nuances of social theory, and his background as both a musician and volunteer with Pittsburgh's DIY show space, the Mr. Roboto Project, it seemed like a no-brainer to put these two gentlemen in touch.

A BRIEF COMMENT ON THE INTERVIEW

This interview was conducted through email. Because of this chosen medium of exchange the discussion that follows is multi-threaded and, to some degree, non-linear. This is no doubt due to the chosen format (a conversational interview conducted online, over the course of several weeks). I believe that, above all else, this interview shows Alan O'Connor, a punk, attempting to put cultural studies and the social sciences in the service of DIY punk rather than using punk as just another stepping stone in the building of socio-cultural theory. In my opinion, this is an admirable position for O'Connor to take, and one that ultimately furthers the project of cultural studies as a socially engaged, interdisciplinary area of scholarly inquiry.

MICHAEL SICILIANO: *So let's start with a few questions about your decision to undertake your relatively recent research on the field of punk record labels.[1] Clearly it's a development of your previous publications on habitus within music scenes, but I think viewed more broadly, I would ask the following: Why study punk in particular? By this I mean, why this particular subculture and not say, the field of hip-hop or electronic music?[2]*

ALAN O'CONNOR: Like many academics who write about punk, I grew up with one foot in the punk scene. Friends and roommates in the 1980s were involved in one way or another. There is a good video about this scene in Toronto called *Not Dead Yet*. I went to a few shows, including one at Larry's Hideway, which is featured in the video. But I wasn't fully part of it because I was in grad school and not on welfare. And I was pretty involved in gay politics. I was a member of the collective of *The Body Politic*, a serious monthly gay news magazine. But I was interested. I bought a few copies of *MRR* – which led me to the fantastic notion that all punks were socialists – a couple of albums by the Dicks (an inspired guess) which are now worth serious money, and, of course, the Dead Kennedys. I would say that I was a political type grad student. Punk looked pretty interesting but I was always busy.

In the 1990s I had roommates from the older anarcho-punk scene. They had a wonderful 4-year old. Little kids really like the Ramones, I discovered. And in the early 1990s I moved from that house to a much younger punk house where everyone was heavily involved in the 1990s underground emo/ straight edge scenes. Shotmaker and Chokehold were friends.

Somehow Martín from Los Crudos and I ended up writing to each other. We've since tried to figure out how this happened and we think a mutual friend who did a queer punk zine gave Martín a letter from this queer punk in Toronto. When Los Crudos were in Mexico in the summer of 1994 (just after the Zapatista uprising in Chiapas) I was visiting a friend whom I met through the community radio scene. And I knew about El Chopo, the outdoor rock market on Saturdays in Mexico City, and wanted to go. Someone brought me and I saw posters for a Los Crudos show and of course I went. I've told that story in print a few times. So the punk collectives in Mexico accepted me (more or less) and I started to spend summers in Mexico upgrading my Spanish at CEPE – a school for foreigners within Mexico's largest university, UNAM – and hanging out with Mexican punk kids. I wrote a handful of pieces about that, mostly because returning to Canada was always a culture shock and I had to write it all down. I guess you might call it participant observation. I found it very hard to find a theme to focus on and I generally starting writing about how different the scenes are in Toronto and Mexico City. I didn't believe what theorists like Arjun Appadurai and Garcia Canclini were saying about cultural globalization. Of course punk didn't start in Mexico, but it sure was very Mexican. It was the differences between Mexico City and Toronto that I found so hard personally. That's why I was writing in the first place…to try to work through those differences. So I didn't buy the idea of some easy hybrid culture. I thought punk in Mexico very Mexican.

MS: *Building from the previous question, I wonder how your recent book, Punk Record Labels and the Struggle for Autonomy: The Emergence of DIY, fits into the overall trajectory of your research. Your work in cultural studies began with a distinct anthropological emphasis on media ownership in Latin America and from there you began to focus on punk and its articulation with political movements against Neoliberalism.[3] To some, writing a book about "the field of punk" and now your more current research on scenes might seem to be a move away from "serious" research by virtue is its emphasis on music cultures. I wonder then, why, at this point in your career, did you choose to shift away from your previous emphases on subjects of inequality and globalization toward this focus on the development of the sub-field of punk within the field of cultural production?*

AO: These articles were in effect a defense of Bourdieu's idea of a habitus. But the research was not systematic; it was ethnography. The book on punk record labels came from a desire to do some systematic research. I wanted something that was less a personal essay and more research that other people could check, or verify, or prove wrong. So I started doing interviews with record labels. I started with four in Spain, I interviewed Martín when he was in Toronto with Limp Wrist, and then a year later on a sabbatical year (but with no research funding) I did a full tour of the USA. I ended up with 61 interviews that I transcribed myself. I did one a day until I got them all done (a few took two days). I even did one on Christmas Day. I started to ask all the questions that Bourdieu asks: what is this field? What are its boundaries? How does it work? What counts as cultural capital? What is the habitus, or family and educational background of the participants? Does this affect how people participate in the field? I would have liked to do 120 interviews, but I just didn't have the time or money. I had to get some help with the Correspondence Analysis, but when the diagrams came back I felt from my detailed knowledge of these [record] labels and the people I interviewed this was a good diagram of the field. Labels that are similar are mostly gathered near each other; labels that are different are mostly far apart. A lot of this had to do with the age of the label. But that is important: which labels survived. I think some of the findings are, statistically not that strong. There is not a very simple relation between social class (measured by father's occupation) and the kind of label people run. But I think there is a fairly evident pattern.

I feel much happier with this book than the articles, though the articles had an important argument. I'd be really happy if more people took up this challenge and did more systematic research on the scene. I love books by participants and have a huge collection of them. But I think social science can contribute too.

MS: *It's very interesting that Martín seems to play a crucial role in your experience as a punk and in your book on the subject. He is certainly a key figure in U.S. hardcore in general and the Latino and queer scenes in particular. As a bit of a side note, I live in the Pilsen neighborhood of Chicago. It has been and continues to be a predominantly Mexican-American neighborhood; it was also the site of some of Crudos's earliest shows (if I'm not mistaken, many of the members were from here or nearby in Little Village, or the Back of the Yards). Recently in a discussion on "authenticity," an urban sociologist asked "Would a punk band from Pilsen be considered 'authentic'?" which suggests that punk does not come from a working class Latino neighborhood.*

In a way this implies that punk, however it is objectively produced and consumed, has the reputation of being white, middle-class, and irrelevant to an urban, working class or poor experience. Though you've said that your data did not provide generalizable observations on the subject, I'd like to pose to you the question of how much Bourdieu's proposition – that aesthetics are always the cloak of a class-based ideology – would hold in the field of punk? Or in popular culture ,generally? Can a fan of Shotmaker ever truly enjoy Warzone?

AO: I think if you look at books (mostly not written by academics) on punk in the 1980s that Hebdige's model [in *Subculture*] just doesn't work. There isn't a single subculture: it splits into all kinds of subscenes such as anarcho-punk, youth anthems, etc. Its different in London and Belfast, not to mention San Francisco and Washington DC. It quickly spreads to many countries mainly through TV coverage of bands like the Sex Pistols, often dies down but then starts up again as a genuinely local scene. I gradually came to realize that Bourdieu's concept of a field works much better than the concept of subculture. A field has boundaries, but they are usually contested. What is punk and what is heavy metal? Is an experimental college band punk? A field is a space where different possibilities exist: anarcho-punk, emo, straightedge, etc. You can participate in a field in different ways: in a band, doing a zine, doing a record label or distro, as a photographer, etc. Fields change. And the concept of field gets away from the researcher coming up with an arbitrary definition of punk (for the purposes of this study punk is defined as...) when that is actually one of the key issues and conflicts in the scene itself. Emo is not punk in Mexico. You call yourself punk? Hey, you go to grad school!

I don't agree with your summary of Bourdieu. I don't think he explains style or aesthetics by social class. It's not that simple. For a start, Bourdieu sees class as a social field: there are many possible positions. It's not just a matter of the working class or the middle class. And second, one's class habitus is a resource for entering different fields such as law school, car sales or punk. It doesn't determine choices. People still, in some ways, make decisions. For example: to drop out of college and go on tour with your band to Japan. It's not a simple cause and effect. That's why you need to interview as many people as possible and why you need a statistical tool like Correspondence Analysis. You can't map the complexities just by interviewing 14 people (at most you might find some differences by gender) or doing ethnography without asking systematic questions.

MS: *I think the first part of your response leads quite neatly into another set of questions I have for you that concern the familiar narrative of punk as cultural resistance, as well as cultural studies and the sociology of culture. So, as you stated earlier, it is very important to take into account the writings of participants regarding their experiences of their social situation. That being the case, essays, histories, and memoirs regarding punk culture are, of course,* *important. Viewing these products (zines, books, records, etc) and the social processes by which they are produced through the lens of cultural studies, or sociology, of course allows one to discuss punk in terms of its place within the broader context of contemporary society. In terms of your work, and the work of many in cultural studies who write about punk, there is a tendency towards partisanship. In a sense, each social scientific text about punk becomes part of the narrative of punk and, as I'm sure you're well aware, quite a bit of the work on punk inherits the preoccupations of the Birmingham school with resistance to cultural hegemony.*

You, on the other hand, seem to be moving away from this interpretation of subcultures. Do you think that these previous interpretations of subculture carry any validity?

AO: I started to question the concept of subculture mostly from my own experiences in the 1990s of the scenes in Ontario, Quebec and the American Midwest. Certainly Hebdige's argument in his classic book, *Subculture,* now seems very dated. Hebdige argues that punk (he seems to mean London about 1976) draws on the postwar period in Britain. Punk is a very odd subculture in the sense that its core style or meaning is actually a refusal of any fixed style or intention. Maybe this fits a very small group of people around the Sex Pistols in 1976. But then Hebdige says that punk has a half-life of about a year before it is recuperated as meaningful, as fashion, deviance, or just good fun.

I really didn't like the idea of post-subcultures when it emerged a few years ago. I thought it was a mistake. I don't think the literature on subcultures is very helpful, especially when people start writing about *the* punk subculture. Anyone who has hung around the scene for any time quickly realizes that there is not one set of meanings. I can remember huge arguments with mostly apolitical people in bands and promoters and what was at stake was they hated my radical politics. There is not a fixed meaning of punk. It is a field in which there are quite contested positions. People have personal and emotional investments in these positions; we've all seen and experienced this.

MS: *Okay, building on that, how do you feel about the issue of partisanship or actively celebrating and enjoying the object of your social-scientific investigation? What problems, personal or professional, has this created for you? More generally, what issues does it pose to researchers?*

AO: I love reading books on punk by participants. I have a huge collection of them. But I do want to step outside all the fights and disagreements in the scene and try to "objectify" it for participants. I think this is the best contribution social science can make. I will never know your local scene as well as you do, but I can help move the scene beyond the debates that go in endless circles. For example, I tried to put together an international research team to look at punk jobs. We were going to each interview about 50 people about their employment history. What jobs do punks get? Do we work in record stores? Used clothing? Stocking shelves at Whole Foods? Are we lawyers? I suspect there are a lot of ex-punk teachers. You know, there is a compilation of punk bands that have teachers in them called *Critical Pedagogy: A Compilation of Teachers in Punk Bands* which has seventeen bands that include teachers such as Jos from Seein' Red and Dave Dictor from M.D.C.[4] But we don't usually ask systematic questions such as, who are the punk photographers? What explains the different styles of doing a record label? Why are so many punks in the USA college dropouts? I wanted my book on record labels to be read by the scene. I tried to make it readable. But it's different from most books on labels; it's not promotion or celebration. It tries to intervene in the debates about "major labels" with some detailed research. The book was intended to help people in the scene talk about the issues in a more informed way. That, I think is the role of an academic punk: one foot in the scene and one foot outside.

MS: *To digress a bit for the purpose of clarification, I did not mean to imply that Bourdieu views the relationship between aesthetic preference (or aesthetic choices on the part of the band or artists) and social class to be deterministic. I believe his philosophical resistance to predictive statistical models illustrates that quite clearly. However I do feel that one need only take a glance at Distinction or Rules of Art to get the sense that the struggles over legitimate practice and over what might legitimately be called "culture" within the cultural field (of which punk is a subfield) are often linked to social position (i.e. the multi-faceted, spatial conception of class determined by possession of various forms of capital).[5] The dominant fractions of the dominant class have a vested interest in maintaining and reproducing their conception of legitimate culture and in a variety of circumstance, both in France and the U.S., the boundary between legitimate culture (institutionalized "high art") and popular arts. This is why, to me, the boundary making in terms of aesthetic and economic practice that you've described continues to fascinate me, especially in the field of popular music production. Here there appears to be so little to be gained in terms of actual capital, yet so much at stake in the symbolic. With so little to gain, I wonder why it is that the struggle in a scene* *is often over maintaining ownership over a cultural form that matters so little in terms of getting a job or succeeding in the "real world"?*

I think that, theoretically, the conceptual device of the field is incredibly useful in approaching punk in the same way that it has been useful in approaching jazz, journalism, and variety of other social phenomena.[6] It allows for the diverse and localized articulations of widespread cultural forms in a way that subculture, at least in the Hebdige sense, does not; while it also, as you so astutely pointed out, accounts for the cross-fertilization between scenes via various forms of media (zines, TV, blogs, etc) in a way that Straw's concept of the "scene" does not.[7] In a way, it prevents you, and potentially other researchers, from committing the symbolic violence of excluding certain fractions of punk from the narrative that academia has been creating for punk over the past 35 years. In fact, it's only relatively recently that academics seem to have moved away from the notion that music scenes or genres have strict, rigid, and relatively unchanging boundaries and formal definitions, yet this is something that any participant (punk or otherwise) in a music scene knows all too well. That's an incredibly difficult idea to convey to both academics and punks alike and you manage to do so very well. That said, your book has been criticized by at least one zine (Razorcake) for having a conception of DIY that "too closely follows the MRR axis" and often leaves out the importance of other zines and intermediaries involved in contextualizing and relaying information on music scenes to punks.[8]

I know that you've responded to criticism on the book within academic circles (in 2010), but what do you make of this criticism from the punk scene itself? Have the labels that participated responded in any way? As you stated before, a zine such as MRR is undeniably left leaning and many of its most vocal writers seem to possess at least some college education. Whose conception of punk benefits from excluding other forms of punk practice from this zine and other similar heavyweights of punk publishing and taste making?

AO: I like your wonderful paragraph on the usefulness of the concept of the field. It drives me nuts to see grad students using terms such as *the* punk subculture, when they as participants in the scene (most of them) know all the differences in music, style, politics, etc. I was really disappointed that *MRR* never reviewed the book. They were sent a review copy but nothing happened. There was a review in *Razorcake* that mostly complained that other zines such as theirs also contribute to the scene and should have been given more weight. Fair enough. What they don't realize is that it is almost impossible to get *Razorcake* in Canada and I only ever saw copies when I traveled in the USA. There was also an online review that had the usual punk skepticism about academic writing, but grudgingly admitted my book might be okay. Actually, this person offered to rewrite his review (in a more positive tone) for *MRR* but they wouldn't accept it because he might just be my friend and they want neutral objective reviewers. Fair enough.

My book is obviously grounded in the debates in *MRR* about major labels, and before that about big bands insisting on large guarantees. I hoped to use what systematic research I could do, and the concept of a field (which really is just a sophisticated way of saying a scene with many possible positions in it) to contribute to a debate that usually just goes around in circles. 'Who cares if Green Day is on a major? They're cool. And anyway they come from working class families and need the money.' If you look you'll see that I am quite angry about Green Day. But if you read the book carefully there are also many people who were associated with *MRR* who have sold out. I wonder if I fell between the cracks because it is just too painful to look at what happened with some of the old crowd.

You'll have picked up on the fact that I think of myself as having one foot in the scene and the other in academia. Maybe that's a bit different from Bourdieu who, until about 1995, very much wanted to be a so-cial scientist and not an activist. He saw too much thoughtless political posing. But I tried to intervene in the 'Major Labels' debate, really as a continuation of the fights we had over this at Who's Emma [DIY info-shop/record store] in Toronto in the 1990s.[9] I do have a commitment and I'm a bit different from Bourdieu about that. But I also want to use his tools to "objectify" the scene, to hold up an objective mirror to it so maybe people will think differently about the issues. I also wanted to add to the ongoing debate in the punk scene about who "we" are (building on some data in *HeartattaCk* readers' surveys). Obviously I'm looking at older people who stuck around because they had a commitment to punk, but also a role in bands, doing zines, doing distros and labels. So who is this "we"? You can look at the data (including raw info at the back of the book) and see that while there is some diversity, "we" are mainly middle class college dropouts. A few, like me, didn't quite drop out.

I really do believe, with Bourdieu, that social science has to be a col-lective enterprise. Most of the work I value in cultural studies also has this quality. In studying punk record labels as a field I'm obviously build-ing on work by Bourdieu and others. I would really love it if other people would join in. I think my findings are interesting but tentative. The work I am doing now with Ian McLachlan and our research team on the un-derground arts scene in Peterborough, Ontario (where Trent University is located) is obviously related. We're asking questions about how the non-commercial theatre and arts scene works in a small city of 60,000 to 70,000 people, located about two hours from a large city such as Toronto. This scene also makes a space for hardcore punk shows. We want to understand the dynamics of this scene; in a small city people move between theatre, art and music. Everyone goes to everyone else's events. In a small city you have to. What we're interested in is how Peterborough may be a refuge that makes non-commercial culture (what Bourdieu calls "restricted production") possible. The rent is cheaper. There is more social support for opting out of legitimate careers. There is a really nice feel about this city. But we are also asking questions about the habitus of everyone involved. Actually, this has been a bit of a struggle in the research team because postmodern theory has done a lot of damage to the idea of social science. But we are now asking the questions about parents' occupations and education, and the interviewee's own education and work experience.

What I think I found in the punk record labels research seems to go against what many Marxist researchers would predict. Because, I found that really alternative labels tend to be run by middle class dropouts – literally dropouts, from college. And there is a tendency for working-class kids (especially an older generation) to treat their labels in a more business-like manner. But then the question that Bourdieu poses (and he always annoys cultural studies people because the question is also meant for them) is how far can you trust middle class dropouts? Or to put it in a more positive way, what support does the hardcore punk scene provide to encourage these dropouts to refuse the temptations of major success (what Bourdieu calls "large-scale production")? This needs more thought and work. My book is quite angry about people who betrayed their youthful ideals, but a lot of other people don't [betray them]. Dischord Records is the heroic example, though they took their own decisions rather than following some template for DIY. The question then for all the middle class dropouts who make excuses for what is in effect unethical behavior is, if Dischord can do it, why can't you?

MS: I'd like to move on to two concluding questions, but first, as this is both an interview and a discussion, I'd like to offer some thoughts on your previous statements. As you said, your book is obviously grounded in the debates that arise internally within punk (specifically in zines such as MRR). While those debates about major labels are, for the most part, simply discursive, they do cause material problems for individuals and companies that seek to bridge this gap between the punk field and the field of music production dominated by multinational media conglomerates. That idea, essentially, was the driving idea behind my own, primarily ethnographic research, on 'indie' labels (some of whom actually fall within the bounds of punk as delineated in your work).

Your brief description of your current work strikes me as immediately understandable based on my experience as a musician in both Pittsburgh and Chicago. In Pittsburgh the scene is a bit closer to how you describe Peterborough. Noise musicians play with indie rock bands, mash-up DJ Girl Talk used to play with hardcore bands, and everyone watches the football and hockey together. I've also felt that, musically, the bands there were a bit more 'out there' in terms of style due to the intersection of these social networks and the fact that the idea of "hitting it big" was generally not part of the creative process. Since arriving in Chicago and playing a decidedly artier form of punk (noise rock a la Amphetamine Reptile Records, essentially), the first question when discussing a band is often "are you doing a record and if so, who is putting that out?" A certain emphasis is on making the numbers and creating hype and that's because in a bigger town that is both an option and, if your goal is to have people interested in your music in such a saturated market, a necessity. Someone recently even talked to me about "branding your band," which as a middle class, Lefty, hardcore punk person with all the ideas about proper practice that tend to go with that, strikes me as a bit crass.

Though I realize that that's grounded in debates within the punk scene, I also feel that such a topic would've never arisen in casual conversation if I were still in a smaller city. Though I'm unfamiliar with the specificities of Peterborough, I'd like to pose this question to you: Based on your research and your experience as a punk, how do you feel about the tendency of punk performance spaces to exist in economically depressed, often working-class, ethnic minority neighborhoods? In a sense, the existence of this subfield of cultural production seems to almost depend upon structural inequality within urban areas. In other words, the middle class can drop out and have its scene, but only because we live under an economic system that produces spaces of poverty with low rents. Perhaps it is different in smaller towns? I realize that to fully engage such a complicated phenomena is difficult, but I'm curious as to what you might think since it seems so linked to your current work.

AO: This is really interesting. When we started Who's Emma it was in a fairly low-rent area of Toronto. Kensington Market has seen wave after wave of migrants to Canada. In the early 1900s it was a Jewish neighbourhood, full of small shops and close to the clothing workshops on Spadina Avenue where Emma Goldman lived when she was forced out of the USA. It then became a Portuguese fish and vegetable market. Today it has a mix of migrants from many parts of the world. But it has also been a punk hangout for the past thirty years; it is featured in the documentary *Not Dead Yet.*[10] I think we were very aware when we started Who's Emma that we were also using this relatively low-cost urban space to start a low-budget punk project. When I was cleaning and painting the first storefront (it was really small) I went across the road to a long-time Portuguese restaurant/bar to get a coffee. The elderly waiter in his white shirt and black tie asked me what the store was going to be. "A punk record store," I replied. "Ah," he said, "dirty punks. Why you bring dirty punks?" But later when his bar turned into a punk hangout – a table of punks in black (the straightedge kids never ventured inside) beside a table of retired Portuguese workers – he would never let me pay for a beer. I'd order a pint and put down a five dollar bill and he'd shove it back at me. For him, I was "the boss" and I'd brought a new life to his bar. It closed a few years later and is now a trendy hangout (but not for punks, because the imported beer is now too expensive).

We've all seen this: the punk house in Detroit that was bought for a song; ABC No Rio in the Lower East Side of New York City. I think we are right to be conscious about this, to think about the consequence for other people who need these low-cost neighborhoods. (I know this is a huge issue in Chicago). But at the same time, Bourdieu describes the conditions necessary for bohemia. You need cheap rent. You need cheap places to hang out. For non-commercial music and art it is essential that people are rewarded in ways other than immediate financial success. These rewards can be free time (to write, to make music), friendship, casual sex or romance, self-respect, a sense of solidarity with people who are doing the same thing, etc. I think the ultimate argument for DIY is that it can be a really fulfilling life. There may be limitations to it, for example if you want to have kids, but the final argument for DIY is that it can be really fun.

MS: *Finally, I'd like to conclude by asking simply: What's your favorite punk band and why are they your favorite?*

AO: I'm not sure why people would be interested in my own musical preferences, but I'll try to answer. The first without a doubt is people that I have known in bands, and seen many times. A good example is Shot-maker. Then, bands that I admire for what they have to say (sometimes people I've also known) like Los Crudos. I'm not going to pretend that I throw Los Crudos on the turntable everyday, but I wouldn't want to lose the 7-inch records, most of which I got from the band at shows. Finally, bands that I like because they're clever. Huggy Bear is a good example, but there are many more. Before we did Who's Emma I had a distro at shows, mostly of anarcho-punk, queer punk and riot grrrl. People would look through my box of records and say, "You have different stuff than anyone else."

NOTES

1   Alan O'Connor, *Punk Record Labels: The Struggle for Autonomy* (Lanham, MD: Lexington, 2008). For examples of his previous work on habitus in music scenes, see O'Connor "Local Scenes and Dangerous Crossroads: Punk and Theories of Cultural Hybridity," *Popular Music*, Vol. 21, No. 2 (2002): 147-58; "Anarcho-punk: Local Scenes and International Networks," *Journal of Anarchist Studies*, Vol. 11, No. 2 (2003): 111-21; "Punk Subculture in Mexico and the Anti-globalization Movement," *New Political Science*, Vol. 25, No. 1 (2003): 43-53; "Punk and Globalization: Spain and Mexico," *International Journal of Cultural Studies*, Vol. 7, No. 2 (2004): 175-195.

2   See Nick Prior's article, "Putting a Glitch in the Field: Bourdieu, Actor Network Theory and Contemporary Music" for an example of work on electronic music that challenges Bourdieu's formulation of a 'field'.

3   Examples of work in these two areas include: *The Voice of the Mountains: Radio and Anthropology* (University Press of America, 2006); "Punk and Globalization: Spain and Mexico."

4   *Critical Pedagogy: A Compilation of Teachers in Punk Bands*, Six Weeks Records, 2000.

5   Pierre Bourdieu, *Distinction: A Social Critique of the Judgment of Taste* (Cambridge, MA: Harvard University Press, 2000); *The Rules of Art: Genesis and Structure of the Literary Field* (Palo Alto, CA: Stanford University Press, 1996).

6   Paul D. Lopes, "Pierre Bourdieu's Fields of Cultural Production: A Case Study of Modern Jazz," in eds. Nicholas Brown and Imre Szeman, *Pierre Bourdieu: Fieldwork in Culture*, (New York: Rowman & Littfield, 2000), pp. 165-185; Rodney Dean Benson and Érik Neveu, *Bourdieu and the Journalistic Field* (Cambridge, UK: Polity, 2005).

7   Will Straw, "Systems of Articulation, Logics of Change: Communities and Scenes in Popular Music," *Cultural Studies*, Vol. 5, No. 3 (1991): 68-388.

8   Todd Taylor, "Punk Record Labels and the Struggle for Autonomy: The Emergence of DIY," *Razorcake*, Nov 19, 2008.

9   For O'Connor's full account of his experience with the Who's Emma DIY infoshop/record store, see "Who's Emma and the Limits of Cultural Studies," *Cultural Studies*, Vol. 13, no. 4 (1999): 691-702.

10   Edward Mowbray and Ruth Taylor, *Not Dead Yet* (Toronto, Canada: Art Metropole, 1984), VHS.

ALASTAIR GORDON

BUILDING RECORDING STUDIOS WHILST BRADFORD BURNED:

DIY PUNK ETHICS IN A FIELD OF FORCE

"THIS IS A CHORD, THIS IS ANOTHER, THIS IS A THIRD, NOW FORM A BAND!"[1]

- SIDEBURNS, 1976

I OCCUPY TWO distinct roles: one as a long-term punk rock scene partici-pant and the second as an academic principally interested in the cultural legacy of UK 1970s punk. Both of these areas of investigation have been central aspects of my life for the last three decades. The undertaking of ethnographic research in this arena has often led to accusations made to me by participants of "selling out" and undermining the integrity of the scene, not to mention my own residual feelings of compromise. To begin, some biographical/contextual information is required.

Long before I became a doctoral student in 2000, I made my first visit to the anarchist punk venue the Bradford 1in12 Club during the summer of 1990. I was traveling with two Nottingham hardcore punk bands, Kings of Oblivion and Forcefed to play a one-day festival at the recently opened building. Also on the bill were two 'ex' member bands from the UK anarcho-punk subculture, Zygote and Kulturo with respec-tive members of Amebix and Antisect. I remember my anticipation and excitement at the prospect of seeing these bands as I'd been a supporter of their nineteen eighties incarnations.

More importantly this was my first visit to the Club. This place was already steeped in punk folklore. It was housed in an old building and worked according to anarchist principles of mutual aid. I was impressed to see the punk ethic of Do-it-Yourself (hereafter DIY) intertwined with anarcho-syndicalist politics to create a space free of corporate control and hierarchical management structures, taking a proud place in a long history of English anarchist resistance cultures.[2] Trawling around the building was an adventure: a venue, a bar floor, a cafe replete with a full-sized snooker table, and the place was full of punks. This place was clearly organised from the grassroots of the Bradford punk scene and meant business. After a great show and the chance to network with people involved in the club, I maintained frequent visits from 1994 onwards, playing with various bands and eventually renting practice room space for my band from 1997. By then however, I was approaching success in procuring a scholarship to undertake ethnographic research on DIY punk cultures.

The background of the underlying philosophy of punk is complicated, but in terms of providing some contextual information, punk arrived onto the UK cultural landscape in late 1976 rendering visible through its DIY philosophy the previously mystified mechanics of music participation, consumption and participation. Punk illuminated UK cultural inequality and economic problems via its musical rallying call whilst offering an opportunity for disenfranchised people to make their voices heard without resorting to the major label music business. The legacy of those now historical events of the Sex Pistols *et al* is constitutive of what is now broadly described as 'early' punk and well documented in both academic and populist terms. What is, however, broadly absent from these accounts – mostly concentrated upon clothing style, musicology, aesthetics, etc. – has been detailed consideration of the daily *ethical* practices that are the core motor for UK grassroots punk cultural activity. This has been summarised in the term: do-it-yourself, which serves to *demystify* previous processes of music production, throwing access open to newcomers, empowered by the de-fetishised punk ethic.[3]

In what follows, I address this oversight via examination of ethnographic fieldwork data detailing the reflexive, contextual constraints and rewards that operate in DIY punk as the basis for creative action against mainstream music production.[4] Intertwined with this account are the tangential yet important issues of undertaking critical insider ethnography in the punk scene. This method is precariously bound up with a number of contextual scene/network power relations that inform wider, associated issues related to ethnographic writing and methodological procedure.

To explore both the historical legacy of DIY punk and the difficult position of doing fieldwork in one's own culture, this article has two principal aims. Firstly, it will illustrate how a thirty-odd year legacy of DIY has crystallised in everyday political punk practice in the UK. Here I will discuss aspects of my ethnographic research undertaken whilst building a collectively-owned recording studio during the summer of 2001. I argue that DIY ethics operate within a framework where the lack of immediate/contextual resources are a *continually* frustrating *yet* equally rewarding part of both the endeavour and the realisation of collective projects.[5] The initial, 1970s romantic descriptions of DIY as 'effortless' and 'immediate' do not resemble the difficult, repetitive struggles evident in the DIY project outlined in this article. Indeed, this is not an essay that portrays DIY culture as a naïve impersonation of mainstream music culture, or, contrary to Henry Jenkins' interpretation of Michel de Certeau, a form of creative practice akin to mere "textual poaching."[6] DIY production is far more taxing, independent and implicitly critical in practice than such accounts would imply. The reality of DIY encountered in this research is that of an uneven endeavour, and one which has its fair share of hardship and struggle factored into the task; though one should not also forget that the fun and satisfaction of involvement – and the completion of a task – is of equal worth.[7] Here the practice of everyday toil with scarce resources has more in common with Alan O'Connor's reflections on co-founding a DIY punk space (in Toronto) as opposed to the catch-all descriptors of punk in the 1970s.[8]

The second aim of the article is to address the personal consequences arising out of undertaking fieldwork as a long-standing, insider member of DIY punk culture. The principal field method for examining this *everyday* DIY punk ethical activity was participant observation informed by critical insider ethnography.[9] The research used field-journal, interview, and diary and club literature to critique populist accounts of DIY as an endeavor requiring little effort. My work can be described as "action research" as the field was permanently changed by my presence and the contributions I made while present.[10] Through this process (and within the larger project from which this essay is culled), I also make my familiar world of DIY punk practice "anthropologically strange"; Hammersley and Atkinson note this is, "an effort to make explicit presuppositions he or she takes for granted as a culture member."[11] Nevertheless, my insider status made for a difficult methodological scenario in terms of potentially overlooking, during the course of fieldwork, the central mechanisms involved in the DIY process and the ways in which DIY operates amidst immediate and external forces (terms I explain below).[12]

The philosophy of DIY involves the ethical commitment to pursuing one's goals not for profit or individual gain but, instead, for the benefit of the club and wider punk network, and to share music and information. The extension of this ethic during fieldwork ultimately meant that *values* were transposed and this, in turn, became of ethnographic interest.[13] The present research operated between the line of both my *personal* DIY values and the process of describing, yet also *constructing*, the field via daily activity and field note writing. There was thus a clash between my ethical standing as a participant and being a researcher involved in both the completion of my doctorate and the development of my subsequent career as a professor. The development of this position can be related to general scholarly anxiety regarding the status of ethnography as a neutral, descriptive tool. My contention is that neutrality is impossible and can only result in compromise. In theoretical terms, the partisan status of ethnographic writing has been historically and geopolitically located and analysed in culturally relativist terms by Clifford.[14] His discussion outlining the "predicament" of ethnography in terms of how, for example, the authority of ethnographic discourse (who speaks on behalf of whom?) evokes, sustains and constructs geographical power relations is both accurate and salient in his much wider discussion of Edward Said and the Western ethnographic representation of the Orient.[15] In specific terms, I found that local power relations were obviously present during my research; this led to tension between my status as both authentic participant and ethnographer in terms of *immediate* scene relations and *external* contextual forces. As an insider, I was in a privileged position in terms of observing activities, though when the data is narrativised through both academic methodology and language, the same power relations of 'who speaks' unavoidably enter the discussion.

To theorise my place as an insider ethnographer, I described such relations in the research as 'immediate and external contextual fields of force.' Principally, the term 'field' is used here in the ethnographic sense and not in the way Bourdieu utilizes the term, though some terminological crossover is possible.[16] The descriptor, 'immediate' explains how general everyday practice in DIY culture is affected by access to resources and other factors that have consequences on the steering of everyday tasks, for example the Bradford riots I describe later. Equally relevant are *external* issues (not directly relative to the field) which affect the subjective ethical status of the ethnographer both during and after the research (in terms of writing, following doctoral degree protocol, and engaging in the process/practice of publishing). In short, I felt the pressure of dual-role existence caught up between the interplay of two contextual 'fields of force' that ultimately presented problems I discuss in the conclusion.

Therefore, in order to address my two central points – the crystal-lisation of DIY in everyday political punk practice, and the tensions of being a punk engaged in an ethnography of punk culture – the article will proceed through five sections. First, I discuss the long-term germina-tion of DIY into the political framework of anarcho-punk, its eventual reproduction via the case study of Studio 1in12, and how I came to be involved in this project as a doctoral researcher. Second, I examine how the recording studio project was steered by an immediate contextual field of force that had consequences on the completion of the task. The third section considers how the immediate political context of the chosen club for the research – the 1in12 Club – was strikingly illustrated during the riots in Bradford, and I then discuss some of the ways the completed studio became a valuable cultural resource for both local punks and the global punk scene in which their records are distributed. Finally, the conclusion speaks to the predicament and consequences of undertaking insider ethnography and action research fieldwork.

'DI WHY?'
THIRTY YEARS OF STRUGGLE AND ELBOW GREASE

Declaration of the emerging DIY punk ethic was first set out in the fanzine *Sideburns* in 1976: "This is a chord, this is another, this is a third, now form a band!"[17] Such statements were expressions of a rebellious, UK punk cultural sensibility forged by grassroots alienation and the frustration of thwarted creative energy. DIY rendered visible the hid-den process of major label musical production and openly scrutinized practices that previously barred people from such opportunities, whether because of talent or resources. Marcus Gray glibly summarised the early punk spirit of DIY: "If you're bored, do something about it; if you don't like the way things are done, act to change them, be creative, be positive, anyone can do it."[18]

The inclusive sensibility of the politically charged punk culture was a sure-fire answer to this problem and opened up new spaces for rebel-lion and resistance to mainstream culture, theorised by Hakim Bey as "Temporary Autonomous Zones."[19] By the early 1980s, DIY was taken on board by a groundswell of leftist musicians, artists, writers and politi-cal activists as an informal ethical code of practice: a radically different yet oddly similar extension of 1960s British countercultural ethics. For example, free-festivals, squatting, and the underground press partly represent the historical antecedents to the present global punk network referred to by O'Connor (following Bourdieu) as a 'field.'[20] Influences from this period also fed into DIY punk as a continuation of radical politics.[21]

A plethora of DIY UK bands, scenes and records crept onto the cultural landscape sending clear messages to the music business that youth did not require the patronising 'assistance' of record companies, nor the rock 'star system' or the 'music' press. Instead, they could release their own records and book shows in spaces they built (for example, in squatted buildings) and in venues they controlled. Furthermore, they could publish their music reviews and cultural commentary in their own version of the music press: the fanzine.[22] In spite of this expansion, elements of the 1970s DIY punk ethic proved to be weak in the face of the music industry and many punk bands did sign to record labels with the accompanying peer accusations of selling out. Toward 1980, with the rise of the independent labels and 'post-punk' music, punk itself was proclaimed (by the music and popular presses) as "dead." This discourse of the death of punk, which was repeatedly employed as a "rhetorical commonplace," resulted in a populist hegemony that totally ignored how the DIY ethic remained active not only within the UK but also across commensurate global punk scenes.[23] Overall, the 'punk is dead' thesis eclipsed the subsequent DIY activity prevalent over the next thirty odd years. Hence, this is an account that serves as an insider academic communiqué from the UK DIY underground.

DIY punk is an example of how participants can control spheres of musical and political activity both within, and outside of, institutions originally geared toward mass production and the accumulation of profit. Rather than surrendering artistic and aesthetic control to record companies, booking agents and advertisers, DIY punk sought to cultivate a non-profit space.[24] Gabriel Kuhn summarises DIY as:

> A principle of independence and of retaining control
> over one's work, DIY (abbreviating *Do it Yourself*) defines
> original hardcore punk ethics and, to many, remains the
> decisive criterion for 'true' hardcore punk; the most tangible
> aspects of hardcore's DIY culture are self-run record labels,
> self-organised shows, self made zines, and non-commercial
> social networks.[25]

In ethical terms, DIY is portrayed as being and remaining authentic. The ethical imperative of authenticity has directly informed DIY punk values and practices over the last thirty years; the 1in12 Club is a clear example of the continuation of this cultural tradition.

ANOK4U2 LAD!
ANARCHO-PUNK AND WEST YORKSHIRE LEGACIES

For the lay reader not familiar with the confusing taxonomy of punk factions, anarcho-punk was both a continuation of the counterculture of the 1960s and a musical genre/scene that amplified the populist embrace of DIY punk by turning it into a political project. At its height in the UK between 1978-84, anarcho-punk was more or less spearheaded by the band Crass, which had its own DIY label (Crass Records) that became the blueprint for, eventually, thousands of other DIY record labels.[26] During the early 1980s there were hundreds of bands (with mostly unemployed band members) squatting buildings and playing in community centres, making anti-war and pro animal-rights political statements, and totally without the support/financial assistance of major record labels. Anarcho-punk was, by default, fundamentally disinterested in profit, privileging the political musical message over self-interest.[27] Broadly, anarcho-punk took the threat of cold-war nuclear annihilation seriously and took aim at both nuclear proliferation and the policies that emerged from the cosy relationship between Conservative UK Prime Minister Thatcher and Republican US President Reagan. Involvement in the Campaign for Nuclear Disarmament (CND), anti-war protests, and general campaigns of direct action were central to the development of anarcho-punk from 1978 onwards and constituted a significant practical political turn in punk culture that forms the historical backdrop for the present article.

While the political actions and music releases of Crass are too wide ranging to document here, their subsequent influence acted as an inspiration for punks to create their own political spaces through squatting and the creation of non-commercial venues.[28] By the early 1980s, Crass clearly established themselves as the centrepiece of anarcho-punk in the UK, with its roots firmly set in an uncompromising reading of the core ethics of DIY punk. Penny Rimbaud, the drummer for Crass, spoke of the ethical catalyst for his band: "When [Johnny] Rotten [of the Sex Pistols] proclaimed that there was 'No Future,' we saw it as a challenge to our creativity – we knew there was a future if we were prepared to work for it."[29] The 'anyone can do it' ethos led to inspired spin-off projects that both cemented networks and created political links, reinforcing anarcho-networks across the globe. The grassroots political example that Crass pioneered in their early, ground-breaking records sparked an ethical shift that came to fruition through the large number of political punk bands that emerged in the late 1970s and early 1980s and continue to this day. It is in this DIY milieu that I make my ethnographic entrance some twenty-one years later, through fieldwork undertaken during 2001 at the 1in12 Club: a self managed venue in Bradford that embraces DIY ethics and reflects the anarcho-punk politics of its members, past and present.

THE ONE IN TWELVE CLUB

The inception of the 1in12 Club – named after the Conservative Government's Rainer report (1980) which stated that one in twelve unemployed claimants in West Yorkshire were committing some kind of fraud on the benefit system – is a prime example of both a British anarchist social club and the continuation of anarcho-punk politics beyond the 1980s. This group of collectively-organised volunteers banded together in the face of Thatcherist attacks on trade unions, the working classes and the unemployed, to link DIY punk and anarchist principles as the cornerstone of their actions. Prior to the club obtaining a building through a grant in 1988, punk gigs were held twice weekly in various Bradford pub locations from 1981 onwards, and this formed the bedrock of fundraising activities which the club would draw upon over the next twenty years:

> The twice weekly gigs held in several city centre pubs provided the embodiment of the 1in12 "way", providing gigs that were cheap, free from sexist, racist and statist hassles, the usual promoters and rip-offs, dress restrictions and bouncer intimidation. The objective was to create a lively and participative social scene, to stimulate a culture of resistance a space under which the control and direction of the membership for entertainment, debate and solidarity.[30]

During the 1980s, the club attracted membership and visitors from those involved in the anarcho-punk scene. Anarcho-punks had attempted on numerous occasions to set up a club in the UK. Sned, a club member, spoke during our interview about collectively run spaces in the 1980s: the 'Station Club' in Gateshead, Sunderland's 'Bunker' venue, and 'the Pad' run by the Scottish Crass-inspired band, The Alternative. Most importantly, Crass helped to fund the creation of a London anarchist centre, Centero Iberico, through the proceeds earned from their 1980 split-single benefit record with the Poison Girls ("Bloody Revolutions/ Persons Unknown"). Following their donation of £12,000, Crass decided to have nothing to do with the centre in order to avoid accusations of being 'leaders' of the scene. Consequently, Centero Iberico collapsed. Rimbaud writes:

> Based in London's Docklands, the centre was open for a
> year or so before collapsing in disarray. From the start,
> conflict arose between the older generation of anarchists
> and the new generation of anarcho-punks. It seemed that
> the only common interest, and that only tenuously, was
> Crass, but true to our agreement we kept our distance. We
> did however play one gig there before the inter-camp bitch-
> ing left me wondering if the thing hadn't been a dreadful
> mistake.[31]

Unlike the short-lived Docklands project, 1in12 successfully avoided closure for thirty-odd years, in spite of manifesting similar 'inter-camp' divisions:

> At no stage in the Club's history has the relationship
> between "ideal" and "reality" ever been straightforward. In-
> deed conflict over whose ideals and which reality has often
> thrown the Club into deep internal conflict. The diversity
> of interests, priorities and expectations of the membership,
> empowered by the open and active process of decision-
> making, has often come at a price. Sometimes members
> have left, disillusioned and occasionally bitter, but this is the
> uncomfortable reality of taking responsibility and control.[32]

The fieldwork detailed in this article was concerned with how the club maintained its DIY activities in the face of such problems, as well as fluctuating membership numbers and a lack of resources. Scarce resources (financial, volunteer and practical skills) are central to the immediate contextual field of force, which can either advance DIY projects to completion or result in conflict. Entrance was secured via my previous relations with the 1in 12 Club and involved daily contact and observation. Due to the number of opportunities for observation within 'the scene,' I also attended DIY punk gigs in nearby Leeds during most evenings, as these were more frequent than the occasional gigs held at the 1in12.

PUNK ETHNOGRAPHY

Upon my arrival at the 1in12 (at a matinee gig on a rainy Sunday in early June 2001), I was informed by Peter, my central 'gatekeeper,' that I would be involved in the construction of a recording studio in the basement of the club, in addition to helping out with other tasks. The club functions under the umbrella of a number of collectives: the peasants (food growing), games, library, gig, drama, and studio collectives. Operational logistics of the club were monitored through membership meetings each Sunday where forthcoming events and day-to-day issues were collectively discussed; at one such meeting I presented the research to outline my project. It was announced that my colleague in the building of the studio was to be John, a caretaker who would offer assistance when time allowed.[33]

The general ethic of DIY, self-management, and collective mutual-aid, is at the heart of the 1in12 Club and is the reason why DIY punk has become a stable method of fundraising. A consequence of involvement in punk DIY activity is the development of individual and group autonomy, control, and empowerment within the immediate field of force. There is a broad resentment to anything considered mainstream, capitalist or corporate, and these sentiments informed the not-for profit rationale for building the studio. More specifically, control of recording and practice spaces is typically dictated by private interest, which results in the majority of DIY musical acts paying inflated costs. This, in turn, surrenders control and recording quality to such interests, it impoverishes band members and labels, and puts added financial pressure on any given project. Thus, the chief aim of building a recording studio in the Club was primarily to develop collective, not-for-profit recording/studio skills and enable bands to record at an affordable price. A further, overarching reason was to provide an authentic alternative to mainstream studios where band members are disconnected from the processes of recording their music and learning such skills is off-limits to the 'customer'; the recording studio would extend the DIY ethic beyond its existing remit of concert promotion, record label distribution, and bands. The project had already been partially realised through the construction of a practice room, from 1998-2000, which resulted in a cheap-to-rent, secure, soundproofed practice space and storage area for bands in the basement of the club; the actual studio was earmarked for construction in an old storeroom, adjacent to the practice space.

In spite of my initial enthusiasm, I encountered frustration from day one. Audiences and general punters are rarely seen outside of Club events which lead to a general and consistent decline in both club volunteers and workers' morale. The immediate lack of volunteers and the paid ground staff of just two people meant that I became isolated during the initial stages of the project; personal initiative and a sense of autonomy became my key allies. For example, when I arrived at the club on the first day of studio fieldwork, I expected to be told what to do. While given prior notice that I would be involved in the studio, I soon found it was *entirely* up to me to get the project moving. Aware that there were three other members of the studio collective (Dave, John and Anthony) I suggested a meeting to formulate a work plan. However, as John was tied up in the running/cleaning of the Club, and Anthony had a full-time job and numerous other Club demands, it was obvious I needed to recruit help to take the project forward. But this was after a number of attempts at kick-starting the project on my own.

The lack of volunteers and staff meant it became virtually impossible, at times, to remain focused on any one specific activity. Hence the early days at the club were *not entirely* involved with work on the studio project. Instead, I laminated membership-cards, cleaned the café, mopped toilets, washed dishes, and assisted with general tasks that all underlay the demands of everyday DIY activity. It is these activities that are the cornerstone of daily survival and the reproduction of the Club. Daily, thankless requirements of volunteers allow the Club to prepare for the demands of large events and gigs, in addition to facilitating its function as an everyday social hub for its three hundred strong membership. Anthony's diary entry reveals his frustration at being drawn into such tasks:

> Saturday 21st Aug 2001
> Drop in early at the club to take pastry out of the freezer to
> thaw, draw some funds from the PA collective (I'd paid for
> some cable and connectors in April with my credit card) – I
> need to pay for the truck parts I'm about to collect. As I'm
> leaving, the brewery arrives with a beer delivery. No one
> else is around so I have to take care of it; as they finish,
> the bar-steward arrives. They're early, or he's late. But the
> job got done anyhow in a spirit of no panic solidarity. Or
> something.

Similar to Anthony, I became drawn into essential tasks in the club and when it came to the studio had to either request assistance or become motivated enough to begin the task myself.

John showed me what the initial tasks of the studio project were. He said I should begin with hanging a door to allow the storeroom to be separated from the main control room. I had no previous experience of undertaking such activity and John was soon called away to another task in the club. I wrote the following in the field-journal once work had stopped because of a defective drill and my fruitless attempts to fix it:

> 18/06/01. John arrived back at the club and managed to get the drill going. The problem was solved by 'banging' the drill on the studio wall. This was not something I was comfortable with, due to the danger of this practice, but after a few 'knocks' the drill appeared to behave itself, though not for long: the work stopped again.

The following week was equally frustrating. At every turn in building the studio I found myself either distracted into other tasks or struggling to complete tasks due to my lack of practical DIY (construction) skills. The sense of frustration began to swell, as did the feeling that I was somehow 'missing out' on the 'real' club activity and that self-observation was pointless: participation was inhibiting observation.

What was apparent was that I would have to make things happen *myself* in order to make any progress. Through my insider status in both the Bradford and Leeds DIY punk scenes I recruited two new studio collective volunteers, who agreed to work for nothing. The first was one of the Club sound engineers, Russ, who had helped construct the Club when the building was purchased and also had long-standing involvement with DIY music. He was a student of sound engineering at a local university and was thus able to use this experience during the summer to expand our knowledge of studio construction. He was ethically clear about why he joined in with the studio project:

> It will be a good space [...] I mean it will be a way, hopefully, of giving people skills. I do hope people will be able to get in there and be able to learn the stuff and make mistakes and gain another rung in the ladder of production. It will make money for the club, hopefully. Use the space that's there, which is what the fucking building is for.

The second recruit, Scotty, was a club member who lived at the Leeds squat-venue known as the '120Rats.' He had been involved in renovating that building from a run-down hovel into a functioning venue. Scotty overheard me voicing my frustration about the studio project in the Club café, and he volunteered his services. John's reaction to Scotty's input was recorded in our interview:

> I had no idea how skilled Scotty was going to be involved: he was just sat in the cafe one day and I was moaning. I was sat there going "fucking hell, I have got to go down that fucking room and sit there. I can't lift stuff and get stuff right." Then Scotty during one lunchtime said "I'll come and give you a hand."

The project then progressed rapidly through the use of the immediate contextual punk scene resources (the field of force). The majority of the tools were of varying quality and were scattered throughout the building. As I noted above, the drill was the first stumbling point. Russ, in reaction to this sad state of affairs, supplied his own drill. The band Chumbawamba donated £500 for the studio project gleaned from their royalties for the popular song "Tubthumping," which they had allowed to be used in a car advert. Cocktail nights organised by the Club raised £100 and, in addition, 1in12 benefit gigs produced equal amounts of project money. Finally, one of the central self-generating funding methods was the hourly-rate charged to bands using the practice room. From various donations to the studio-project (via benefits, etc.), we now had a small amount of money to purchase tools and these were procured at various stages during construction. The project also had existing funds for essential building materials that came from sources within the immediate DIY punk network.

NAZIS AND THE BURNING OF ROME

As construction advanced towards the conclusion of my fieldwork, the immediate field of force both inhibited and advanced the project during an alarming event. Work was ongoing during the day of the Bradford riots of July 7th 2001, when the British National Party (BNP) attempted to march through Bradford and met with stiff opposition from anti-fascist groups and local protestors.[34] On the Saturday of the riots, the club was a staging post for Leeds Anti-Fascist Action and the café was open and very busy. Club security was doubled, with members and volunteers also posted on the top floor in order to scope out visitors before permitting them entrance via the door buzzer system. Studio collective members agreed to be present at the club due to Internet threats from the BNP, posted on the Club website. Upon my arrival that day, I discovered that there had been an attempt to set fire to the club by pouring engine oil on one of the exterior walls and igniting it. The atmosphere in the club that day was tense in light of both the failed arson attack and the riots. Club members were in and out of the building, returning with occasional reports of events during the run-up to the riots. Whilst this was happening, work on the studio proceeded as usual. But in contrast with the project's previous work, a number of new people got involved; four newcomers assisted to help complete of a section of the studio. The audible backdrop to that day's work was the sound of police helicopters, breaking glass, and sirens. John commented that we were "building a studio whilst Rome burned."

Overall, the riots ironically aided the studio project's progression, though fear was very much evident in the general atmosphere that day. Specifically, the Club was inspirational to newcomers who learned of its activities. Here John was explicit:

> Loads of people came in. People had come from London to resist the NF and were going "Oohh, this place is great." I imagined I was in a World War I soup kitchen, on this sort of wagon, a few hundred yards away from the front, 'cause people kept coming in talking about what was going on and then having their burger and going out again. Mobile phones were ringing and stuff and I was just, like, serving food which is, sort of like, kind of mundane really, but it was obvious that they needed to be fed and they did think that the place was great.

What one can also observe here was the intersection of mutual aid with the immediate fields of force, as the DIY community and club members banded together in the face of a threat to the club, both to build the studio and to protect the building from potential attack.

OUTCOMES AND POSTSCRIPT

My research observation at the club was completed by August 2001. Scotty and Russ focused their attention elsewhere and the project stalled. Without the volunteers and I, interest waned until Anthony and other Club members picked things up later that year. That the studio project halted for a time is evidence of the way the Club functions within the immediate field of force. Uneven access to resources, both financial and human, made for a slow conclusion to the project. But eventually, studio equipment was installed in 2002 and two years later in 2004, the studio project was up and running with a number of bands successfully recording material that has since been released on DIY labels as vinyl, CDs or free downloads that all stand as a testimony to the mutual efforts of everyone involved. I returned there to record three 12-inch records with my band during 2006-8, and the recordings were done at a fraction of the cost of any commercial studio. As of mid-2011, 'Studio1in12' (as it is now known) is exceedingly busy and has over twenty recorded albums to its credit.

Though the process of building the studio stirred feelings of frustration at the lack of progress, it is important to note that they were counterbalanced with feelings of determination, success, fulfillment and satisfaction. However, this sense of achievement was not equally shared amongst all members. Here John is candid:

> I haven't got the same sense of achievement building the studio as I had building the practice room because it is like having your second kid or something. It's like you have done it once. Obviously it's exciting but it's not the first time it's happened. I think when I actually hear a recording [...] it will hit me the most.

Whilst John notes the lack of feeling fulfilled, he was enthusiastic about the potential for the Club to achieve things that were deemed previously impossible:

> That sense that you can do what you want, really. Sort of freedom, within reason, you know. It's like today we can just go, "Alright. We are going to build a recording studio."

The Club provides spaces to achieve such goals and represents just one example amongst a global network of DIY ventures that are practical applications of DIY punk ethics. Projects are gradually accomplished if people are prepared to persevere within the demanding, immediate contextual field of force. But of equal importance in this case was the sharing of new skills between Club members. The DIY ethic had been *practically* extended: Club members and participants in the UK punk scene could now record cheaply and effectively, though this was certainly not an easy undertaking. The significance this project represents in terms of extending DIY cultural production is the shift from merely releasing and distributing records independently, to taking *physical* control of the recording process itself. This was unprecedented in the English DIY punk scene. Sned's comments reflect the more local effect of this success:

> I think the practice room and the studio have definitely improved the club. I am really looking forward to when our band can record in the studio that has been built by friends. I mean, that is everything that I am about with the band [...] If we could have just pressed the fucker [the record] there it would have been even better. But I mean that's one amazing, inspiring growth thing.

The frustrations of the project also serve to illuminate how DIY day-to-day practices operate within an immediate field of force. The constant reproductive tasks central to the survival of the Club mean that there is high turnover of volunteers, a perennial scarcity of resources and a lack of motivation, especially as the completion of essential daily tasks distract and remove members from achieving goals swiftly. This factor of 'struggle' leads to member burnout. That said, the extra revenue the studio and practice room now bring in provides a welcomed addition to the skeleton funding of the club. Indeed, my November 2006 recording session witnessed a collapse of the Club's sewage pipe from strong winds, and our studio fees directly paid for its repair (Dave also donated his fee to the Club). Whilst such acts are largely *ad hoc*, and operate under the anarcho-syndicalist badge of mutual aid "by all means necessary," the feelings of achievement (however sporadic) that spring from the successful completion of a DIY project are chief motivational factors in the DIY punk scene.

ETHNOGRAPHY AND CONTEXT

So what of the external, contextual field of force? In this case, it is a balance between the requirements of the academy (scholarship and research), the ethical context of the culture, and the participant status of the researcher. There are three dilemmas evident in undertaking a participant observation of one's own culture; I offer a short discussion of these by way of a conclusion.

First, in terms of undertaking the ethnography there was a conflict of interest regarding my use of a university scholarship (public money) to conduct research. Whilst the other club-members were toiling wage free in that studio, I was in receipt of a generous research grant and thus partially removed from the pressures of daily survival.

As a club member and long-time scene participant, this raised ethical issues for me: ones that have left a prolonged sense of guilt. Was I gaining, career-wise, from this undertaking, or was the club gaining from free labour power? Second, the fact that my long-term career prospects were secured by my research on the DIY punk scene has left me feeling ethically uneasy about the work. Have I indeed used this whole process as a career stepping-stone and potentially lost my scene credibility as a result? My immediate reaction to this question is "No," but the question persists. I also find it very difficult to now turn off my "ethnographic imagination" when participating in DIY activity; this is an occasional source of mental discomfort and anxiety.[35] Consequences of fieldwork have had a profound effect on my way of 'seeing' both my daily existence and my standing within the punk scene. Somewhat uncomfortably, I cannot easily switch off the role of fieldworker in non-research social situations. Third, in terms of the external context alluded to above, the narrativisation of club members into an academic discourse to which they are not privy, leaves me with an equal feeling of discomfort. Transferring the struggle of DIY daily practice into academic concerns and debates places me in the precarious position of both a participant and a commentator with reflexive positions of control in terms of the power of representation. With the institutional connections and financial support of my fieldwork have I indeed, and ironically, 'sold out'? This is a serious question that has had a long-standing impact upon both my sense of self and my standing in a scene based upon equality. To wit, I am now, post-viva, frequently referred to (by some of those involved in the research) as "Dr. Punk": a rather patronising, yet equally disciplinary term.

These personal dilemmas, or ones like them, seem unavoidable if one is to generate authentic data though fieldwork in one's own 'backyard.' Hypothetically, one solution to avoiding such feelings would be to employ a participant with no previous insider-experience in punk culture to conduct the field research on my behalf. The researcher could enter the field a 'stranger' and remain much closer to the external, contextual academic field than the community under observation. Both financially and practically, this is unrealistic. But more to the point, what one gains in critical distance one necessarily loses in detail *and* the opportunity to offer an authentic description of DIY punk. Generally then, the solution to this dilemma is the one I employed: suffer an uneasy trade-off in which, on the one hand, my ethical integrity as a researcher and the authenticity of the research were both preserved, but at the same time, the uncomfortable personal consequences of the research were accepted, leaving me uneasy about my status as *both* an academic and a long-time participant in the DIY punk scene.

Herein lies the unresolved "ethnographic predicament," previously identified by Clifford, which stems from researching one's own culture.[36] Ethnographic writing produced within the immediate and external contextual fields of force is hitherto *always* a careful balance between methodological platforms. Engaging in participant observation of a culture in which one has long-standing links and commitments will often raise a host of potential problems related to both professional and personal integrity: some of which have long-term residual consequences.

NOTES

1   Jon Savage, *England's Dreaming: Sex Pistols and Punk Rock* (London: Faber and Faber, 1991), p. 281.

2   See George McKay, *Senseless Acts of Beauty: Cultures of Resistance Since the 1960s* (London: Verso, 1996); George McKay (Ed.), *DiY Culture: Party & Protest in Nineties Britain* (London: Verso, 1998); Brian Edge, *924 Gilman: The Story So Far* (San Francisco: Maximumrocknroll Press, 2004); Berger, *The Story of Crass* (London: Omnibus Press, 2006).

3   See Alex Ogg, *Independence Days: The Story of UK Independent Record Labels* (London: Cherry Red, 2009), p. iii.

4   Keith Negus, *Producing Pop: Culture and Conflict in the Popular Music Industry* (London: Edward Arnold, 1992).

5   This is one aspect of DiY culture that has transferable potential for any researcher seeking to examine this ethical legacy in commensurate fields, for example hip-hop or political activism.

6   Michel de Certeau *The Practice of Everyday Life* (Los Angeles: University of California Press, 1984), p. 176; Henry Jenkins, *Textual Poachers: Television Fans and Participatory Culture* (London: Routledge, 1992), p. 24.

7   See Alan O'Connor, *Who's Emma: Autonomous Zone and Social Anarchism* (Toronto: Confused Editions, 2002).

8   See Alan O'Connor, *Punk Record Labels and the Struggle for Autonomy: The Emergence of DiY Culture* (Plymouth: Lexington, 2008).

9   Karen O'Reilly, *Key Concepts in Ethnography* (London: Sage, 2009), pp. 51-56.

10   Ibid, pp. 109-118.

11   Martyn Hammersley and Paul Atkinson, *Ethnography: Principles in Practice, 2nd Edition* (London: Routledge, 2006), p. 9.

12   Analytical problems of field-data analysis were addressed by following Glaser and Strauss's "grounded theory" method. Such procedure also

involved engagement with Strauss and Corbin's model of the "conditional matrix," that frames how ethnographic accounts are written up by taking into account contextual inhibitors such as resources, events and consequences. The conditional matrix is a component of Strauss and Corbin's grounded theory data analysis technique; it is principally used in the present research as a tool to incorporate wider cultural intervening factors, such as the Bradford riots. The conditional matrix is described as, an "analytic aid, a diagram, useful for considering the wide range of conditions and consequences related to the phenomenon under study. The matrix enables the analyst to both distinguish and link levels of condition and consequences" (Strauss and Corbin, p. 158). However, such accounts say little of the general legacy of writing ethnography by an insider and this is an issue for further discussion. See Anselm Strauss and Juliet Corbin, *Basics of Qualitative Research Techniques and Procedures for Developing Grounded Theory* (London: Sage Publications, 1990), pp. 158-175; Barney Glaser and Anselm Strauss, *The Discovery of Grounded Theory* (Chicago: Aldine, 1968).

13   As noted by Hammersley and Atkinson: "values refer to the human potential that is built into the unfolding of history," p. 15.

14   See James Clifford, *The Predicament of Culture: Twentieth Century Ethnography, Literature and Art* (Cambrdige, MA: Harvard University Press, 1988).

15   Clifford, 1988, pp. 255-276; Edward Said, *Orientalism* (New York: Pantheon Books, 1978).

16   Pierre Bourdieu, *The Field of Cultural Production* (Cambridge: Polity, 1993). For examples of this terminological crossover, see O'Connor, 2008.

17   Savage, 1991, p. 281.

18   Marcus Gray, *The Clash: Return of the Last Gang in Town* (London: Helter Skelter, 2001), p.153.

19   Hakim Bey, *T.A.Z The Temporary Autonomous Zone, Ontological Anarchy, Poetic Terrorism* (Camberley: Green Anarchist Books, 1991), p. 1.

20   O'Connor, 2008; Pierre Bourdieu: *Distinction: A Critique of the Judgment of Taste* (Cambridge, MA: Harvard University Press, 1984); Bourdieu, 1993.

21   See McKay, 1998, pp. 1-53.

22   See Elizabeth Nelson, *The British Counterculture 1966-73: A Study of the Underground Press* (London: Macmillan, 1989); Stephen Duncombe, *Notes from Underground: Zines and the Politics of Alternative Culture* (London: Verso, 1998); John Downing with Tamara Villarreal Ford, Genève Gil and Laura Stein, *Radical Media: Rebellious Communication and*

Social Movements (London: Sage, 2001); Christopher Atton, *Alternative Media* (London: Sage, 2002).

23 Michael Billig, *Talking of the Royal Family* (London: Routledge, 1992).

24 Peter Golding and Graham Murdock, "Culture, Communications, and Political Economy," in eds. James Curran and Michael Gurevitch, *Mass Media and Society* (London: Edward Arnold, 1991), pp. 60-83.

25 Gabriel Kuhn, *Sober Living for the Revolution: Hardcore Punk, Straight Edge, and Radical Politics* (Oakland, PM Press, 2010), p. 15.

26 See O'Connor, 2008.

27 Ogg produced a robust study of the history and legacy of the UK independent record label. Whilst anarcho-punk and its legion of subsequent projects have similarities to corporate production houses, there is a fundamental difference worthy of note. Broadly, independent labels still operate within the confines of the profit motive and equally within the organisation frameworks of major labels. By contrast, anarcho-punk and DiY record labels operate within the schema of complete control of the space of cultural production, thus keeping to an absolute minimum contact and engagement with major label or capitalist music institutions.

28 See Penny Rimbaud (aka J.J Ratter), *Shibboleth: My Revolting Life* (Edinburgh: AK Press, 1998); McKay 1996; Berger, 2006; John Robb, *Punk Rock: An Oral History* (London: Ebury Press, 2006); Ogg, 2009; Chris Daily, *Everybody's Scene: The Story of Connecticut's Anthrax Club* (Harrisburg: Butter Goose Press, 2009); Ian Glasper, *Trapped in a Scene: UK Hardcore 1985-1989* (London: Cherry Red Books 2009).

29 Rimbaud, p. 62 (emphasis is mine).

30 *What is the 1in12?*, (1in12 Twelve Pamphlets, 1995).

31 Rimbaud, p. 124.

32 *What is the 1in12?*, p.3.

33 For a complete discussion of the recent layout of the US DiY label system and associate field, see O'Connor, 2008.

34 The Bradford Riots ended with the Manningham area (of Bradford) in flames, with millions of pounds of damage inflicted. A car showroom and the Labour club were firebombed, with both white and Asian businesses finding themselves under attack by over a thousand Asian youths who were disgusted at the proposed march of the BNP through Bradford. Over 500 people were injured, 83 premises and 23 businesses were damaged at an estimated cost of £7.5m. (*BBC News,* October 15, 2007).

35 For detailed discussion of this issue see Paul Willis, *The Ethnographic Imagination* (Cambridge: Polity, 2000).

36 See Clifford, 1988.

GROWING UP CLICHÉD

IT SEEMS, DESPITE my best wishes otherwise, that I grew up somewhat clichéd. To be more precise, I grew up somewhere in suburban or ex-urban Pennsylvania, in an area populated by a curious collection of back-water rednecks and ex-New Yorkers trying to escape urban blight. It was, and still is, a location where a decaying economy served as fertilizer for flowering of discontented youth, but one that expresses this discontent through what is perhaps not an all too imaginative arsenal of expression.

For me, the space of discontent found to be most welcoming was the local punk scene, to the degree that there was one. Maybe less of a musical scene in any sense that would be recognized as one, but more a conglomeration of marginal social identities and forms (punks, goths, performance artists, literary types, etc.). Given that, it is not so surprising that I ended becoming involved and thinking about radical politics and art, starting through a series of what, in retrospect, would be described as less than mind blowing punk bands. In these short lived projects, aside from trying to bastardize together forms of music that did not always fit, I thought that if I managed to write a song that had just the right progression of chords and composition, the state itself would fall apart and some form of a glorious revolution would occur. In case you didn't notice, this didn't happen.

Some years after that, I found myself in the streets of New York for the worldwide protests against what was then the impending war in Iraq. In this case, it seemed that somehow, if we managed to get enough bodies in the streets, this would reach some critical point that would translate into the war not happening. This same idea was not confined to anti-war demos but fed through other forms of protest action, where it often seemed that if there just enough bodies, enough mass built up, then whatever particular questionable institutional or social arrangement (the IMF, capitalism, lack of health care, treatment of animals, etc.), would ultimately be transformed.

Both of these examples are connected by a magical conception and understanding: The idea that a certain set of actions or gestures would, by themselves, accomplish an outcome far exceeding what would reasonably be considered possible (if you actually thought about it for more than a few seconds). But if both of them are underpinned by magical conceptions, is that really such a problem? I'd suggest not, because even if in both situations what was hoped for did not actually come about (revolution spurred on by music, prevention of a war or effecting massive social change through a protest manifestation), these efforts put into action other forms of social energies and collective becomings. Other social relations became possible, composed through the performance involved.

And this is what I've learned most from punk, as a radical pedagogical apparatus for conveying ideas, shaping social relations and building communities. Punk is important precisely for how it finds ways to marry together political content in context and social relations. Or to put it another way, I learned just as much through the kinds of cooperative relations created through self-organizing shows, zines, musical projects and releases as I did by reading the liner notes of *Yes, Sir I Will* by Crass or thinking about the Gang of Four's lyrics. Punk, as a technology of rebellion, works most effectively (and affectively) when the process of artistic composition exists through a process of social composition, of bringing together and enacting other ways to live and be together in the world; ways not based on the values of capitalism or other forms of social domination and exclusion.

In the years after I started to become more interested in radical politics and organizing, I moved to New York City and got involved in the anti-globalization movement as well as various autonomous media projects. Since then, I have been very inspired by the tradition of radical politics most commonly known as autonomism, which focuses on both the kinds of social compositions that radical politics brings together, and also understanding how these composed forms of social relations have a primary role in shaping the world we live in. When I encountered these kinds of ideas they made sense to me through what I had already experienced with DIY organizing. Punk creates not just moments of excessive noise, but also moments of sociality excessive to capital: interactions and relations that are pushed beyond the commodity form and the domination of wage labor. And I don't think I was by any means the only person for whom punk was a gateway into radical politics, and for whom it represented what the autonomists would call a self-valorization of cooperative practices and relations. The same networks underlying and connecting the infrastructures of the DIY punk scene fed through, and supported, the formation of other projects and forms, like Food Not Bombs, Reclaim the Streets, and what eventually became known as the anti-globalization movement. This is the same trajectory that the folks who are now involved in the militant research and organizing project, Team Colors, followed: from the organizing of shows and social centers – which were understood as holding the potential to move beyond capital – to teasing out a radical politics starting from these relations.

Given how shitty it is in most of what the world population experiences as their working lives, a pressing problem to address once you've started to move beyond punk-as-pure-negation, is the question of what might be another way to organize economic relations cooperatively. This fed into a project I was involved in for several years: a worker-owned and -run record label, Ever Reviled Records. ERR produced and released music not only by punk bands, but from bands across a wide variety of genres (folks, blues, etc); the label was formed more around the idea of continuing to build a politicized counterculture. The purpose and method of ERR was a form of propaganda, but not only through the ideas contained with the music released and events organized, but also through the idea that creating cooperative forms of social relations and self-organization were themselves forms of propaganda. We understood what we were doing as direct action. Direct action not in the sense that it was any kind of direct confrontation or contestation, but that through creating self-organized forms and means for ourselves was to act directly, and without mediation or recourse to the state.

But creating forms of self-organized communities and cooperative relations are not enough in themselves. One of the main things I have learned from autonomist politics and analysis is that the problem of recuperation is inevitable, but this is not such a problem, or the problem that it appears to be. Recuperation in the sense meaning the process through which an idea or politics that was formerly radical or subversive becomes adapted into existing forms of power, whether by forms of state power, or more commonly by being turned into a commodity form, and sold back to us. And this presents itself as an obvious problem, as we're constantly confronted with any new idea, art form, or energy of social vitality being turned into another marketing campaign or something worse. But what I have learned from autonomist politics is that this happens constantly because it is capitalism itself that is parasitic and can only thrive and develop through its ability to render these social energies into new forms of capital accumulation and governance.

But recuperation is also not the problem it is often thought to be. The fact that it occurs does not mean that it is the end of radical politics.

Rather it means that any radical politics will face the problem, and maintain itself and its subversive potentiality by working through and against these dynamics. Recuperation thus offers new points of intervention for rethinking and rearticulating the very nature of radical politics. This is perhaps the greatest illustrative value of post-punk and no wave, in how they put forward one approach to recuperation. What does post-punk have to with the problem of recuperation? It's simple. Post-punk was for those who weren't in the right place or time to take part in the overly fetishized media version of 'the rise of punk.' But not being there at the 'right' moment doesn't mean there is no social energy or potential in punk. Rather, it just means you have to rip things up and start over again.

This is the creative recombinant dynamics of post-punk that Simon Reynolds explores in his book on it. You have to rip it up and start again both because of the problem of recuperation and that of falling into creative stasis and stagnation. Post-punk arises at the moment where the open space, creativity, and anger unleashed in the space opened up by punk became reduced to self-parody, formula, and unintended recuperation. People who weren't lucky enough to be in the metropolitan areas where punk originated found ways to turn the conditions of post-industrial cities and the ex-urban decay into materials for starting again. Things had just become stale and uninspiring. Ripping it up and starting again isn't necessarily a nihilist gesture, or pure negation, by breaking forms and practices up so that an open and creative space can be maintained. And this is what post-punk bands did, borrowing from the history of avant-garde experimentation to create new forms of dissonance, or working between social alliances of bohemian elements and working class kids to enable new forms of social cooperation and being together in the world.

Punk then is not a moment but a territory, something that creates a space for other forms of being together and mapping out a space for bringing about another world in common. It is, to borrow an idea from Deleuze and Guattari, a refrain. In the way that a child sings a song to herself to create a safe space in the dark, we too sing songs, both by ourselves and together, to create a space for ourselves in a world is indeed dark and troubled. It is the melodies and vibrations that compose a territory as they resonate through us in the territory we find ourselves in, and through that change that territory. This is punk not as a manic burst of energy that declares itself and then putters out after three minutes (or both sides of the 7"), but the creation of plateaus of energies and vibrations, of ways of relating and being together, that branch out into other projects and vibrations. Punk isn't punk because of the arrangement of chords, the speed of the songs, or a layer of crust in appearance, but in the way it breaks through the layers of social stagnation in everyday life and builds something else in its cracks.

In the new intro to the reprint of *Last of the Hippies*, Penny Rimbaud (the drummer for Crass and member of many other artistic-political projects during the past forty years), makes two comments that have really stuck with me as being important. The first is that most academics writing about punk totally miss the point, precisely because they end of focusing on the media spectacle of it (the Sex Pistols, news scandals, puking punks in gutters) rather than the forms of radical politics that grow around and through it. And secondly, the kinds of social antagonism and rebellion that found their expression in anarchist punk were by no means new, but just one incarnation of the almost timeless desire to subvert social domination in all its forms and embody more cooperative ways of living and being in the world.

ESTRELLA TORREZ

PUNK PEDAGOGY:
EDUCATION FOR LIBERATION AND LOVE

"LET ME SAY, WITH THE RISK OF APPEARING
RIDICULOUS, THAT THE TRUE REVOLUTIONARY
IS GUIDED BY STRONG FEELINGS OF LOVE. IT
IS IMPOSSIBLE TO THINK OF AN AUTHENTIC
REVOLUTIONARY WITHOUT THIS QUALITY...THEY
CANNOT DESCEND, WITH SMALL DOSES OF DAILY
AFFECTION, TO THE PLACES WHERE ORDINARY MEN PUT
THEIR LOVE INTO PRACTICE."[1]

THE ABOVE STATEMENT made by the revolutionary icon, Ché Guevara, encapsulates my experiences as both an educator and hardcore kid.[2] Understanding, accepting, and internalizing our own love, while allowing it to guide our daily interactions, reinforces respective humanity. It unites us with others, with our community and with our environments, constructed and natural. Following Paulo Freire, I believe that it is acting out of love when truly revolutionary acts happen. After years of involvement in hardcore, it was my strong belief in this concept of "love" that eventually moved me out of the hardcore scene completely. Having internalized the spirit of an emotionally filled environment, which at one time was so compelling, I walked away from hardcore. This essay, a lamentation of sorts, chronicles my simultaneous experiences attempting to create a university course situated in *punk pedagogy* and my struggles to understand punk as a pedagogical tool.

As a teenager, hardcore's undeniably anger-drenched, politically charged music drew me in and plunked me into a group of kids that were eager to question hegemonic ideologies. Its overtly emotional allure paralleled the countless injustices that my family, a settled migrant farmworker family in rural America, had come to view as normalized. For the first time in my short life, I saw that it was acceptable (and even expected) to be outwardly angry with the microaggressions directed by the predominantly white community toward my Mexican family. For once, my questions did not raise eyebrows or stop a conversation in its discursive tracks. What an energizing feeling to be part of a conversation, rather than simply the receiving end of a whispered conversation. In the rural Midwestern community where I was raised, the conciliatory apparatus given to young Latinos allowed navigation of the rural town's social landmines, while suggesting that we silently accept the racism that riddled our lives. This, of course, was a formal survival mechanism. While I accepted these words of wisdom from my family, I secretly screamed in frustration at our self-imposed silence. In response to our familial silence, hardcore (both the music and the subculture) inversely expected that I scream aloud. What an incredibly liberating feeling for a young Xicana feminist raised in a patriarchal, racist, and classist society.

Unfortunately, after a number of years, countless shows, festivals, and workshops, I took notice of the over-representation of white, middle class boys (not quite men) propagating the sorrowful lives of white suburbia. As a former farmworker, personally living the atrocities of American capitalism, the lyrical content felt insincere and naive. Moreover, it did not reflect my own lived reality. Regrettably, the world began to feel empty once again (a good time for the emptiness of *emocore* to enter my life). While white boys on stage jokingly stripped naked, their songs stopped resonating with me. Girls spent too much time looking *straight edge* and the frequent critiques of my choice to pursue higher education solidified my personal desire to leave a scene that at one point had been my only solace.

Those who vehemently sung lyrics raging about social inequities did not act upon the injustices embodied within their music and it became disappointingly apparent that the musical rage was purely performance without action. This once liberating and liberated space where *education* had occurred had instead become a site for *schooling*, a socializing space to train youth to be more punk than the next kid. I decided I wanted no part of this stagnant system. In the spring of 1998, I thanked hardcore for its role in my life and left my last show as frustrated as I entered the musical scene.

However, as my life continued, it became apparent that while you can take the kid out of the scene, hardcore will always rage within. At some point, it will once again emerge in our daily actions. In the following essay, I endeavor to describe my attempts, as a thirty-something straight edge Midwest Xicana vegan scholar and mother to bridge punk pedagogies within a university setting. However, as you proceed through this essay, do not be misled in that this is a 'how-to' manual. Do not assume that I flawlessly execute punk pedagogy, or even that I know exactly what punk pedagogy is. Instead, what follows is my attempt to create meaningful environment within the university based on a teaching philosophy which I began to call *punk pedagogy*. Based in my own hardcore youth, as well as my training within critical pedagogy, these attempts are couched within Freire's acts of love, passion, and fear – much like the very backdrop of hardcore itself.

CRITICAL PEDAGOGY

In *Pedagogy of the Oppressed*, Paolo Freire argues "Freedom is acquired by conquest, not by gift. It must be pursued constantly and responsibly."[3] In this way, we must actively pursue freedom rather than believe it is simply an entitlement that will be given to us. However, we cannot reach this point without first recognizing our role in the ongoing relationship of oppression oscillating between oppressor and oppressed. In this dialectic relationship, a clear division is commonly drawn between teacher and student based on a false notion of objectivity. The current educational systems holds steadfast to the notion that teachers are the owners of knowledge, while students are empty receptacles into which knowledge is poured. From this perspective, known as the banking model, education is a process of transferring information in a linear manner, rather than the dialogic production and transformation of knowledge.

I believe that education is a fundamentally empowering, liberating, and healing cycle of reciprocity between teacher and learner. Many university classrooms are shaped by a neoliberal agenda pushing for "educational policy to be centered on the economy and around performance objectives based on closer connection between schooling and paid work."[4] Consequently, as learning institutions struggle to maintain funding and turn to business-like models of generating entrepreneurial scholars, *punkademics* must fight to preserve counter-hegemonic sites of education within the corporate university. It is our individual responsibility to reclaim spaces of learning, despite pressures to propagate a degree-factory ethos.

Personally, I envision education and schooling as very different processes. In fact, the distinction between the two is quite obvious once outlined by Ivan Illich. *Schooling* is an institutionalized space meant to socialize individuals into societal norms, while *education* is a fluid process by which knowledge is transmitted, contextualized, and transformed.[5] Accordingly, education is a space where "knowledge emerges only in invention and reinvention, through the restless, impatient, continuing, hopeful inquiry human beings pursue in the world, with the world and with each other."[6] Unfortunately, as research indicates, these spaces are declining at an alarming rate, particularly as universities shift their focus from nurturing humanistic development to nurturing corporate relationships. As individual states in the US diminish funding for higher education, universities scramble to fill the financial gap by pressing faculty to go after foundation dollars in a process that at times removes them from their duties as educators.

Through this process, many universities are transformed into corporations, not places of education. Criticality and a praxis-based relation to knowledge production is void within this model, with faculty frequently unable to carve autonomous spaces for this process to emerge. In K-12 education, *No Child Left Behind* continues to supplant testing for assessment, which also suppresses the creative and activist impulses within education at the elementary and secondary levels.[7] In this environment, students become raw material to be processed, inculcated with false notions of meritocracy, alienated from their own development as human beings, and spit out as apathetic products. Despite my position as a faculty member who feels the tenure-system pressure to pursue an entrepreneurial trajectory, I remain steadfast in my belief that university education should emerge from intentional forms of critical pedagogy.

Through critical pedagogy, students and faculty alike endeavor to think about, negotiate through, and transform the relationship between the schooling institution, the production of knowledge, and its relationship to civil society.[8] Furthermore, as Joan Wink identifies, critical pedagogy "teaches us to name, to reflect critically, and to act," skills I once thought were at the foundation of hardcore.[9] While critical pedagogy has no singular definition, I evoke its applicability in an attempt to discuss a methodology that is grounded in the contextual intricacies that are neither static nor void of human experience.

PHILOSOPHY OF PUNK

As many books and documentaries have publicized, punk became an identifiable youth subculture vis-à-vis the expressions of working class white youth in the UK. For these marginalized kids, punk was manifest in a form of nihilistic and destructive aesthetic attacking mainstream ideologies. In these nihilistic explosions, punk enraptured disdain. Unbeknownst to many outside punk and hardcore scenes, the subculture's historical roots predate cultural icons, such as the Sex Pistols. Punk is not torn-and-tattered clothing held together by safety pins or brightly colored mohawks. Although the media (and *Hop Topic* capitalists) would have us believe that punk is a fashion statement paralleling a brief period of teenage rebellion. In fact, hardcore is both an epistemology (worldview) and ontology (nature of being). It is more than a lifestyle, even if it has an ideological stance. Punk is the everyday embodiment of anger and alienation. It is a critique of hegemony and the advocacy against conformity. To be punk, one must not only reject complacent consumerism but simultaneously question why she yearns for the material objects that occupy the spaces in our lives meant for love toward humanity. To be punk is to recognize how commodity fetishism supplants the spaces that allow us to work toward a just world, a world where we actively listen, respond, and dialogue.

As Craig O'Hara recognizes in *The Philosophy of Punk*, "punks question conformity not only by looking and sounding different, but by questioning the prevailing modes of thought."[10] Punk philosophy is an amalgamation of early punk goals that expressed "their rage in a harsh and original way" and whose "most hated thing in the world was someone who was willing conformist."[11] In this fashion, DIY (do-it-yourself) ideals call upon punks to stop relying on capitalist institutions by creating alternative means of production (whether it be music, fanzines, clothing, or even knowledge), thereby determining our personal and collective realities. While dominant education alienates youth from their individual life-worlds, punk pedagogy requires that individuals take on personal responsibility (anarchist *agency* in the face of capitalist *structuralism*) by rejecting their privileged places in society and working in solidarity with those forced on the fringes. By doing so, we strike to undo hegemonic macrostructures.

A WORKING DEFINITION OF PUNK PEDAGOGY

While punk philosophy frames how we interact with outside society, it likewise shapes our position as educators and the manner by which we construct the classroom (and other sites of knowledge sharing) as a learning environment. It is this particular pedagogical approach, influenced by our lived realities as punks, that we are able to establish a punk pedagogy. Punk pedagogy is a manifestation of equity, rebellion, critique, self-examination, solidarity, community, love, anger, and collaboration. It is space where the teacher–learner hierarchy is disavowed and the normative discourse of traditional education is dissembled. This particular pedagogy is, for me, a teaching practice that attempts to extrapolate the individual dimension from the social being. In a conversation with Myles Horton, co-founder of the Highland Folk School, Paulo Freire asserts that, "we cannot be explained by what we do individually, but undoubtedly there is a certain individual dimension of the social realization."[12] There is an undeniable relationship between our individual actions and our collective possibilities.

As "formally" trained educators, we are frequently led to believe we are "experts" and in turn carry ourselves as such. It is in this misguided belief that we internalize the false notion of "complete" self, which has little to learn from anyone other than fellow "experts." When describing Freire's work in democratic education, Carlos Alberto Torres asserts, "Democracy implies a process of participation in which all are considered equal. However, education involves a process whereby the 'immature' are brought to identify with the principles and life forms of the 'mature' members of society."[13] As a punk, I wholeheartedly oppose the idea of being an "expert," particularly when this is applied to individuals creating and disseminating a form of knowledge completely disengaged from the communities it is meant to represent.

Punk pedagogy requires individual responsibility for social actions, while invoking continuous reflexivity in our quotidian actions upholding supra institutions of oppression. While critical pedagogy is traditionally known to circulate in the walls academe, and punk ideologies are often times associated with youth counter-cultures, it is my belief that these two parallels can and do meet once punks begin to claim space within the academic world. It is my contention that we, what Zack Furness calls *punkademics*, carry with us the vestiges of punk culture into our pedagogical and classroom practices. If this is the case, the question becomes: once punkademics enter the university, can we merge punk ideology with a localized critical pedagogy in an institution that proliferates capitalism as the dominant economic modality?

MOVING TOWARD A PUNK PEDAGOGY

What does punk pedagogy mean? How does one engage in a punk pedagogy in the classroom, particularly if that individual is untenured? How can we, as punkademics, pursue a pedagogy committed to truly challenging the "hidden curriculum" that is threatening to dismantle higher education? In an era when apathy has become increasingly rampant and the school system is on the brink of a nationalized curriculum, can punk pedagogy reclaim the political space of the classroom? In my experience, I find these counter hegemonic spaces can and do exist, regardless if faculty members consciously pursue a punk pedagogy. As I stated before, this chapter is not intended to be a how-to manual or even a functional model, rather this text is meant to begin a discussion of how our individual and collective experiences as punks influence our teaching in the academy.

Recently, I taught a course focused on youth subcultures' linguistic and cultural practices as forms of resistance. The course objectives challenged students to interrogate and deconstruct their ideological positions on rebellion, complicity, and social roles in a dominator-culture.[14] One such core objective was for the students to consider the cultural significance in what Dick Hebdige terms *mundane objects,* those objects that symbolize self-imposed exile.[15] For Hebdige, these subcultural objects become icons, representations of forbidden identities or sources of value. The course's objectives interrogated the shift occurring when mundane objects, icons of consumer culture rejection, become sublimated by dominator-culture. What happens when these mundane "punk" objects are sold in department stores, such as *Hot Topic,* inevitably transforming these counter-cultural items into capitalist fodder.

In retrospect, the course had many difficulties. Honestly, the course became a painful experience stored away in the deep recesses of otherwise successful teaching experiences. As I write this essay, my stomach twists, begging me not to dredge up and return to those excruciating sixteen weeks of class. The course was riddled with issues from the onset. Pedagogically, the intent was to structure the course providing students maximum flexibility and ownership over classroom content and course design. However, my own training to be an "expert" overtook my ideals, resulting in a well-developed syllabus, complete with pre-selected foundational readings and an instructor-designed final project, including an adjoining analytical paper.[16]

My vision was to have a course where students thoroughly enjoyed the readings, arriving at our weekly seminars ready to engage in discussions examining our individual and social responsibility to heal an ailing society. Instead, the course transpired in a way that the readings confused the students, many of whom desired one-dimensional lectures. In turn, seminar conversation was often stagnant and uninformed. My initial attempt to create a "punk classroom," where we moved "from being

passive consumers of ideology to active participants in their cultures,"
fell painfully flat.[17] Perhaps, more lectures presenting the readings' chief
arguments could have made the students more comfortable; however,
lecturing seemed antithetical to the very structure of the seminar, which
was based on the collaborative construction of knowledge. Whereas,
I unreservedly reject the "banking model" of education that assumes
knowledge is seen as a gift bestowed upon students from those more
knowledgeable to others who are considered to know nothing; students
were uncomfortable in such a learning environment.[18]

During the semester, we covered multiple youth subcultures around
the world, beginning with Chicano zoot suiters and ending with nerdy
girls, each section focused on a subcultural group which rebelled against
the society that marginalized their respective communities based on class,
race, gender, sexual orientation, etc. Course discussions examined the impetus of each respective subculture, including its core ideals, attitudes, language usage, and in-group visual markers. The goal, as I envisioned it, was
to engage in meaningful dialogue critiquing the preconceived notions of
subcultures, factors contributing to those preconceptions, and the historic
significance of subcultures within the US. Moreover, I intended the class
to illustrate how youth were not always apathetic or complacent in the social constructs restricting their development as human beings. As O'Hara
notes, "there is a current feeling in modern society of an alienation so powerful and widespread that it has become commonplace and widespread…
It is as if we have all been brought here to function for ourselves in a way
that does not include others."[19] One such objective was to investigate how
global youth, out of contumacy, reject their socially constructed destiny by
participating in direct or in-direct action.

For example, the section on nerdy girls called upon students to interrogate the existence of rebellion and what constitutes a rebellious act.
Here, I wanted students to reflect on their own gendered ideas of rebellion, commonly limited by masculine constructions of resistance, actions such as open acts of misguided anger, property destruction, brick
throwing, and "punk fashion" as true markers of rebellion. Inversely, self-
identifying nerdy girls revolt against the conventional adage that to be
"cool" women must disengage their bodies from their intellects and occupy themselves with particular cultural material markers, friend choice,
and social practices.[20] Mary Burcholtz observes,

> For girls, nerd identity also offers an alternative to the
> pressures of hegemonic femininity-an ideological construct
> that is at best incompatible with, and at its worst hostile to,

female intellectual ability. Nerd girls' conscious opposition
to this ideology is evident in every aspect of their lives..."[21]

Their brightly colored dress reflects their affinity for fantastical creatures and positive attitude. Consequently (after much cajoling), the class
decided that although, nerdy girls did not listen to Bikini Kill and wore
primary colors, they were, in fact, intentionally participating in rebellion.

Even if the students eventually began to critically think about these
concepts, the class was an uphill battle and ended in poor instructor
evaluations (hopefully this is not indicative of my actual abilities as a
professor). In these documents, students commented that the professor
did not "lecture enough" and that I was "unorganized," to use only two
prominent themes. Upon readings the evaluations, I was emotionally
and pedagogically crushed, even if I also knew when the individual class
sessions failed. I spent the rest of the day curled up in the fetal position.

What the hell happened with the class? Where, exactly, did it go
wrong? The syllabus was laid out in such a way to encourage student
input and I explicitly described our collaborative roles in the course, both
teachers and learners in the process. As I began to think through the
semester, my initial defensive response was that students were clearly not
ready for taking responsibility for their learning, and were instead more
concerned with a grade rather than engaging in their *education*.

But then, after a few weeks of disappointment, it finally came to me.
What really went wrong was that we did not jump the hurdle of learning
as an act of liberating love; rather it was simply an obligation for degree
requirements. After an entire year's worth of self-reflection and numerous
discussions with my peers, both punkademics and non-punk academics,
I realize that my anger was misdirected. It was misguided to expect students to unreservedly accept the Freirian perspective where "education
[is] the practice of freedom." Without directly engaging students in the
discussion of democratic and liberatory education, I preempted course
objectives before the cycle of teaching-learning even began.

Not recognizing that university students have lived through more
than thirteen years of schooling fashioned on the "banking model," it
was my mistake to throw them into a class completely contrary to what
they were accustomed. In attempting to teach a course out of *love*, I
blindly disregarded their expectations of my role as a professor. My un-
certainty in creating such an environment was clearly demonstrated in
the course's organization. It was unwise to structure a course based primarily on student input, without having the students participate in this
from the onset. Why would they understand the course objectives if they

were asked to jump in at the back end of the process?

It is at this point when I concretely relate this teaching anecdote to the construction of punk pedagogy. The foundations of the course were imagined to emulate a show, where "band members were no different than audience members."[22] For those of us reared in hardcore, we are familiar with the expectations that bands and audience were involved in every facet of the show, from organizing the event to getting up on the stage to singing along. The punk style, similar to critical pedagogy, tears down the standard barriers present in the performer–viewer relationship, as well as educator–learner. By embracing this loving act to dismantle hierarchical forms of domination, the educator–learner understands the importance in practicing counter-hegemony as a necessary act for liberation.

My pedagogical approach to the course aimed for the same goal. I began the course by presenting my relationship with the theme and my interest in examining the material through an "academic" perspective. Furthermore, I stated that my background was not in cultural studies and therefore this was new course material for me. I hoped my sincerity would illustrate that I would be learning alongside the students, and that, in fact, there was not an "expert" in the room. In this way, we were both band and audience in the punk classroom, both working through the process of teacher and learner. The stage (in this occasion, a university classroom) was an open forum that everyone occupied, jumping on and off whenever the mood struck us. Through the frame of punk pedagogy, where the teacher–learner roles are dismantled, we shared the stage screaming lyrics of injustice was not manifest with non-punk students. Unfortunately, the show did not work as intended.

CONCLUSION

Even if my course did not function as smoothly as I would have liked, this does not suggest punk pedagogy can or does not exist in the university. I understand the point of this chapter was to layout what punk pedagogy is, but this task is incredibly daunting and an almost presumptuous undertaking for an individual. How can I define something that I find so completely personal and reflective of one's life experiences? How can I define something that seemed to fail me when I try to imply it? In the end, my experiences as both a punk and educator have intersected at various times, diverged at others, and mapped onto one another countless times during my time as both student and professor.

So what did I learn through this experience? I learned that punk pedagogy and critical pedagogy are incredibly similar. While critical pedagogy was created with the old bearded men in the academy and punk pedagogy began with marginalized youth on the streets, both emerged in response to poverty, capitalist injustices, and global inequality. My experiences as a punk in the academy have opened a space where I may bridge both my understanding of critical pedagogy and punk practices. This particular theoretically infused anecdote suggests that reclaiming such a space needs concerted effort and strategic planning merged with a DIY ethic.

To be a *punkademic* is both frightening and alluring, particularly because once we are identified as such, our politics become definable. While I find it a mark of pride to identify as a *punkademic*, I am nonetheless terrified to not live up to such a designation. How can I truly be a *punk educator* when I work within the university? Aren't these contradictory, as other punks let me know years ago? Can I, as a punk and professor, truly be likened to those other revolutionary practitioners when working in dominant institutions? Regardless of my own doubt in successfully maintaining a punk pedagogy, it nonetheless serves as my ultimate goal within the classroom; therefore, it becomes an eternal struggle to attain such an environment.

I continue grappling with creating a balance between these two roles, teacher and learner, in the class. In those learning spaces when I begin with a brief lecture, students industriously write notes without making eye contact. It is during these moments when I feel utterly alone in the classroom, a sensation that is antithetical to my reason for pursuing higher education in the first place. The front of the class is an isolating place, especially when speaking without being heard, as only a women of color can attest to. Regardless of the number of times we will discuss the lack of freedom when education is reduced to the regurgitation of "truths" or "facts," I sense it is nonetheless still what students want or understand education to be (even if I would call this schooling). Therefore, it our responsibility, as punkademics, to scream out in anger and frustration as the neoliberal and entrepreneurial model overtakes learning spaces. We must work collaboratively and collectively with others in revolutionary acts of love. If we find the space to teach in such a way, then we have found a punk pedagogy.

NOTES

1   Ché Guevara, as cited in Jon Lee, *Che Guevara: A Revolutionary Life* (New York: Grove, 1997), pp. 633, 637.

2   Although, I am clearly not a teen, I consider myself a hardcore kid. For all intents and purposes in this text punk and hardcore will be used interchangeably.

3   Paulo Freire, *Pedagogy of the Oppressed* (New York: Continuum, 1970), p. 47.

4   Michael Apple, *Ideology and Curriculum* (New York: Routledge, 2004), p. 74.

5   Ivan Illich, *Deschooling Society* (New York: Harper and Row, 1971).

6   Freire, 1970, p. 72.

7   See Peter Lichtenstein, "Radical Liberalism and Radical Education: A Synthesis and Critical Evaluation of Illich, Freire, and Dewey," *American Journal of Economics and Sociology*, Vol. 44, No. 1 (1985): 39-53.

8   Peter McLaren, *Life in Schools: An Introduction to Critical Pedagogy in the Foundations of Education* (New York: Longman, 1998).

9   Joan Wink, *Critical Pedagogy: Notes from the Real World* (New York: Longman, 1996), p. 3.

10 Craig O'Hara, *The Philosophy of Punk: More Than Noise!* (Oakland: AK Press, 1999), pp. 27-28.

11 O'Hara, p. 27.

12 Myles Horton and Paulo Freire, *We Make the Road by Walking: Conversations on Education and Social Change* (Philadelphia: Temple University Press, 1990), pp. 9-10.

13 Carlos Alberto Torres, *Democracy, Education, and Multiculturalism: Dilemmas of Citizenship in a Global World* (Oxford: Rowman & Littlefield, 1998), p. 162.

14 In *Teaching Community*, bell hooks states that dominator-culture keeps society bound in a state of fear and encourages homogeneity (particularly in thinking) rather than diversity. See bell hooks, *Teaching Community: A Pedagogy of Hope* (New York: Routledge, 2003).

15 Dick Hebdige, *Subculture: The Meaning of Style* (London & New York: Routledge, 1979), pp. 2, 66.

16 The latter was a reluctant contribution, but developed after pressure from squeamish students uneasy with the idea of allowing their projects to organically develop.

17 Seth Kahn-Egan, "Pedagogy of the Pissed: Punk Pedagogy in the First-Year Writing Classroom," *College Composition and Communication*, Vol. 49, No. 1 (1998): 100.

18 Freire, 1970, pp. 71-86.

19 O'Hara, pp. 21-22.

20 Mary Burcholtz, "Why be Normal?": Language and Identity Practices in Community of Nerd Girls," *Language in Society*, Vol. 28, No. 2 (1999): 203-223.

21 Burcholtz, p. 213.

22 O'Hara, p. 153.

MARIA ELENA BUSZEK

HER LIFE WAS SAVED BY ROCK AND ROLL:

TOWARD A FEMINIST PUNK ETHIC/ AESTHETIC

MY WORK TO date as scholar of contemporary art has largely revolved around attempts to historicize feminist uses of pop culture toward political ends – and the trouble with which these efforts have consistently been met, in relation to generational, intellectual, and class issues. From Elizabeth Cady Stanton to Alice Paul to Gloria Steinem to *BUST* magazine, when young feminists have held up their pop-cultural savvy as an expressive or recruiting tool for their era, they have also had to wait at least a generation for this approach to be considered with any seriousness by established thinkers both within and outside of the feminist movement. (At which point, inevitably, the media begins salivating over the impending catfights they might exploit between this generation of leaders and the inevitably-painted overly-optimistic, over-sexed, under-appreciative behavior of the generation coming up behind them.) So, what begins – with popular imagery, music, fashions, languages, or media employed toward reaching out to new audiences – as a gesture of inclusion becomes divisive. The persistence of this phenomenon, I argue, reveals the short-term, or at the very least selective, memory of feminist history.

But, the problem is a much bigger one in my field. Too frequently feminism is viewed in my particular discipline of art history as an *interpretive tool* rather than an *activist movement*. And art historians, regardless of age, specialization, or political engagement, are generally a library-dwelling species: so much so that those who write about contemporary art are often viewed by our colleagues with suspicion for what is perceived as the insufficiently "scholarly," and often social quality of our field. I work on – and thus research, write about, and deign speak to...even, perhaps, form friendships with – living artists responding to a living, constantly evolving culture. Because this culture is engaged in a dialogue with the popular as well as scholarly sources these artists reference means that critics of contemporary art must be as willing to track their artists' references to the street as to the studio, where these references are not as neatly confined and, thus, classified. Art historians' frequent mistrust of contemporary art in general, and pop culture in particular also speaks more broadly to the academy's fear of the personal, the phenomenological, the physical as somehow existing in opposition to the objective, the empirical, the intellectual. Time and again, I am blindsided by the responses of my colleagues for whom the pop-cultural influences I discuss alongside contemporary feminist art – many times, work with which they are familiar – are viewed as a shocking discovery or questionable diversion.

Such responses are disheartening, if only because it is in the realm of pop culture that one arguably finds the most visible, vibrant, and persuasive reflections of emerging feminist art today. Contemporary independent music in particular is loaded with examples of out-and-proud feminist artists, most of whom actually have direct ties to the international art world, such as Le Tigre, Tracy + The Plastics, and Peaches. All of these artists create cutting-edge music inspired by punk, metal, and hip-hop, and do so with overtly feminist lyrics and consciousness – but fly almost completely under the radar of feminist art criticism, regardless of the fact that these same women have been included in exhibitions at such highly visible venues as Deitch Projects, the Whitney Biennial, and the Venice Biennale. Yet arts professionals whose attention to the media rarely strays from established, mainstream print magazines, newspapers and academic journals are under the mistaken impression that young women championing feminist issues and demonstrating a deep familiarity with feminist history do not exist, because they are rarely reported upon, much less given opportunities to speak for themselves – or when given the chance (from the 1998 *Time* magazine cover on "Ally McBeal feminism" to Susan Faludi's November 2010 *Harper's* cover story on young women's "ritual matricide" of feminist mentors), young women are overwhelmingly and sensationistically portrayed as rejecting feminism.[1]

This oversight leads us to the critical perception of not just young women, but youth itself by the academic institutions from which much feminist art scholarship is generated. Ever since the very notion of a "popular culture" emerged with Industrial Revolution technologies and economies, the perception has been that pop culture, and especially popular music, is a young person's game. And, of course, youth culture has consistently been perceived, like youth itself, as both temporary and oversexed: so completely and unabashedly pandering to its audience's intemperate pursuit of pleasure that even the most detached and objective scholar risks becoming personally implicated in the orgy. Unless it is firmly embedded in a study of the past (and, better still, used solely to illuminate one's understanding of an "important" historical painting, sculpture, or print by a blue-chip artist), popular culture is kept at arm's length for fear of what it reflects upon the scholar who dares analyze it.

Which brings us to the class issues surrounding the discipline of art history, from which most scholars come. For decades now, art scholars, curators, and critics alike have generally been expected to pursue or possess a PhD, of late a degree only valuable when derived from one of about a dozen, mostly private institutions valorized by art history programs around the globe (themselves, increasingly populated solely by faculty from these same dozen institutions). And – consciously or unconsciously – art criticism and scholarship seems to increasingly share the academy's obsession with the (blue) bloodlines of these exclusive institutions. Indeed, universities and museums alike still often rely upon the assumption that its art historians will have the means to supplement low salaries or unpaid internships with independent wealth. Even when engaged with issues of class (through Marxist, postcolonial and, yes, feminist methodologies), art history has yet to meaningfully confront the elitism at the very foundation of the discipline's history, methods, and professional practices.[2] And so, the idea of studying popular culture – which, for many populations throughout the world represents "culture," period – remains, like the working class and underprivileged populations to whom it is directed, largely outside of the purview of art-historical inquiry.

Personally? I think that art history – and especially feminist art history – needs its own Lester Bangs.

I spent the first several months of my job at the used record store where I worked during my high school and undergraduate studies, engaged in the thankless task of sorting and pricing a solid, floor-to-ceiling-full room of music magazines that had piled up over the course of nearly two decades. It was here, a lone girl in the dusty stacks of Dirt Cheap Records (frankly, doing more reading than working), that I discovered Bangs' writing. From his earliest reviews in *Rolling Stone* and *Creem* in the late 1960s until his death from an accidental overdose in 1982, Bangs wrote some of the twentieth century's most informed and innovative criticism of popular music. Bangs gleefully skipped from rock history (such as his persuasive efforts to recuperate novelty acts like The Count Five and the Mysterians) to defenses of both the avant-garde (Kraftwerk and The Clash) and guilty pleasures (in particular, the Swedish pop of ABBA), to political commentary (his "White Noise Supremacists" arguably remains the punk era's most responsible insider analysis of the scene's sexism and racism), in a style that never buried the pleasure at the root of his partisan positions – positions that constantly shifted as the years went on. He unapologetically acknowledged and analyzed his revisions in a manner that readers granted him because of the deeply personal place from which all his criticism came.[3]

Reading Bangs' work for the first time, still in my teens, I was surprised to find parallels between his simultaneously joyful, critical, and insistently embodied approach to pop culture and my own. Having grown up in Midwestern communities where the closest thing to a "library" in my neighborhood was my musician father's enormous record collection, I began collecting records myself at around age 9 and learned to bond with my father by instigating what eventually became deep and frequently contentious debates about music history. The stacks in which I dug, shopped, and eventually worked were my first education in the "archive," where I learned and loved the same sort of information safaris that I later applied to my earliest research in art history. Coming up in this informal but informed, as well as overwhelmingly male-dominated culture of record collecting also nurtured my feminism, as I grew up well aware of the phenomenon whereby I needed to be twice as demonstrably knowledgeable as my male counterparts to be considered half as smart. My burgeoning feminist voice found inspiration in Bangs' unique, self-aware style; as his critical practice developed, he grew quicker to point out the frequency with which the "ironic embrace of the totems of bigotry crosses over into the real poison" in the same pop culture that simultaneously fueled and frustrated us both. Bangs offered that the growing sense of responsibility that emerged in his later music criticism came about "not because you want to think rock and roll can save the world but because since rock and roll is bound to stay in your life you would hope to see it reach some point where it might not add to the cruelty and exploitation already in the world."[4]

But, this was where Lester and I differed: I believed, and still believe, that rock and roll *can* change the world. It certainly changed mine.

My own path to becoming a feminist, art historian, and educator was forged not by my formal education, but from my immersion in the popular culture with which I grew up – in the first wave of hip-hop, the second wave of punk, and the third wave of feminism that emerged in the tumultuous 1980s – amid the postmodern theory, AIDS crisis, "Sex Wars" and, most importantly, voices of queer activists and feminists of color that would name these "new waves" of popular and protest culture. While my mother's generation may have looked to heroic feminist literary predecessors like Simone de Beauvoir and Betty Friedan, and activist contemporaries from Gloria Steinem to Angela Davis for inspiration, my generation enjoyed the luxury of looking to models a little more earthbound and a lot more diverse, fashioning themselves after the models that best resembled young women's cursory, and highly individualized ideas about the women's movement: Poly Styrene, Lydia Lunch, Pat Benatar, Grace Jones, Siouxsie Sioux, Joan Jett.[5] I was able to take its teachings for granted not just in the literature and legislation for which the movement fought, but in unsanctioned and even critical reflections of feminism in youth culture.

As cultural historians Joanne Hollows and Rachel Moseley have argued, unlike previous generations, for whom there had always been an "outside world" that those inside the feminist movement were invested in challenging and infiltrating, those growing up in its third wave "never had a clear sense of, or investment in, the idea of an 'inside' or 'outside' of feminism:" feminism could be, and often was, just about everywhere.[6] This constellation of pop-culture icons would later merge with the culture of our feminist predecessors in what would become the most visible organized movement of the third wave, Riot Grrrl. This international movement first coalesced on the high school and college campuses of the United States in the late 1980s at a point when feminist thought – both overtly and covertly – was becoming a regular part of most students' curricula. Riot Grrrl was the brainchild of young women who, like me, strove to pair up and analyze their twin interests in pop culture and feminist thought in ways that the culture surrounding each often didn't realize was possible.[7]

Riot Grrrl activists joined veteran feminists in organizing reproductive-rights marches, volunteering at Planned Parenthood and rape-crisis centers, and creating alternative art and performance spaces, but they also argued for the activist potential of founding their own bands, 'zines, record labels, festivals, and eventually websites to spread the word of this generation's continued resistance to constraining gender expectations – expectations that many young women often argued had been as narrowly defined by feminist predecessors as their sexist antagonists. They also spoke directly to the need for diversity in the movement, incorporating an awareness of feminism's historical heterosexism, classism, and white privilege into its discourse and action, and insisting that male and genderqueer feminists had roles in the movement alongside biological women.

In the twenty years since the birth of Riot Grrrl, its growth on many different levels is apparent in the evolving work of movement leaders like Kathleen Hanna: where her pioneering band Bikini Kill analyzed feminist issues through songs dedicated to the intimate, personal details of girls' lives in hard-driving punk singles and Xeroxed and stapled 'zines, today her scope and media have broadened; and her current band Le Tigre communicates through its website, which includes links to Judy Chicago's and Laurie Anderson's homepages, sites offering support for transgender activism and domestic violence victims, and an entire section dedicated to how you can make, record, and distribute your own music using inexpensive or free gear, and songs like the band's instant-dance-classic "Hot Topic" name-check figures from Modernist poet Gertrude Stein to transgender artist Vaginal Davis, to a sampled vintage-R&B backbeat, accompanied online and in live performances by a similarly-sampled, digital-collage video by artist Wynne Greenwood.

Greenwood's own, one-woman-band Tracy + the Plastics is another excellent example of Riot Grrrl's ongoing influence and evolution in the contemporary art world. Greenwood similarly uses popular music as a vehicle for self-expression and community-building, and treats the growing accessibility of digital media as an important evolution in feminism – as much for how these media are shifting young peoples' perceptions of reality as their ability to communicate. Greenwood argues that new media like digital recording and technological developments like Web 2.0 encourage "deliberate edits to reconstruct an empowered representation of reality. One that not only allows for but demands inquiry, challenge, talk-back, yelling, waiting, and joyful understanding between the 'viewing' individual and at least one other person, possibly a lot more, and maybe even the media makers."[8] The "members" of Tracy + the Plastics – slightly bossy front woman Tracy, contentious keyboardist Nikki, and spaced-out percussionist Cola, who "play all the instruments and sing" on the band's albums – appear in live performances as Greenwood performing as Tracy onstage, who interacts with Nikki and Cola as pre-recorded video projections.

Greenwood has written of the band's underlying goal: "A Tracy and the Plastics performance attempts to destroy the hierarchical dynamics of mass media's say/see spaces by placing as much importance on the video images (the plastics) as the live performer (tracy)."[9] And, between the awkward, silence-laden on-stage "banter" of Greenwood in her various permutations and the pointedly open stage set-up, wherein the performance occupies a space that bleeds out into the seating, this "hierarchy-destroying" approach extends to artist-audience dynamics as the viewers are similarly encouraged to blur the line between who is there to "say" and who is there to "see." As Greenwood explained at a recent performance at The Kitchen in New York, Tracy + the Plastics explore feminism through an exploration of inhabited space, asking: "What does it mean for me, a feminist lesbian artist, to take up room?"[10] At this three-night engagement, "the band" performed in an elaborate living-room setting (right down to the beige pile carpeting ubiquitous in homes built or remodeled in the 1980s or '90s) that pointedly blurred the distinctions between the audience, performer/s, and projected imagery.

More recently, Greenwood has collaborated with the LTTR collective, through which she has furthered her experiments with the line between artist and audience, self and community. Originally founded as "Lesbians To The Rescue" in 2001 – a collaborative print and web 'zine of writing, artwork, and new media – the group has since annually changed its acronym (to such evocative names as "Lacan Teaches to Repeat, "Let's Take the Role," "Listen Translate Translate Record") and evolved into a sprawling collective of individual contributors and curators putting together installations, exhibitions, screenings, protests, music, and workshops, (most recently, alongside the traveling blockbuster exhibition *WACK! Art and the Feminist Revolution,* and in the work of several individual members included in the current Whitney Biennial).[11] Greenwood has articulated the appeal of the collective (saying): "LTTR can be seen as a body, a person, an 'individual' and expresses the idea that our community can stand next to us, the individual, the one person," which I hope to relate to the sensibility that LTTR co-founder, artist and curator Emily Roysdon recently coined "ecstatic resistance."[12] Art historian Julia Bryan-Wilson – the lone scholarly voice who has approached the group's work – has approvingly defined LTTR's political practice as "critical promiscuity" generating unexpected connections across genres and media as well as the generational, ethnic, gender, and sexual identities of the artists who contribute them.[13]

While Greenwood and LTTR explore the feminist possibilities of critical promiscuity, Peaches...well, I suppose she's just plain exploring the feminist possibilities of promiscuity. While Peaches is a legend in the electronic music scene, members of the contemporary art community may recognize Peaches from Sophie Calle's sprawling installation at the 2007 Venice Biennale's French Pavilion, *Take Care of Yourself.* In this powerful, hilarious piece Calle turns a statement of rejection – a break-up e-mail from a long-term boyfriend – into a statement of affirmation, using 107 other women's voices and experience to re-read, reinterpret, and recover from the message. It seemed significant to me that Peaches was chosen by Calle as the last reader/interpreter of the letter considering the ecstatic, if silly sexuality of Peaches' music. Peaches is the final woman in Calle's *Take Care of Yourself* with a song she composed and sings using fragments of the letter's text. Unlike the largely vindictive or dismissive readings of the rest of the participants – proof-readers, editors, artists, actresses, psychoanalysts, schoolgirls, a judge, a clown, a clairvoyant – Peaches' confident, abstract, musical take ends on an elliptical, but optimistic, even edifying note, with an (utterly transformed) phrase from the email: "I will always love..."[14]

Born Merrill Nisker in North York, Canada, after a decade in the Toronto lesbian-folk scene and teaching preschool-aged children music and theater, Peaches invented her outrageous on-stage persona – named after one of the "Four Women" in Nina Simone's haunting song of the same name – and began collaborating with (the now, chart-making) singer-songwriter Feist, composing music and experimenting with hip-hop beats toward what would eventually become her groundbreaking album *The Teaches of Peaches* in 2000 – a showcase for Peaches' wild musical and performative mash-up: comedic, over-the-top-sexual braggadocio in the tradition of R&B diva Millie Jackson; tinny. old-school hip-hop beats and rhymes; and fuzzy, glam-rock riffs and get-ups, all (in her words) "made, mixed, and mutilated" by this androgynous former folkie one reporter described as "aggressively unpretty."[15]

What could have been a novelty act, however, evolved over Peaches' next several albums, where the gender-bending, queer sensibility that pervaded her first evolved into a more clearly feminist one – what began as foul-mouthed effort to freak out the squares seemed to take on more explicit political connotations in subsequent albums, videos, and performances, and in venues such as the Toronto Biennial and ArtBasel Miami as well as rock clubs. Acting out the most spectacular, shock-rock clichés – metallic outfits with matching platforms, straddling guitar necks with attendant crotch thrusts, "on the left/on the right" sing-a-longs – Peaches simultaneously embraces the stupid fun of a rock show and dismantles the notion that only straight men could pull it off admirably. Indeed, her metal-inspired song and video for "Boys Wanna Be Her," sampling AC/DC's anthemic "Dirty Deeds," addresses the subject head-on. Peaches has spoken of what inspired the piece in an interview (saying): "I was thinking how men seem to find it really difficult to look at a powerful woman and say, 'Wow! I wish I was you.' The inspiration might have been [...] any of those songs where it's like 'The boy comes to town! Lock up your daughters!' I mean, why is it a guy who gets to play the Antichrist?"[16]

So, my question is: where in art scholarship has there been room for the feminist potential of the Antichrist? Or, at least the shock-rocker? Calle's brilliant, surprising use of Peaches as the transcendent end to the journey of *Take Care of Yourself* seems to happily suggest a place at the table. But, queer activist, filmmaker and critic Bruce LaBruce is the only arts writer to date to tackle the subject, writing: "In pop cultural terms, the intelligent, quirky, female icons of the '70s (Karen Black, Sissy Spacek, and, well, for better or for worse, Helen Reddy), with normal bodies and obvious flaws, have been replaced by the likes of Britney Spears, Jessica Simpson and Pamela Anderson, the shaved and plucked, air-brushed, plastic blow-up doll triumvirate that we know and hate today. Peaches takes up where the kind of militant, subversive, and sexy feminism of the '70s left off."[17]

But, really? Helen Reddy? Well, for better or for worse...Reddy's feminist-lite anthem "I am Woman" surely helped more women in the 1970s consider the acceptability of feminism in the wake of the popular backlash against the second wave than purchased the works of Shulamith Firestone, Kate Millet, and Robin Morgan combined in that same decade. But, in a decade that *also* introduced the world to the *truly* "militant, subversive, and sexy feminism" of Lydia Lunch, Cosey Fanni Tutti, Martha Wilson and DISBAND, and Linder Sterling – just to name a few women directly tapped into both the music and art worlds of that very decade – LaBruce's slight demonstrates the limited scope of even the best-intentioned art criticism, brought about in large part because of the narrow histories and subtle prejudices by which scholars so frequently confine themselves, and which my next book will attempt to redress.

How many members of the feminist community know about the rock criticism of artist Lorraine O'Grady, director Mary Harron, or journalist and Redstockings co-founder Ellen Willis? Willis wrote deliciously of her own juxtaposition of rock and feminist rebellion in the 1960s and '70s, in a way that perpetually inspires me: "Music that boldly and aggressively laid out what the singer wanted, loved, hated – as good rock'n'roll did – challenged me to do the same, and so even when the content was anti-woman, antisexual, in a sense antihuman, the form encouraged my struggle for liberation."[18] It is striking to me that the album that led Willis to this revelation in her essay "Beginning to See the Light" was the Sex Pistols' album *God Save the Queen*, which she had fought hard not to like – for the same racism, sexism, and fascist imagery that riled Bangs – even as she ultimately submitted to what she called the "extremity of its disgust" as both a catalyst to and a strategy for action.[19]

That feminism expresses itself these days perhaps most tangibly on the dance floor seems relevant to me as a feminist art historian, as it is a profound reflection of what it means for feminist thought to have evolved into a generation of emerging artists without "the idea of an 'inside' or 'outside' of feminism." And such popular expressions of feminism also reiterate the pressing need for feminist scholars to address the power of pleasure, joy, and embodiment as activist strategies. A politics of pleasure has emerged in the work of feminist artists choosing to engage with popular culture – one that, more than ever, deserves a feminist art criticism to recognize, broadcast, and analyze its goals. And this work, these women deserve feminist scholars willing to both historicize these strategies and use them as a model for their own. Not just because contemporary feminist interventions in popular music and performance are an education in the ever-evolving nature of the women's movement, but because they also resemble those, largely unsung, by predecessors like Willis in the second wave of the women's movement. I certainly have Helen Reddy in my record collection – but wonder how many others who do *also* own CDs by Le Tigre or Peaches...not to mention what thrilling new forms feminist discourse might take if this was the case.

NOTES

1   I address the problem and history of such media portrayals extensively in Maria Elena Buszak, *Pin-Up Grrrls: Feminism, Sexuality, Popular Culture* (Durham: Duke University Press, 2006), pp. 325-364.

2   While the subject of classism in the discipline of art history is one far too complex, contentious, and undocumented to possibly be given its due here, I would guide readers to the succinct, excellent analysis of the problem of elitism in the professional practices of art and academic institutions in David Graeber, "Army of Altruists: On the alienated right to do good," *Harper's Magazine*, January, 2007, pp. 31-38.

3   Much of Bangs' writing remains in print, available in anthologies such as (Ed.) Greil Marcus, *Psychotic Reactions and Carburetor Dung* (London: Serpent's Tail, 2001); and (Ed.) John Morthland, *Main Lines, Blood Feasts, and Bad Taste: A Lester Bangs Reader* (New York: Anchor Books, 2003). Many thanks to Raphael Rubinstein, whose visit to the Kansas City Art Institute campus in 2005 instigated a conversation on the subject of Bangs that I relish the opportunity to follow through upon here.

4   Lester Bangs, "The White Noise Supremacists," *Village Voice*, December 17, 1979, reprinted in *Psychotic Reactions*, pp. 275 and 282.

5   For a more detailed account of my misspent youth, see Maria Elena

Buszek, "'Oh! Dogma (Up Yours!):' Surfing the Third Wave," *thirdspace: A Journal of Feminist Theory and Culture*, Vol. 1, No. 1 (July 2001). Online at http://www.thirdspace.ca/articles/buszek.htm

6   Joanne Hollows and Rachel Moseley, "The Meanings of Popular Feminism," in (Eds.) Joanne Hollows and Rachel Moseley, *Feminism in Popular Culture* (London: Berg, 2006), 2.

7   I discuss the history of feminism's third wave from an art historical perspective in chapters 7 and 8 of my book *Pin-Up Grrrls*, which is itself indebted to Astrid Henry's excellent, book-length study of the subject from a literary and activist position, *Not My Mother's Sister: Generational Conflict and Third-Wave Feminism* (Bloomington and Indianapolis: University of Indiana Press, 2004).

8   Tracy + The Plastics, "TRACY by Wynne," from the liner notes to *Culture for Pigeon* (Troubleman Unlimited, 2004), CD.

9   Tracy + the Plastics, liner notes to *Forever Sucks EP* (Chainsaw Records, 2002), CD.

10 Gallery materials quoted in Leigh Anne Miller, "Tracy + The Plastics with Fawn Krieger at The Kitchen (New York), *Art in America*, Vol. 93, No. 6 (2005): 180.

11 See http://www.lttr.org.

12 Greenwood quoted in Amy Mackie, "*Hot Topic* Curatorial Statement" (Annandale-on-Hudson, NY: Bard College, 2006). Online at http://www.bard.edu/ccs/exhibitions/student/2006/theses/hottopic/. Also see Emily Roysdon, "Ecstatic Resistance," (2009). Online at http://www.emilyroysdon.com/index.php?/hidden-text/er-text/

13 Julia Bryan-Wilson, "Repetition and Difference," *Artforum*, Vol. 44, no. 10 (2006): 109.

14 See the documentation and films from this piece in the book/DVDs from Sophie Calle, *Take Care of Yourself* (Arles, FR: Actes Sud, 2007).

15 Credit line derived from *The Teaches of Peaches* (Kitty, Yo Records, 2000); Caroline Sullivan, "Filthy and Fury: For Peaches, the famously X-rated rapper, the personal just got political," *The Guardian*, July 24, 2006, p. 23.

16 James McNair, "A Decidedly Fruity Lady: Peaches dresses like a porn superhero and has a lot to say about gender politics," *The Independent (London)*, July 21, 2006, p. 15.

17 Bruce LaBruce, "Peaches: Word to the Fatherfucker," *C:International Contemporary Art*, March 22, 2004, pp. 16-18.

18 Ellen Willis, *Beginning to See the Light: Sex, Hope, and Rock and Roll* (New York: Knopf, 1981), p. 99.

19 Willis, *Beginning to See The Light*, p. 99.

PUNK THEORY MIX TAPE, SIDE B

DANIEL S. TRABER[1]

L.A.'S 'WHITE MINORITY':
PUNK AND THE CONTRADICTIONS
OF SELF-MARGINALIZATION

GONNA BE A WHITE MINORITY
ALL THE REST'LL BE THE MAJORITY
WE'RE GONNA FEEL INFERIORITY
I'M GONNA BE A WHITE MINORITY

WHITE PRIDE
YOU'RE AN AMERICAN
I'M GONNA HIDE
ANYWHERE I CAN

– BLACK FLAG, "WHITE MINORITY"

PART OF POPULAR music's allure is that it offers fans tools for identity construction. Lawrence Grossberg argues that musical choices open sites for people to negotiate their historical, social, and emotional relations to the world; the way fans define and understand themselves – what they believe and value – is intertwined with the varying codes and desires claimed by a taste culture associated with a specific genre.[2] An example of claiming social and cultural difference through music occurs in *Dissonant Identities*, Barry Shank's study of the Austin music scene. In explaining her impetus for joining the punk subculture, a fan states, "[I]t really had something to do with just wanting to do something different. With in a way being an outcast but then being accepted...And you were sort of bound together because the other people hated you. I think that [sic] might be part of the attraction, too, is being in a minority. Being in a self-imposed minority."[3] This tactic of self-marginalization to articulate a politics of dissent is central to the Los Angeles punk scene from (roughly) 1977 to 1983.[4] To resist metanarratives they found static and repressive, in order to form an independent sense of self, a small fringe group of youth pursued a life based on that inner-city underclass denied access to the American dream, an identity I will call the "sub-urban."

The racial and class facets of the sub-urban identity are deployed by L.A. punks to re-create themselves in the image of street-smart kids who are skeptical about the trappings of bourgeois America. In doing this they hoped to tap into a more "authentic" lifestyle – equivalent to "real," "hard," "tough," all those qualities associated with a life on city streets – than the one they thought themselves being forced to replicate. However, it is the contradictions in punk's practice of tapping into the aura of the Other that will be the crux of this essay. Underpinning punk's appropriation of otherness is the theory that social categories are fluid constructs that can be accepted, rejected, or hybridized at will, and this belief disrupts the notion that identity is fixed, that there is anything natural or concrete about one's subjectivity. But in using markers classified as subordinate, this voluntarist self-exile is laden with the baggage of preconceived social categories. Punks unconsciously reinforce the dominant culture rather than escape it because their turn to the sub-urban re-affirms the negative stereotypes used in the center to define this space and its population. I consider punk rockers who move into the sub-urban site, but I am also interested in the general celebration of this identity by those who remain at home. While noting the specific positive effects of this border crossing, I analyze punk's lofty subversive goals as a paradoxical mixture of transgression and complicity for reasons the participants themselves overlook.

I will elaborate on the theory of the underclass later; for now, I want to address labeling this space as "sub-urban." The term is more than a pun on the word suburbia, for sub-urban denotes an existence unlike the typical depiction of city life's everyday difficulties. It is important at the onset to emphasize that the sub-urban is multiracial (poverty is not just a "nonwhite" problem), but it does constitute a very specific class position, one that must confront the utmost levels of poverty, hunger, inadequate housing, and the constant threat of physical danger and death. Sub-urbanites are forced to negotiate their environment simply by surviving it as best they can, and it is this "extreme" way of life that punks of the period chose for their hard-edged bohemianism. I do not wish to trivialize the circumstances many of these kids faced, such as dysfunctional homes, being kicked out by their parents, or the economic downward mobility middle class families suffered during this period; still, we will see that a good number of the earliest punks present themselves in a way that is rooted in the often romanticized existence of the down-and-out. The choice starts to lose its thrust as a commentary on the parent culture's own litany of naturalized beliefs upon closer examination: that success is the result more of hard work than the privilege accorded to race and class (is it not such privileges that give them the option *not* to succeed?); that material wealth is synonymous with freedom (how can it be thought otherwise when these subjects have the freedom to come and go?); that their way of life constitutes the highest level of progress (then why else reject it by going "downward"?). Punk's adoption of marginality as a way to experience "real life" proves to be a belief in something transparent, thus they manipulate their identities in the name of choosing one they situate as less contaminated by middle class illusion and conformity. This dissent and social critique are further contradicted and weakened since L.A. punk remains complicit with America's dominant social values by privileging the individual.

Although problematizing L.A. punk's strategy of rebellion, I want to emphasize that their self-marginalization is not lacking in subversive promise. The punk movement did not achieve an outright transformation of society's dominant truths, but it did at least change the minds of many people. It established a permanent alternative to the corporate apparatus of the music industry by returning to a system of independent labels (originally used to distribute the postwar "race music" that influenced the white rockers of the 1950s). It also enabled a form of political community as witnessed by the numerous punk scenes throughout the world that share their music and ideas. Nonetheless, the foundations of L.A. punk's politics are shaky, and its liberatory spirit needs to be reconsidered. This subculture claims to desire dissonance and destabilization, but it depends on boundaries and regulatory fictions staying in place to define itself as oppositional. This does not mean the subversive energy completely dissipates, but it cannot be theorized as a trouble-free dismantling of identity categories because it relies uncritically on the dominant for its difference and forces the subordinated into the role of being an alternative. Punks are actually uninterested in abolishing those restrictive lines of cultural and social demarcation, and any act of denaturalization in this gesture starts to appear accidental. Instead of tearing down the boundaries, they use them to sustain a false sense of autonomy – like those in the center, without the Other they cease to exist.

In making this argument I do not strive to give an account of the way "it really was" in the L.A. punk scene. Instead, I aim to make sense of the way we are *told* it was by interrogating the narratives, discourses, and practices used to position Los Angeles in the punk movement by considering how participants and their supporters voice the merits of becoming like the sub-urban Other. To do this I turn to published interviews, historical reportage about the scene, and the music itself as a means for articulating shared ideas. What I have for evidence, then, is information culled from the punks' own cultural production (music and fanzines), documentary films, academic texts, and general historical accounts that all attempt to theorize what punk "is" from its stated intentions and performed acts. In short, along with the music I have a collection of statements received secondhand that I want to piece together, analyze, and critique.

L.A. punks intend to transgress the fixed order of class and racial hierarchies by crossing the boundaries of their inherited subjectivities as privileged white youth. The animosity they direct toward straights is commonly traced to their socialization experience: "Many punks had come from social situations where they had been the outsiders. Having escaped suburbia, having been outcasts, they now had their own group from which they could sneer and deliver visual jolts to the unimaginative, dumb, suburban world."[5] For many kids, the subculture's sense of anger and unrest came out of southern California communities where post-sixties children were searching for something to pierce the boredom of their lives and express their sense of social and political marginality. The ability to choose your own narrative, to live according to a worldview that you have authorized for yourself, is an act of self-empowerment, and the ideology of punk advocates just such a reinscription through an identity different from the majority. In *Subculture*, Dick Hebdige describes how these subjects desire to annihilate their past: "the punks dislocated themselves from the parent culture and were positioned instead on the outside...[where they] played up their Otherness."[6] L.A. punks react against the image-conscious mentality of Los Angeles by presenting a contrary image: celebrating ugliness in contrast to beauty, depression instead of joy, the sordid over the morally approved; in short, opting for the city's gritty underbelly over its glamorous face. It is by using a version of L.A.'s own tricks (e.g. making themselves into something to be looked at, the logic of self-(re)construction, a belief that history can be erased and rewritten) that they attempt to open a space for social critique.

Their strategy of segregating themselves from the status quo in an antithetical style extended itself beyond fashion and music for the core

L.A. fans. In early 1978, a run-down apartment complex named the Canterbury Arms became the living quarters for several punks. Craig Lee (guitarist for the Bags) lists a catalog of their new neighbors that relies on racial and class markers to indicate its stark difference from home: the hotel was "occupied by black pimps and drug dealers, displaced Southeast Asians living ten to a room, Chicano families, bikers from a halfway house, in addition to various bag ladies and shopping cart men."[7] In discussing the Canterbury with Jeff Spurrier, Trudie repeats Lee's roster of marginal figures: "When we first moved there, the whole building was full of criminals, SSI people, hookers, bikers, and pimps."[8] This site constitutes a form of existence delegitimated in dominant American political discourses and the popular media...Particular signifiers of race and class are used, often mapped onto each other, in establishing this rebel credibility to invent an inner-city subjectivity denoting genuine otherness.

Land and location are central to L.A. politics as they maintain the spatial hierarchy that allows some people access to the "good life" while keeping others out. For middle class punks to banish themselves from "paradise" is a transgression of the American dream. Even as their parents fought battles over taxes, property values, and neighborhood boundaries to prevent the influx of inner-city populations, this subgroup of youth (who were the public justification for the parents' politics) rejected the planned utopias to live among the very people the folks back home claimed to be protecting them from.[9] It is a choice about a certain way of life: immersing oneself in urban decay and the asceticism of harsh poverty. This border crossing becomes, quite literally, an act of deterritorialization (to use Deleuze and Guattari's term for escaping repressive social structures) in that changing one's physical environment facilitates a change in the ideological framework of one's personal psychic space. The lifestyle works as an inverse form of social mobility; in their own social formation punks earn status by becoming tougher and going "lower."

One L.A. punk divulges the code: "Everyone got called a poseur, but you could tell the difference: Did you live in a rat-hole and dye your hair pink and wreck every towel you owned and live hand-to-mouth on Olde English 800 and potato chips? Or did you live at home and do everything your mom told you and then sneak out?"[10] Here austere living is configured as virtuous because it is a sign of honesty and devotion to the subculture's values. A similar example of this occurs in Penelope Spheeris's 1980 documentary *The Decline of Western Civilization* (hereafter *Decline*) when Chuck Dukowski, a college student, narrates becoming a punk as his "search" for an answer to the meaning of life: "I did this because I felt like to set myself aside and make myself different, maybe, maybe, [the answer] will just come to me."[11] All the more suggestive is that he delivers this conversion narrative from a room brimming with signifiers of extreme poverty. As the camera pans to follow Ron Reyes (the Puerto Rican singer for Black Flag, adding a nonwhite subject to the picture) giving a tour of his apartment, we see the rest of the band and a few hangers-on (all of them white) lounging on decrepit furniture, drinking cheap beer, surrounded by walls covered with spraypainted band names and profane slogans. It turns out that Reyes pays $16 a month to sleep in a converted closet since he owes money to all the utility companies. This scene establishes a connection with the "just getting by" life(style) of the sub-urban subject. Reyes's attitude about his living conditions teeters between realizing there is something troublesome here – he shows how some people actually live in America – and exhibiting a resigned, digni-fied posture – this is how "we" live as compared to "you."

Another voice on using self-marginalization to achieve a sense of hard "realness" comes from the eighties. From 1981 to 1986, Henry Rollins was the singer for Black Flag. In *Get in the Van* Rollins explains why he was attracted to the lifestyle of the band upon first meeting them:

> They had no fixed income and they lived like dogs, but they
> were living life with a lot more guts than I was by a long
> shot. I had a steady income and an apartment and money
> in the bank…The way they were living went against all
> the things I had been taught to believe were right. If I had
> listened to my father, I would have joined the Navy, served
> and gone into the straight world without a whimper.[12]

Rollins later describes his new life after joining the band and moving to Los Angeles:

> I was learning a lot of things fast…Now the next meal was
> not always a thing you could count on…Slowly I came to
> realize that this was it and there was no place I'd rather be.
> As much as it sucked for all of us to be living on the floor
> on top of each other, it still was better than the job I had
> left in D.C.[13]

Rollins defines himself in terms of his origin in middle class stability, but also as proudly contesting that existence to live a life beyond the wall the bourgeoisie has built around itself. By adopting a life in contradis-tinction to his natal social environment, this kind of punk articulates the discourse that autonomy can be achieved by disengaging from the ruling social order. [...] It is rare to find in L.A. punk anything like an outright lament for the loss of white privilege, while critiques of suburbia's very values and desires are ubiquitous. These punks do not resolve their problems by deciding to work harder; instead, they say "fuck it" to the whole idea of desiring a suburban middle class lifestyle. [...] References to one's necessary freedom from coercion are overwhelming in their number and variety in punk rock, but they are hardly deployed in the name of upholding the "free market" doctrines of competitive individualism. Rather, they are concerned with free will and autonomy in thought, values, and identity and being unencumbered by external constraints. In *Decline* Malissa tells the interviewer that punks are striving "to be accepted any way we want to." And Jennipher advises the audience that "everyone shouldn't be afraid to be as different as they want to be."[14] This autonomy of conscience and action also gets distilled through a logic of artistic originality as the right to be unique instead of a conformist adhering to clichéd form. The earliest scene makers became disenchanted as the punk scene shifted to the hardcore style. The Weirdos' John Denny opines, "[Punk became] more macho, jock, aggressive. The whole individuality thing began to dissipate, and it just became more fascistic."[15] That is ultimately the passkey for grasping how individualism functions in punk subculture: one is either independent and unique, or acquiescent and ordinary. [...] The self becomes the property that they protect and aggrandize with the Other manipulated and objectified as a means to that end, thus, denied his/her own individuality and freedom. The ultimate implication of this negligence is that punk unwittingly repeats the *ideological* patterns of the dominant culture by privileging the importance of the self and self-interest, thus treating the Other as an object to be used for their own desires. Despite the call to be free from external influence, what L.A. punk shows is that without critically questioning our notions of the individual we take those discourses of the center with us everywhere we go. And this finally weakens punk's transgressive potential, for the individualism at punk's core forecloses the possibility of collective action that could more effectively challenge the problems they are protesting...And as the U.K. variant of punk traveled back to America, Los Angeles is one of the places where The Clash's call to have a "white riot" is taken up enthusiastically, and it is by fitting themselves into public discourses surrounding nonwhites that they hope to realize their version of white insurgency.

The impulse behind this self-fashioning and its class politics is the rejection of a specifically conceived racial identity; namely, whiteness as a specific social, economic, and cultural formation. In denying the benefits of their race, these kids are in effect attempting to critique the entire system upon which the United States was founded and truly functions. Elaine K. Ginsberg explains the political benefits whites gain by choosing nonwhite marginality in their identity construction: "the decision to 'pass' as [an Other], to self-construct an identity perceived by a white majority as less desirable, disrupts the assumptions of superiority that buttress white privilege and self-esteem. [Consequently,] challenging racial categories threatens those whose sense of self-worth depends on their racial identity and the social status that accompanies it."[16] Additionally, Eric Lott's work on the racial logic of blackface minstrelsy as "love and theft" – simultaneously a desire for and racist disparagement of black culture – locates this form of entertainment in the "American tradition of class abdication through...[a] cross-racial immersion which persists... in historically differentiated ways, to our own day."[17] This situates L.A. punk as a link in that chain, and by turning to the sub-urban this treason is amplified by going against the dominant white social class buttressing suburbia. But in setting its sights on this particular form of whiteness – based on a conflation of racial and class categories – an unintended contradiction develops as punk drifts toward essentializing both whiteness and nonwhiteness by ultimately situating a version of bourgeois middle class whiteness as the norm against which all is compared (which also perpetuates a stereotype of whites), such that it is sustained as the nation's dominant ideology. This paradox will be addressed more fully later; for now, I want to establish how whiteness is defined and deployed by these subjects.

In *Another State of Mind*, a 1983 documentary/tour film on L.A. hardcore, it is notable that during this later phase of the subculture's history the kids interviewed all pick out preppies, rather than hippies (the earlier middle class youth group punk targets), as the opposite that helps them grasp their identity as punks.[18] In other words, preppiness is the alternate subjectivity open to them. Like punk, preppiness is itself a distinctive way of life – clothes, behavior, and worldview – but one immersed in a notion of affluent whiteness. Now, one can find nonwhite preppies and those who do not wholly subscribe to tenets of conservatism and elitism, but in punk's social landscape it is a style thoroughly associated with "acting" and "looking" white as well as "acting" and "looking" wealthy. In punk, whiteness is configured as the subject position of the center, and punk's border crossing calls attention to its "invisible" ideology that permeates society and evaluates as an inferior "Other" all that does not meet its standards. By associating whiteness with the suburb, punk comments on the (mis)representation of white racial and class subjectivities, i.e., the invisibility of whiteness and the attendant privileges it is awarded.

This can be interpreted as a move toward fulfilling David Roediger's claim that "consciousness of whiteness also contains elements of a critique of that consciousness and that we should encourage the growth of a politics based on hopeful signs of a popular giving up on whiteness" by "exposing, demystifying and demeaning [its] particular ideology."[19] The Black Flag epigraph about being a "white minority" both labels whiteness as a specific race and resists the homogenizing pressures of that culture – to be bourgeois, mundane, conventional, in a word: uncool. As the lyrics propose, the only viable alternative for white kids uninterested in the American dream is to reject the privilege of their skin color by emulating the lifestyle of marginalized subjects – safe from outside control to the extent that they can remain hidden from and ignored by the larger society like other "oppressed" social groups.[20] So if, as Roediger argues, the "very claiming of a place in the US legally involved... a claiming of whiteness," punk's cultural practice becomes even more politically weighted as a refusal of the ruling perception of legitimate Americanness itself.[21] The rewards of whiteness are rejected in their new identity through a conscious "disaffiliation," to use Marilyn Frye's term, from the racial and class groups in which they are supposed to desire membership.[22]

To implement this strategy, class and racial difference are sometimes conjoined by punks to distinguish how cut off from the mainstream they now are. There is a deep investment in the idea of difference (as well as white middle class homogeneity) that easily lapses into essentialist formulations. The romanticized naturalization of marginality that slips into their understanding of the sub-urban is a primary element of the contradiction I discuss later, but I want to be clear on the matter of racial and class diversity in L.A. punk subculture. As with preppies who break the stereotype, one finds nonwhites participating in the L.A. punk scene, paralleling Los Angeles's multicultural population as whites, blacks (Black Flag's producer Spot), Chicanos (the Zeros, the Plugz, and Suicidal Tendencies), Asian Americans (Dianne Chai, bass player for the Alleycats, and Kenny, a teenage fan interviewed in *Decline*), and others gather in the same social spaces. Yet, it must be conceded that the great majority of this subculture consists, quite overwhelmingly and without a hint of doubt, of white people.

It is more unwise, on the other hand, to generalize the subculture's class background (with the larger groups being lower and middle) because the audience not only was made up of suburban teenagers and runaways but included college students, artists, and older fans like Ray Manzarek of the Doors. In spite of this broad population, it is still the social space of suburbia that keeps drawing punk's contempt. To depict the suburbs as populated by only the middle class is incorrect, for the working class lives there, too (and many who joined the middle class retained working class inflections after the rise in social status and real estate values). Still, suburban punks are raised seeing what they are supposed to envy and achieve with their lives. The clear visibility of economic divisions and the desires they produce are the means by which the middle class perpetuates itself. Punk uses one's geographical location to determine identity, reading one's presence in suburbia as a telltale of one's desire to climb the next rung of the social ladder. The common themes of the music and fans' enunciations are focused on the perceived threat of a petty bourgeois lifestyle and their consequent rejection of it. Even those white punks not from the middle class can be read as reacting to their race as the passport to such a life, rebelling against the very expectation that suburban comfort is what they desire.

The music reveals a strong discursive investment in depicting "true" fans as either coming from such a mainstream environment or refusing to compete for its dangled rewards. And this protest is repeatedly framed as a privatized concern with the self's personal desires and problems. The Descendents' "Suburban Home" does not express an overt class politics as much as a fear of losing to the forces of conformity. Similarly, the Adolescents ("Creatures"), Middle Class ("Home is Where"), and Social Distortion ("Mommy's Little Monster") are just a few other groups dealing directly with the issue of one's relation to a suburban identity.[23] These texts take a critical view of a culture people are born into but find hollow and unfulfilling. The appropriation of sub-urbanism becomes a powerful political statement given that the middle class wants to move up rather than down, indeed, that it treats that mobility as an unspoken birthright. Albeit not the central theme for every band or song, one can apply the anti-suburban discourse to L.A. punk since its general politics critique those who are not dispossessed.

Yet American punk was berated as "inauthentic" because it supposedly lacked the more "serious" political realities considered a necessary source for making a truly oppositional music. Los Angeles in particular is censured as the final promised land of hyperreality where false surface is treated as reality…Nonetheless, one should not discount the underlying political impetus of this emerging culture. Rather than being born into a life of poverty with nothing to lose, these malcontent descendants of the American dream made a conscious decision to experience a different sense of affect by joining the ranks of the disenfranchised "underclass."

This is a debated term, coming into vogue in the 1980s, but it is used commonly enough to suit our purposes.[24] The concept categorizes poverty, and the cultural lifestyle associated with it, by splitting the poor into two groups: those who are either deserving or undeserving, worthy or unworthy. This division was central to conservative strategies for dismantling social programs they claimed had "created a culture of dependency in a population which explicitly denies the norms and values of the society to which they notionally belong."[25] The undeserving poor are stigmatized as enemies of the state who neglect their civic duty and swindle decent citizens of their hard-earned money because they lack the moral fiber and self-motivation to help themselves. Here we have a group framed as so base they warrant no help whatsoever. What is stubbornly ignored by the pundits manipulating this scapegoat portrait are the structural inequalities at the root of poverty – racism, unemployment, and dwindling employment opportunities for those unable to leave the urban centers for jobs relocated to outlying suburbs.

This inaccurate, malicious portrayal of poverty opens a way for thinking about the roots of L.A. punk's political imagination. Conservatives represent the underclass as a counterculture "who stand – in terms of values, behavior or life style – in some sense outside 'the collectivity.'"[26] Punks take this discourse of the underclass and turn it into a badge of honor. This attitude is central to statements Jeff Spurrier collected in his 1994 interviews with people from the original scene who lived in the sub-urban:

> Geza x: I was on SSI – about $600 a month. That was like the artist's subsidy. Nobody worked, everybody was broke, but everybody just fed each other. It was like a tortilla-and-no-beans diet.

> KK Bennett: They fed themselves by raiding an ice-cream truck that was parked in the alleyway. They stole about twenty gallons and ate it for weeks [...] And there was a liquor store...that took our food stamps.[27]

These statements encode the survival techniques of extreme poverty – living by one's wits – as part of an alternate truth system, an ethic of living that rejects the standard patterns. These memories are layered with the rhetoric of community and improvisational negotiations of hardship, yet, ironically, they fit the dominant culture's negative depiction of the underclass. Punks accede to and incorporate the racist assumptions of underclass theories by engaging in the "pathological" activities attributed to that group. Both Geza X and KK ennoble the kind of behavior conservatives brandish for their periodic inner-city witch hunts. Punks act this way because they think it is how the sub-urban Other is "supposed" to behave. What is revealed is the way L.A. punks rely on the center's discourses for their sense of marginality. This dilemma should be read as a cultural negotiation – a practice and rhetoric built on the conflicting mixture of belief systems the punks are working through – but that qualification must be accompanied by an attempt to critically theorize the contradiction arising when punks adopt a stereotype and posit it as sincere rebellion. [...]

[P]unk's appropriation of otherness exhibits a significant transgressive shift in the ideological investments of this group. Their self-marginalization is enacted in opposition to the conservative vision of American life where people adhere to those values of the proper American: self-reliance and self-sacrifice directed toward material success. But punk's desire for a disjuncture between dominant and subordinate cultures gets complicated when race enters the picture. The lower position most minorities are forced to hold prevents full participation in the nation's politics or benefiting from its promises. This helps to account for why suburban punks were so drawn to the image of the sub-urban to spurn the complacent life of American conservatism: to be associated with a nonwhite underclass fulfills their logic of being disconnected from the norms and free from the direct control of institutional power. Barry Shank's discussion of punk's subterranean nature [...] emphasiz[es] the connection to marginalized racial groups a punk lifestyle opens:

> This rock'n'roll truly challenged people. It was not safe to
> like it; you could get beat with a billy club; you could get
> arrested. The ability to derive pleasure from punk rock gave
> an instant aura of danger, independence, and power to
> any individual... [Being a fan of punk] seemed to produce
> momentary experiences for middle class [whites] akin to the
> everyday life of Blacks or Hispanics.[28]

This circles us back to Black Flag's song, seeing how punk's strategy is to flip the binary of majority/minority. Minority status is the privileged element for this group as they valorize it into a condition to be appropriated. This recognizes the structural racism in American society, yet it does so by essentializing the nonwhite Other into a victim role – romanticizing nonwhites into all that is simultaneously threatening and threatened. [...] What aims to be a critique of repression in L.A. punk ends up an agent of it, for its rejection of the dominant culture relies on adopting the stereotypes of inferior, violent, and criminal nonwhites.[29]

Punks attempt to re-create themselves by slipping on their conception of the life(style) and appearance of a marginal group, and this new self is one that seemingly disrupts all certainty of an original core being.[30] The suburban identity is revealed as just another ideological construct of normalcy imposed on its youth to contain them in the dominant symbolic order. By shifting identities and donning what they regard to be the image of the subordinate, they are engaged in an implicitly subversive act that transcends a simple disaffected teenage rebellion as it disrupts the entire system that has formed both themselves and the Other. In effect this act destroys the hierarchy of meaning so that binaries – the method by which bodies and products are judged, separated, and contained – are shown to be arbitrary and empty. Such a positive treatment of punk's control over identity formation neglects the problematic assumptions underlying how this subjectivity is actually achieved. In short, these "real" punks choose an existence based on poverty, addiction, and random sex and violence – what they consider to be the American *reality* rather than the American dream. Ultimately, they are working from a particular *image* of that reality by playing out the authorized stereotypes they associate with that habitus and expect to find there.

This chosen life of social marginality depends on its relation to what the suburban bourgeoisie decides to include and exclude from the center. The cultural practice of punk's subject formation comes to take on another quality: a colonial appropriation of the sub-urban life through a specific "look" and behavior. Punk's border crossing can be read as a commodification of the Other that aestheticizes identity for capital in a symbolic economy of signification. Some are bothered that punk's counterhegemonic power ultimately cannot escape cooptation in the material economic system, but the truth is they employ that same logic against those they intend to posit as the newly privileged element. They exploit the sub-urban to produce a product marketed through the channels of their own bodies and cultural production, and while I do not accuse them of a "failed rebellion" because they cannot get outside that system, I *do* reject treating this contestation as if the agents are completely aware of the contradictions within which they move. There is simply too much being invested in this public image that wants to be taken quite seriously as a cultural intervention.

The most obvious way to problematize this appropriation is by considering the option of (re)escape waiting for some participants back home. Although one must be wary of generalizing the disparate economic statuses and life options of white L.A. punks, we must also recall that this rebellion, as framed by middle class punks, is a rejection of the desires and social values *causing* the sense of economic anxiety their parents and mainstream peers feel. These kids left a parent culture that believed their lifestyle could survive if the proper political steps were taken – hence the sweeping turn to conservatism – so there is still a sense of hope for the future. And those values that attempt to maintain a middle class lifestyle, which punks ran from, are still waiting for them. Besides, any transition away from a sub-urban life will seem all that much easier because the next level appears all that less grim. Even the Chicana Alice Bag of the Bags, who left her east L.A. barrio to live in the Canterbury, has a better place to run as the first phase of L.A. punk is dying in late 1979. Disheartened by the changes in the subculture, she "moved back home and had quit [the punk scene] and was getting ready to go back to school."[31] By contrast, for "true" sub-urbans this life is one with very real threats of hunger, disease, and death that are firmly rooted in a systematized inequality from which they are unable to easily free themselves.

Admittedly, this border crossing increases the aura of "credibility" attached to punks because they *are* living this life, but that status is just another essentialist version of true identity. Postmodern parody and decontextualized signifiers cannot adequately account for this cultural practice because these subjects *want* context – they move *into* the sub-urban and are utterly invested in it, otherwise they are mere "poseurs." This pursuit of authenticity, no matter how sincere, is as insulting a gesture as playacting when compared to those who cannot escape. That they would freely opt to live like oppressed groups formed by historical and social conditions they cannot claim says much about the political dedication of some punks, but it also speaks to how people of their social status understand their relationship to the notion of freedom. As Grossberg proposes, mobility and access can be configured spatially, for where one is placed on the map of the social totality "define[s] the forms of empowerment or agency...available to particular groups."[32] Such places are constituted in a way that can offer either emancipation or further repression – a large number of punks enjoy the former. The crushing realities of racial and/ or economic subjugation are trivialized in their search for autonomy. They become mere adornments for differentiation to be discarded when no longer useful to the new subjectivity – just one more brand in the supermarket of identities. Punks attempt to be associated with a group that is ignored and swept away from public acknowledgment [...] but that oppressed status is complicated by being presented in a way that requires, that begs for, the shocked gaze of the conservative masses.

If we return to the Canterbury apartments, that physical and social space chosen for its qualities of extreme otherness, only seven months after a contingent of punks moved in, we find a growing tension between the "real" sub-urbans and the new initiates. Craig Lee describes the changing state of the hotel and the negative reaction of the non-punk residents to their neighbors:

> The halls smelled like shit, someone constantly pissed in the elevator…one girl was raped at gunpoint, cockroaches were everywhere, and another girl had an angry neighbor throw a pot of boiling soup on her face. Racial tensions were high. The basement rehearsal room had been padlocked, little fires were breaking out and punks started to flee. What had been envisioned as L.A.'s equivalent of the Chelsea Hotel [in New York] was no longer hospitable to kids playing Wire and Sham 69 full blast at four in the morning.[33]

The punks treated the Canterbury the way they thought it deserved. They behaved like spoiled kids who refuse to clean up after themselves and showed no respect for a place some are forced to live in because they lack a choice. This is more than the "snotty teen" pose punks affected. Here we see them using the sub-urban identity but refusing the possible multiple desires of people in that habitus. The sub-urban subject is exoticized, forced into a preexisting stereotype that further stabilizes a monolithic view of marginality. Gayle Wald's account of this problem (with reference to Janis Joplin) is accurate: it "borders on a reactionary romanticization…and a reification of the notion of racial [and class] difference."[34] […] Lee does not elaborate on the cause of the "racial tensions" at the Canterbury, but one might assume they grew out of a feeling that the punks "don't fit in" here and have no respect for "us."

Any conceptualization of punk identity that equates the suburban and sub-urban as having comparable opportunities for subject (re)formation is problematic. "True" sub-urbans have considerably less control over their life choices, least of all over the identities they can afford to wear or the places where they can show them off. Punks ignore how some have the freedom to explore different identities while ontological mobility is restricted for others – "white subjectivity [is equated] with a social entitlement to experiment with identity."[35] Denaturalizing both suburban and sub-urban identities is a worthy objective, but then what? This is not a plea for returning to a naive conception of authenticity, it simply acknowledges that suburban punks crossing racial and class lines come from a position where they are allowed to speak and act, where they have more options. All identities are performances of approved categories (ways we are either taught or adopt) so punks are trying on a particular subjectivity to accomplish a transgressive goal. Yet something lingers, something that intimates complicity, when kids coming from comfortable lives earn hipness by playing dress "down" – a version of symbolic capital acquisition in the economy of youth culture.

By framing these practices of signification within an economic metaphor, we see that punk exhibits a colonizing impulse in its border crossing. It exploits the condition of sub-urbans by mimicking a "way of life" others must negotiate in order to survive. What can be considered the sub-urban's labor (i.e., what they "do") in the economy of signification is to look and act "poor," and this is turned into a form of prestige by punks: *being* different by *acting* poor, which is all the more troublesome since they believe there is such a way of behaving that is then totalized. Acquiring symbolic capital is how the appropriation of otherness "pays," and it becomes the imperializing gesture in punk's tactic of escape…This is a re-othering because those in the margin are made to conform to preconceptions that are a product of the center. Punks totalize their chosen marginal subjects according to their own narrative of honorable poverty; they force the Other into a fixed identity to empower themselves. The assumption that the life of the underclass is open to appropriation objectifies them in a model of emulation, while conveniently ignoring how these people may want to escape from the degradation of this life.

By treating them as an exploitable object enabling punks to achieve their own desires, this re-othering allows the center to continue speaking for the Other. By eliding the heterogeneous hopes existing in the sub-urban, they silence the marginal subject's own viewpoint on marginality. By proposing that they have joined a different cultural formation by adopting a certain lifestyle, punks further naturalize that subject position in a binary relationship to suburban life that is also (re)naturalized. The power of whiteness is recentered and buttressed as the norm through a logic of stereotyped racial and class difference – those sought-after characteristics of otherness that are actually products of dominant white discourses – to give a substantive meaning to their cultural practice. I wish to avoid duplicating the punks' theft of voice, but it is highly dubious that anyone located in the sub-urban – for a reason other than free will – would consider this life a just and good consequence of the unequal distribution of wealth.

This incongruity between positive social intentions and negative ideological underpinnings rarely appears in the enunciations of L.A. punks.

The result is that living on welfare becomes more like a game than a necessity, daily navigating danger is a source of excitement rather than terror. Although punk situated itself as a self-conscious reaction to the commodification ubiquitous in late capitalism – realizing that even as it berated corporate rock it could not sell its product without replicating its processes – it appears neither capable of, nor interested in extending, that critique to its own cultural practices at this level. Too many suburban L.A. punks seem to believe they can achieve an identity free of their past personal history by moving to this social space and positioning themselves as a taste culture on the boundaries of mainstream consumption. Ironically, it is this system of differentiation that limits the effectiveness of punk's politics. Those subjects adopting a sub-urban "lifestyle" are, in essence, duplicating the methods of the group they publicly vilify to realize their rebellion. They leave the parent culture to form their own "lifestyle enclave" by producing an identity different from others according to certain patterns of belief, dress, and leisure activity, all framed as a vanguardist movement occurring in underground venues for people of the same inclination.[36] To escape the group mentality, they build their own group; one purposefully designed to appeal to certain types of people while keeping others out. As a subculture of secret meanings and codes for dress, bodily movement (be it dancing, walking, or posing), and attitude, the identity produced is an exclusionary one; therefore, in the end they are not unlike their parents. Although intended to function as a counterhegemonic alternative to the center, punk remains less a threat to institutions of authority than merely another option because it must maintain the center's standards to position itself...[Thus] it is really "Punk" itself that replicates the dominant by using the same basic ideology and social patterns as the parent culture. The transgressive potential of their strategy for rejecting America's reigning ideologies is enervated since it is quite complicit with such beliefs. And this is due to that stringent faith in the primacy of the individual – one of the key discourses America and Americans use to justify coercive and oppressive acts – so central to punk's conceptualization of resistance. Any economic and social injustices punk rails against are an effect of the logic of individualism. An ideology rationalizing the withdrawal into private concerns – be it financial or spiritual or aesthetic fulfillment – by advocating self-interest is the one taken up as the foundational tenet of punk politics.

Punk's discourse finally becomes an extension of the parent culture's belief system; an unconscious affirmation of the materialism and political self-interest this "counterculture" claims to oppose...The late capitalist alienation these subjects feel is due to their investment in a version of autonomy that perpetuates that sense of isolation by privileging an insular individuation over a collectivity that will allow the inclusion of non-punks. They force themselves into a solipsistic cocoon wherein they cannot affect the conditions they claim make them unhappy, and this adds the finishing touches to their sense of alienation. As a music and culture produced by postmodern subjects, punk may best be understood in terms of a Foucauldian micropolitics: the localized effect of crossing boundaries contains the potential to spread. This possibility is severely limited, though; punk is too far in the margin, due to its own actions and those of society at large, to be heard by the kind of mass audience a more subdued music can (or is allowed to) reach. Perhaps, however, that is all that can be asked of it.

My intention has not been to police ontological boundaries of race and class as they have been traditionally demarcated. The point is hardly that punks fail to achieve a thing called authenticity, a "true" and whole self; nor is it that they fail to meet an impossible injunction to exist in either "pure 'autonomy' or total encapsulation."[37] The point is to ensure that people deploying "subversive" narratives and practices maintain the skepticism that initially prompted the decision to transgress. Punks prove themselves highly adept at criticism, including themselves, but more typically of those positioned as outside themselves. Yet I have shown the borderline that could not be crossed in Los Angeles, the discourse they refused to treat with critical vigor. For those punks who join the sub-urban and those simply celebrating it as the Other of suburbia, their means of self-construction remain entrenched in the logic of individuality as it is practiced by the enemy: the bourgeoisie they claim to reject. Despite the possibilities for engaging in denaturalization, their contrarian version of "reality" and the "good" succumbs to the illusion of a whole self, and the home where they choose to cultivate that subjectivity is based on stereotypes circulated by the dominant power formation. Although attempting to create a free self on their own terms, L.A. punks forgo critiquing their complicity in denying freedom, thus getting further entwined within the system they despise to the point that the paradox becomes so accepted – like the unseen whiteness in the center – that it is rendered all the more invisible to themselves.

NOTES

1   This chapter is an edited and abridged version of an article that was originally published as Daniel S. Traber, "L.A.'s 'White Minority': Punk and the Contradictions of Self-Marginalization," *Cultural Critique*, No.

48. (Spring, 2001): 30-64. Thanks to University of Minnesota Press for granting permission to reprint the text.

2   Lawrence Grossberg, "Another Boring Day in Paradise: Rock and Roll and the Empowerment of Everyday Life," in *Dancing in Spite of Myself: Essays on Popular Culture* (Durham, NC: Duke University Press, 1997), p. 31.

3   Barry Shank, *Dissonant Identities: The Rock'n'Roll Scene in Austin, Texas* (Hanover, NH: Wesleyan University Press, 1994), p. 122.

4   My bookends encompass the points from which punk becomes a recognized scene in Los Angeles to its transformation into hardcore and final wane into cliché. There is typically a line drawn between punk and hardcore that places the latter in the 1980s, depicting it as faster, more violent, and less interested in the artistic motivations of the first phase. Hardcore is all of these in its different guises, but several of the so-called "later" punks had been interested and active in the scene well before any official demarcation was imposed. Black Flag is a band associated with hardcore who existed since the beginning; in fact, "White Minority" was first recorded in January 1978, well after the Germs' first single but *before* Dangerhouse issued the *Yes L.A.* compilation of "properly" punk bands. Stories of the changing scene – that hardcore pushed out Hollywood art-rockers with younger, dumber, rougher suburban kids – rarely mention that the hardcore bands had been blocked out of the scene by the key clubs, so it did not occur as suddenly as historians tend to frame it. Thus hardcore is best understood as an emerging culture within an emerging culture.

5   Peter Belsito and Bob Davis, *Hardcore California: A History of Punk and New Wave* (San Francisco: Last Gasp Publishing, 1983), p. 17.

6   Dick Hebdige, *Subculture: The Meaning of Style* (London: Methuen, 1979), p. 120.

7   Belsito and Davis, p. 22.

8   Jeff Spurrier, "California Screaming," *Details* (December 1994), p. 122.

9   See Mike Davis *City of Quartz* (New York: Random-Vintage, 1992) on the development and political mobilization of L.A.'s suburbs, especially chapter 3. George Lipsitz gives a detailed history of the Federal Housing Administration's racist practices in making home loans that resulted in the overwhelming white demographics of postwar suburbs in *The Possessive Investment in Whiteness: How White People Profit from Identity Politics* (Philadelphia: Temple University Press, 1998).

10   Spurrier, p. 126.

11   *The Decline of Western Civilization*, Penelope Spheeris, Director (Atlantic Television, 1980).

12   Henry Rollins, *Get in the Van: On the Road with Black Flag* (Los Angeles: 2.13.61, 1994), p. 8.

13   Ibid, p. 11.

14   *The Decline of Western Civilization*, Penelope Spheeris, Director (Atlantic Television, 1980).

15   Spurrier, p. 126.

16   (Ed.) Elaine K Ginsberg, *Passing and the Fictions of Identity* (Durham, NC: Duke University Press, 1996), p. 15.

17   Eric Lott, *Love and Theft: Blackface Minstrelsy and the American Working Class* (Oxford: Oxford University Press, 1993), p. 51.

18   *Another State of Mind*, Adam Small and Peter Stuart, directors (Time Bomb Filmworks, 1983).

19   David R. Roediger, *Towards the Abolition of Whiteness: Essays on Race, Politics, and Working Class History* (London: Verso, 1994), pp. 3, 12.

20   Greil Marcus attacks "White Minority" as a song about hatred of the Other, that person or thing which is the not-I (*Ranters and Crowd Pleasers: Punk in Pop Music, 1977–92* [New York: Anchor, 1993], p. 185). His censure is based on misunderstanding the song's lyrics: what he reads as "breed inferiority" is actually "feel inferiority" (p. 184). This is not an attack on the Other, it is a call to *become* Other, to "hide anywhere" you can so as to escape that center legitimizing itself through "white pride." Discarding social centeredness for a life on the periphery allows one to sidestep the dominant power formations and to forestall being incorporated into their system of reality.

21   Roediger, p. 189.

22   Marilyn Frye, "On Being White: Thinking toward a Feminist Understanding of Race and Race Supremacy," in *The Politics of Reality: Essays in Feminist Theory* (Trumansburg, NY: Crossing Press, 1983).

23   Descendents, "Suburban Home," *Somery*. (1982, rereleased, Lawndale, CA: SST, 1991), LP; Adolescents, "Creatures," *Adolescents* (1981, rereleased, Sun Valley, CA: Frontier, 1990), LP; Middle Class, "Home Is Where," *A Blueprint for Joy, 1978–1980* (1980, rereleased, Los Angeles: Velvetone, 1995), LP; Social Distortion, "Mommy's Little Monster," *Mommy's Little Monster* (New York: Time Bomb, 1983), LP.

24   Christopher Jencks, "Is the American Underclass Growing?" in (eds.) Christopher Jencks and Paul E. Peterson, *The Urban Underclass* (Washington, DC: Brookings Institute, 1991), p. 28; Lydia Morris, *Dangerous Classes: The Underclass and Social Citizenship* (London: Routledge, 1994), pp. 107–10. See also Micaela di Leonardo, *Exotics at Home: Anthropologies, Others, American Modernity* (Chicago: University of Chicago Press, 1998) and Francis Fox Piven and Richard A. Cloward, *The New*

Class War: Reagan's Attack on the Welfare State and Its Consequences (New York: Pantheon, 1982) on the underclass debate. See Michael Katz, *In the Shadow of the Poorhouse: A Social History of Welfare in America* (New York: BasicBooks, 1986) for a history of welfare in America, including the tropes used to discuss it.

25 Morris, p. 3.

26 Ibid, p. 79.

27 Spurrier, pp. 120, 122.

28 Shank, p. 110.

29 Punk's challenge to whiteness is further conflicted by the music itself. Its investment in the label "whiteness" has been transformed, yet, in a sense, it calls attention to and plays up its race through the music...Some imagine punk bleaching out rock's "blackness," but this should point us toward recognizing the problem of trying to attach the name "whiteness" to punk music: at its root it remains a style of rock and roll – indeed, a self-conscious bricolage of its very history – replete with the deep grounding in African-American culture that helped to give birth to rock... [Punk's] own interests echo the attributes typically deployed to explain what rock learned from African-American traditions (and thereby naturalizing the cultural as racial difference): "honest" expression, energy and emotional passion, and articulating dissent through music.

30 One may consider Judith Butler's work on performativity where she turns to Mary Douglas's theory of the margins to propose that the "pollution" ingested by going there will "contaminate" normalized discursive practices inscribed in subjects (*Gender Trouble: Feminism and the Subversion of Identity* [London: Routledge, 1990], p. 132). The sub-urban existence, with its status as the reviled, is chosen as a means for articulating opposition to the centralized discourses read as "white" by punks, with all that racial designation implies to them (often within essentialist paradigms) about social privilege and bland conformity. What Butler calls the "operation of repulsion" is capable of weakening the boundaries that are "tenuously maintained for the purposes of social regulation and control" (p. 133)...We also see the possible danger in Butler's theory, for punk's rejection of the dominant culture relies on adopting the stereotyped connotations of inferior, violent, and criminal nonwhites invented by it. In Butler's defense, I have left underdeveloped her idea of parody because the notion of parodic play in L.A. punk is untenable...For the most part, punk would have to wait for the riot grrrls movement for anything resembling a truly parodic manipulation of regulatory identities (see Joanne Gottlieb and Gayle Wald, "Smells Like Teen Spirit: Riot Grrrls, Revolution, and Women in Independent Rock," in (eds.)

Andrew Ross and Tricia Rose, *Microphone Fiends: Youth Music and Youth Culture*, [London: Routledge, 1994]; and Neil Nehring's *Popular Music, Gender, and Postmodernism: Anger Is an Energy* [Thousand Oaks, CA: Sage, 1997]).

31   Spurrier, p. 124.

32   Lawrence Grossberg, "Identity and Cultural Studies – Is That All There Is?" in (eds.) Stuart Hall and Paul du Gay, *Questions of Cultural Identity* (London: Sage, 1996), p. 102.

33   Belsito and Davis, p. 31.

34   Gayle Wald, "One of the Boys? Whiteness, Gender, and Popular Music Studies," in (ed.) Mike Hill, *Whiteness: A Critical Reader* (New York: New York University Press, 1997), p. 158.

35   Wald, p. 153.

36   Robert N. Bellah, Richard Madsen, William M. Sullivan, Ann Swidler, and Steven M. Tipton, *Habits of the Heart: Individualism and Commitment in American Life* (New York: Harper, 1985), p. 335.

37   Stuart Hall, "Notes on Deconstructing 'the Popular,'" in (ed.) John Storey, *Cultural Theory and Popular Culture: A Reader* (Athens, GA: University of Georgia Press, 1998), p. 447. Johan Fornäs argues that debating authenticity is pointless. Authenticity should be seen as an act of contextualized self-reflexivity such that it "appears as an option and a construction rather than as a given fact" (quoted in Nehring, *Popular Music*, p. 63). Identity is formed according to localized "rules" that create the boundaries defining authenticity, and sense is then freed from a romantic conception of "natural" origin or purity.

TAVIA NYONG'O

THE INTERSECTIONS OF PUNK AND QUEER IN THE 1970S[1]

NO FUTURE...FOR YOU!

A PLAUSIBLE STARTING point for exploring the relationship between punk and queer is the shared vocabulary of "rough trade," the phrase denoting the easily recognized casual and sometimes commoditized sexual exchanges found in both subcultures. In Rob Young's excellent new history of the germinal punk music store and record label Rough Trade, he reprints a cartoon that economically summarizes that relation. In it, a cherubic, London-born Geoff Travis hitching through North America pauses to think: "Toronto was pretty cool...that band 'Rough Trade' must know the phrase means gay hustlers. That's even trashier than 'Velvet Underground.'"[2] This particular origin story for the label and store's name begs the question: does its founder Travis know that the same etymology of the phrase *rough trade* is also true of the word *punk*? As James Chance bluntly informs viewers of Don Letts's recent documentary *Punk: Attitude* (2003), "originally punk meant, you know, a guy in prison who got fucked up the ass. And that's still what it means to people in prison."[3] At one level, then, queer is to punk as john is to hustler, with both words referencing an established if underground economy of sexual favors and exchanges between men. That Chance could announce his definition as a ribald revelation suggests, however, that the subterranean linkages between punk and queer are as frequently disavowed as they are recognized. This suggests that alongside the "frozen dialectic" between black and white culture that Dick Hebdige famously noticed in British punk, there is also a less frequently noticed but equally furtive set of transactions between queer and punk that is hidden, like Poe's purloined letter, in plain sight.[4]

Punk may be literally impossible to imagine without gender and sexual dissidence. But the secret history, as Chance's comment suggests, also records a history of antagonisms between punk attitude and a male homosexual desire variously cast as predatory and pitiable. In a recent interview, for example, the journalist and author Jon Savage responded to the query about whether or not punk was "a sexy time" by arguing, "No. I thought punk was quite puritan, really. I didn't have a very good time during punk. I spent a lot of time feeling I was worthless...it still wasn't great to be gay in the late Seventies."[5] The phrasing of the question, and the whiff of pathos in Savage's response, suggests both a queer eagerness to identify with punk, as well as the hostility with which this desire was frequently met. We might consider as another example of this "53rd and 3rd" (1976) by the New York punk rockers the Ramones, in which Dee Dee Ramone recounts his hustling days at that notorious intersection on the east side of Manhattan and asks his audience, "Don't it make you feel sick?"[6] That line, ironically, is rhymed with "You're the one they never pick," suggesting Ramone's doubled abjection of failing even at being rough trade. But by contrast, Cynthia Fuchs, Mary Kearney, and Halberstam have argued that the affinities between lesbian, feminist, trans, and gay people and the punk subculture was immediate, definitive, and far more enduring.[7]

In a 2006 exchange with Edelman, Halberstam observed that his provocative title, *No Future*, was also the original title for the 1977 Sex Pistols' single, the one known more commonly today as "God Save the Queen." In the chorus to that song, the band front man, Johnny Rotten, snarled that there was "no future in England's dreaming," a line from which Savage drew the title for his celebrated history of British punk.[8] In Halberstam's opinion, Edelman's queer polemic does not stand up well in light of its unacknowledged punk predecessor. "While the Sex Pistols used the refrain 'no future' to reject a formulaic union of nation, monarchy, and fantasy," she argues, "Edelman tends to cast material political concerns as crude and pedestrian, as already a part of the conjuring of futurity that his project must foreclose."[9] Edelman, like Oscar Wilde with his rent boys, stands accused of using punks and then snubbing them as "crude and pedestrian," like the waiter whom Wilde famously, at his trial, denied kissing, dismissing him as "peculiarly plain" and "unfortunately, extremely ugly."[10]

Halberstam's comparison between the political stakes of "No Future" 1977 versus *No Future* 2004 bears some discussion. While rock stars may seem unlikely objects on which to pin our hopes for the expression of material political concerns, historians like Savage and Greil Marcus have situated "God Save the Queen" in a context of political, economic, and cultural crisis, one in which both conventional politics and the countercultural ethos of the sixties appeared exhausted and a time during which the anarchic antipolitics of punk therefore signaled something new.[11] Marcus in particular persuasively susses out the resonances, real and feigned, between anarchism proper and the anarchist poses and iconography of punk shock tactics. The offensive gestures of bands such as the Sex Pistols, the Clash, and Siouxsie and the Banshees, documented in films like Don Letts's *The Punk Rock Movie* (1978) and Julien Temple's *The Filth and the Fury* (2000), sometimes communicated a rejection of political action as traditionally conceived on the Left. But their very popularity inspired attempts, by both the Right and the Left, to appropriate punk attitude for political purposes. Paul Gilroy has given perhaps the definitive account of the contradictions involved in such attempts to incorporate punk, reggae, dancehall, dub, and other genres associated with alterity into a new cultural front in the late 1970s.[12] The absence of formal political incorporation, Gilroy notes, does not immediately negate the possibility of a political reception or deployment.

Furthermore, cultural critiques of the political meanings ascribed to punk often elide the class context of British punk, a component of the subculture that is often missed in the United States where the *sub* in *subculture* seems to stand more often for "suburban" than "subaltern" and where punk is typically read as a mode of middle class youth alienation. The submerged context of class struggle for British punk, however, comes to the fore in *The Filth and the Fury*'s astonishing footage of Rotten, Sid Vicious, and their bandmates smiling and serving cake to the children of striking firemen in Huddersfield, England, in 1977. Amid the moral panic, physical assaults, and public bans that had followed their incendiary early performances and record releases, the Sex Pistols played a Christmas benefit for the strikers and families. In the film, the Pistols are seen smearing themselves and the children with cake, and then performing, almost unbelievably, "Bodies" – an intensely graphic song about an illegal abortion – as the children and their parents bop around deliriously. Such a truly shocking conflation of the sentimental and the obscene, the perverse and the innocent, produced a moment of saturnalia that served as an outright rejection of the manufactured consensual fantasy of the queen's jubilee year. That moment was political in spite of, or even because of, the absence of a formalized politics among the callow, gangly lads that the pop Svengali Malcolm McLaren had cannily spun into cultural terrorists. Like Patti Smith, the Pistols in Huddersfield did not outright reject the mainstream scenarios of family, child rearing, and workingclass politics. Rather, they insinuated themselves into the very space that their rebellious stance ostensibly foreclosed to them. In both cases, Smith's and that of the Pistols, there is a countersymbolic charge to such a performative enactment that cannot simply be subsumed as antisocial behavior.

For Edelman, however, such a countersymbolic charge goes mostly unappreciated. Edelman has objected that the Pistols' "God Save the Queen" "does not really dissent from reproductive futurism," and he has argued that punk rebellion is merely caught up in the Oedipal dynamic of the young claiming the future from their corrupt and complicit elders: "No future…for you!" Instead of with the *sinthome*, Edelman associates punk anarchy with the derisive category of kitsch, ever the mandarins' term for that which the masses take seriously but which they consider intellectually or politically puerile. "Taken as political statement," Edelman argues, "God Save the Queen" is "little more than Oedipal kitsch. For violence, shock, assassination, and rage aren't negative or radical in themselves." While Edelman concedes that "punk negativity" may succeed "on the level of style," he takes such success to reinforce rather than undermine his position on the grounds that stylistic revolt is best achieved through the "chiasmic inversions" of his erudite polemic. Edelman warrants that the punks – and Halberstam in her critique – have confused "the abiding negativity that accounts for political negativism with the simpler act of negating particular political positions." We cannot preserve its negativity by making "the swing of the hammer an end in itself," as Edelman puts it, but only if we "face up to political antagonism with the negativity of critical thought."[13] Johnny Rotten, meet Theodor Adorno.

Punk as a mode of revolt indeed begins in fairly blunt affects such as stroppiness and rage. But to reduce its message to the negation of particular political positions (such as repudiating the queen's jubilee) means that Edelman accounts for the Pistols' song only at the level of the lyrics and neglects a consideration of punk in the context of performance. This is a shame, as punk performers are highly cognizant of precisely the challenge of abiding negativism that Edelman raises. In the case of the Pistols, this challenge emerges at least in part from the original negation of musical skill and technical virtuosity that had occasioned punk's three-chord breakthroughs in the mid-1970s. Letts's documentary *Punk: Attitude* reflects retrospectively on the problematic prospect of a virtuoso punk rebellion. If punk rock dissented in part by rejecting musical virtuosity for pure attitude and ecstatic amateurism, how precisely could it sustain that stance? The more committed to punk one was, the quicker one acquired precisely the expressive fluency the genre ostensibly disdains. Either that, or one transforms into a cynical parody of adolescent fumbling such as that exhibited by former Bromley Contingent member Billy Idol, the bottle blond who transformed Vicious's wild snarl into the knowing smirk of eighties megastardom. Punk, like adolescence, quickly becomes its own archival specter, and for many purists, the moment was over almost as soon as the first punk singles were released. Simon Reynolds explores the extremely fruitful terrain of "post-punk" music (some of which preceded punk proper, or developed adjacent to it) that rose to prominence almost as soon as the style of punk had congealed into a recognizable, repeatable form.[14] The challenge of an abiding negativism, whether or not one agrees with the various solutions proposed, is a core feature of punk performance. Punk and postpunk styles are anything but the static, generational revolt caricatured by Edelman's analysis. The punk spirit cannot be decoded from a single lyric, song, or band, no matter how iconic the text or performer seems to be.

Part of this spirit, of course, is the traceable charge of erotic frisson detectable in much of the seemingly hostile overlap between punks and queers, which are often mirrored in the social and economic dynamics that crystallize the relationship between john and hustler. Those dynamics derive from a history of attitudes toward male homosexuality; but it strikes me that 1970s punk represents the moment at which those specifically male homosexual associations lose their exclusivity and punk becomes a role and an affect accessible to people within a range of gendered embodiments who deploy punk for a variety of erotic, aesthetic, and political purposes. The asymmetric, hostile, and desirous relations preserved in punk from the dynamics of rough trade do not always produce an open, inclusive punk community. But the forms of exclusivity punk has historically produced tend to fail abjectly at the reproduction of hegemonic and identitarian logics, even when they seek to engage in it.

For this reason it may prove useful to acknowledge and meditate further on the historical switch points between punk and queer. Let me offer two that would bear a more extensive analysis than I have space for here: a 1975 photo session of the Sex Pistols done by Peter Christopherson, a member of the legendary performance art and music group Throbbing Gristle, and Derek Jarman's 1977 film *Jubilee*. Christopherson, whose early work, by his own description, was "of white trash kids, a bit like Larry Clark's work," was contracted in the summer of 1975 by McLaren to photograph the Sex Pistols. This was at a time when

McLaren and his partner, Vivienne Westwood, ran the famed SEX shop on Kings Road in London that featured men's and women's street fashions inspired by S-M, gay porn, and various fetishes, like bondage trousers, that were both intentionally shocking and knowingly Warholian. But wearing the iconography or style of the homosexual – such as the gay cowboy T-shirts the Pistols would sometimes sport in concert – was apparently not the same thing as subjecting oneself to the stigma of being perceived as homosexual, or being willingly identified as "gay for pay." When Christopherson posed the Pistols to resemble rent boys in a YMCA toilet, McLaren was apparently shocked and threatened by the explicitly homoerotic images, and he turned down the pictures.[15] The photos nevertheless reside as one archival switch point between the queer and punk seventies.

Similarly, Jarman's *Jubilee* is considered by some the first punk movie, and to make it he recruited a number of nonprofessional actors from the punk scene, including Jordan (Pamela Rooke), Adam Ant, and (in a cameo) Siouxsie Sioux. According to Chuck Warner, the punk Steve Treatment guided Jarman through the punk scene, vouching for the gay outsider when necessary.[16] The film, originally intended as an impressionistic documentary of punk London, evolved into a powerful depiction of urban dystopia as seen from the fantastic vantage point of a time-traveling Queen Elizabeth I. A historically and theatrically erudite iteration of the Pistols' "God Save the Queen," *Jubilee* literalized the disjunction between present-day reality and an anachronistic monarchy by juxtaposing Elizabeth with the anarchic punks. The film proved prophetic in a number of ways, but it was not universally well received at first, with Westwood delivering her review on (where else?) a T-shirt: "The most boring and therefore disgusting film…a gay boy jerk off through the titillation of his masochistic tremblings. You pointed your nose in the right direction then you wanked."[17] Westwood's rhetorical condensation of Jarman's camera – first onto his nose, then onto his penis – made particularly explicit the structures of cruising and slumming that made the production of the film possible. And yet to freeze the queen/queer at the other end of a voyeuristic lens would prematurely foreclose the transmissions of desire and affect that were clearly at play in both directions, and to which *Jubilee* stands as an important testament. As Peter Hitchcock notes, while "slumming is an ideologeme of class discourse…the slummer also fantasizes what the culture must otherwise hide, the ways in which the porous conditions of class augur the concrete possibilities of change."[18] Rough no doubt, but trade no less.

NOTES

1   This chapter originally appeared in Tavia Nyong'o, "Do You Want Queer Theory or Do You Want the Truth? The Intersections of Punk and Queer in the 1970s," *Radical History Review*, No. 100 (2008): 102-119. Thanks to Duke University Press for permission to reprint this excerpt.

2   Rob Young, *Rough Trade: Labels Unlimited* (London: Black Dog, 2006), p. 11.

3   For more on *punk* as a keyword, see Tavia Nyong'o, "Punk'd Theory," *Social Text*, Vol. 23 No. 3-4, 84-85 (2005): 19–34.

4   "For, at the heart of the punk subculture, forever arrested, lies this frozen dialectic between black and white cultures – a dialectic which beyond a certain point (i.e. ethnicity) is incapable of renewal, trapped, as it is, within its own history, imprisoned within its own irreducible antimonies." Dick Hebdige, *Subculture: The Meaning of Style* (London: Routledge, 1979), p. 70.

5   Alex Needham, "Jon Savage," *Butt*, Winter 2006, p. 62.

6   The Ramones, "53rd and 3rd," on *The Ramones* (1976), Audio CD, Sire.

7   Judith Halberstam, *In a Queer Time and Place: Transgender Bodies, Subcultural Lives* (New York: New York University Press, 2005); Mary Celeste Kearney, "The Missing Links: Riot Grrrl – Feminism – Lesbian Culture," in ed. Sheila Whiteley, *Sexing the Groove: Popular Music and Gender* (New York: Routledge, 1997), pp. 207–29; Cynthia Fuchs, "If I Had a Dick: Queers, Punks, and Alternative Acts," in ed. Thomas Swiss, John Sloop, and Andrew Herman, *Mapping the Beat: Popular Music and Contemporary Theory* (Malden, MA: Blackwell, 1998), pp. 101–18.

8   Jon Savage, *England's Dreaming: Anarchy, Sex Pistols, Punk Rock, and Beyond* (New York: St. Martin's, 2002).

9   Robert Caserio et al., "Forum: Conference Debates; The Antisocial Thesis in Queer Theory," *Proceedings of the Modern Language Studies Association* 121 (2006): 824.

10 Michael S. Foldy, *The Trials of Oscar Wilde: Deviance, Morality, and Late-Victorian Society* (New Haven, CT: Yale University Press, 1997), p. 17.

11 Greil Marcus, *Lipstick Traces: A Secret History of the Twentieth Century* (Cambridge, MA: Harvard University Press, 1989).

12 Paul Gilroy, *"There Ain't No Black in the Union Jack": The Cultural Politics of Race and Nation* (London: Hutchinson, 1987).

13 Caserio et al., "Forum," p. 822.

14 Simon Reynolds, *Rip It Up and Start Again: Postpunk, 1978–1984* (New York: Penguin, 2006).

15   Simon Ford, *Wreckers of Civilisation: The Story of Coum Transmissions and Throbbing Gristle* (London: Black Dog, 2000), pp. 4–10, 5–13. Some of the photos are reproduced in Savage, *England's Dreaming*.

16   Chuck Warner, personal conversation with author, August 13, 2005.

17   Quoted by Tony Peake in "Derek Jarman's *Jubilee* (1977)," an essay accompanying the Criterion Collection release of *Jubilee*. Online at http://www.criterion.com.

18   Peter Hitchcock, "Slumming," in eds. María C. Sánchez and Linda Schlossberg, *Passing: Identity and Interpretation in Sexuality, Race, and Religion* (New York: New York University Press, 2001), pp. 184-85.

RUBÉN ORTIZ-TORRES

MEXIPUNX

WHO WERE THEY? What did they do? How did they sound or what did they look like? If they were anarchists, I was one of them...

The hillsides ring with "Free the people"
Or can I hear the echo from the days of '39?
With trenches full of poets
The ragged army, fixin' bayonets to fight the other line
Spanish bombs rock the province
I'm hearing music from another time
Spanish bombs on the Costa Brava
I'm flying in on a DC-10 tonight

-The Clash, "Spanish Bombs"

The Spanish civil war was lost by Spain and civilization but it was won by Mexico when thousands of intellectuals and other political refugees were given asylum and turned up on its shores in 1939. Among them was the Andalucían anarchist teacher, José the Tapia, who realized that freedom had to be taught at an early stage before social pressures to conform settle in. He founded an alternative experimental utopian grammar school that I was so privileged to attend. "Anarchism is not a fashion or an A inside a circle, it is morals" he told me later on.

* * *

Diego was fourteen when he came back to Mexico City from visiting his mother's family in England, in 1978. He told us in school about some crazy guys called punks that puked, wore ripped clothes with pins, had green hair, and insulted the Queen. Such strange natives of exotic distant lands seemed of interest, as did their resistance to authority. One day Leonardo invited Diego and me to his house and asked us to stay because his older sisters where going to have a party and a "punk" was going to come. With high expectations we stayed late, spying from the second floor in pajamas until a guy showed up sporting short light hair, wearing an orange suit, pointed shoes and a tie. He did not have green hair, ripped clothes, or behave in any recognizable anti-authoritarian way, but he certainly stood out among the longhaired crowd with jeans and sneakers. In fact, he was the guy from the record shop close to my house, where my father used to take his sound system to be fixed. His name was Guillermo Santamarina. They call him "Tin Larín," the name of a popular candy, because his suits looked like the ones worn by the cartoon characters in their advertisements. They also called him "La Holandesita" (the Dutch girl) because apparently he had spent time in Holland where, according to the legend, he became the first Mexican punk, or whatever he was.

I used to play baseball in little league and would come back from training on the bus. I would get off in the San Angel neighborhood in the South of the City and walk to Yoko Quadrasonic, the record shop where I would browse at the records and imported magazines. Whenever I would buy a record, usually recommended by Guillermo, he would throw in a free skateboard magazine or a *Heavy Metal* comic book. This did not happen often because the imported American LP's cost twice as much as they would have in the US, and English, Japanese, and other European records were even more rare and expensive. Rock concerts and other mass youth events were usually not allowed after the government of the institutionalized revolution massacred thousands of demonstrating students in the plaza of Tlatelolco in 1968; jazz and blues concerts were about as close as it would get. We would go see films of concerts as if they were the real thing. I remember a memorable screening of *Woodstock* in the film club of the national autonomous university where people danced naked, so stoned they didn't notice the horrible quality of the scratched print and the sound.

* * *

'Ronnie Tampax and the Tampons' were based on a comic strip I drew. The name seemed punk but we played blues and Rolling Stones' covers because we did not know any better. We debuted in an event at my high school. I could not rehearse my singing properly with the band because we did not have a microphone. I owned two different recorded versions of "Jumping Jack Flash" and in one, it seemed like Jagger shouted, "Want You" and in the other "Watch it." My English was very basic. Confused, I shouted "Watcho" in some kind of Spanglish, embarrassing my bilingual band mates. Singing in English (even precariously) also did not go over particularly well in a high school whose directors had sympathies with the Communist party, which was full of political exiles from the military dictatorships in South America. The guitarist, Martín García Reynoso, who is now well known as a musician in Buenos Aires, was so embarrassed that he decided not to face the audience and played backwards. Nevertheless, the aura of rock and roll must be bright and powerful because even we were able to get some groupies, including a few precocious intellectual Argentinean girls who had escaped the dictatorship with their parents, and my mom, who hated rock.

There was only one rock program on the radio other than the daily hour of the Beatles and the show featuring Credence Clearwater Revival (the "Crrreeedens Clearrrwaterrr Rrrrreevival," according to the DJ). It was called "El Lado Oscuro de la Luna" (The Dark Side of the Moon) and it was produced by the then young writer, Juán Villoro, and broadcast on public radio. He even translated some lyrics of songs and published them as poetry. His program was an oasis in the desert of disco and bad cumbias that was commercial radio. The pinnacle of the program was a series called "La Rebelión Gandalla" (The Jerk Rebellion). Finally, I was able to hear the dissonant cords of the Sex Pistols, The Ramones and the like. They were the shot of adrenalin that finally made me feel I was part of a generation and not the nostalgia of my uncles and the Sixties. My father, who used to play in a Latin American folk band called Los

Folkloristas and loved classical music, worked at the same radio station broadcasting live concerts by the symphony orchestra. Despite his almost absolute ignorance and rejection of rock – based on Latin American nationalist and ideological principles – he took me there to meet Villoro. As a result, I was invited to play my records once or twice! Another, more unintended consequence of our meeting, was a character in a book of short stories he later wrote about different generations of rockers: the character was called "Rubén" and he just so happened to be a punk son in conflict with parents who were into Latin American folk music.

* * *

A couple of blocks from my high school in Colonia, the record shop 'Hip 70' organized a burning of disco music records. Kids with leather jackets, sunglasses, spiky hairdos and shoes imitated an event that happened elsewhere. The argument was that disco was "fresa" (literally "strawberry," a local version of square and yuppie). However, those early Mexican punk kids were privileged enough to travel in order to import their style, and they sang in English – stuff like "I want to kill your mother with my finger tonight," which was from a song by Illy Bleeding, the singer of the band 'Size' and one of the first Mexican punks. Disco was indeed commercial and its appeal transcended the expensive international discotheques in Acapulco and Mexico City and reached populist, massive sound systems in urban streets and rural towns. There were also some racist overtones for its hatred, considering that disco was mostly black music.

* * *

My friend Miguel told me I had to meet another anarchist artist. I had to. He introduced me to "El Vox." Paco López Morán, known as "El Vox," was swimming while wearing a tie in the pool of a suburban house in the south of the city. His little brothers also had straight long blond hair and fish faces like him, with the exception of Bernardo, who had curly dark hair and was better looking. Paco played the organ and did art with a Dadaist and Surrealist affinity. In fact, he played his experimental compositions on the organ at one of his brother's first communions, scaring the priest and the rest of the family. He was known for doing an opera in his high school where he released little chicks into the surprised audience; people ran hysterically, stepping on them. His parents imported Spanish wine and did very well. When the devaluation of the currency was imminent they decided to invest in Canada and bought a hotel in Mississauga, close to Toronto. Paco married his sweetheart Alejandra, who was 15 years old, so she could go with him to Canada. There, the winters and the nights seemed endless.

Paco went beyond punk: his mohawk hairdo was gigantic, he designed his eccentric clothes, got tattooed, wore a lot of make up, and played in a band called 'Jesus and the Mutants.' When they would visit Mexico during Christmas and the summer, traffic would stop and everyone would stare into the street or the mall, waiting to see if this unknown breed of living creatures were hostile. At a party, a drunken older woman encouraged by her exhibitionist eccentricity decided to undress and masturbate in front of us, before being kicked out. I decided to take photographs and Super 8 films of these encounters with an old Yashica camera that belonged to my father. In the hotel, we experimented with the television, the lamps and the elevator; the images were grainy and black and white. In the television images of atomic bombs, poor starving third world kids and primitivist art appeared as if they were part of the narrative. There is a particular image of Paco and Alejandra, partially blurred from a long exposure, but sharp in a frozen moment by the flash: they appear like beautiful strange ghosts in a cheap restaurant in downtown Mexico City, decorated with a painting of the last supper over a jukebox. The composition is hieratic and symmetric, and they are drinking a glass of milk. They seem to fit, and simultaneously be perfectly out of context, in this version of "Mexican Gothic."

From a roll of film, I printed eight images to meet the number of photographs required to participate in the biennial of photography. My knowledge of photography at the time probably came more from album covers than anywhere else; among my favorites were Patty Smith's *Horses*, shot by Robert Mapplethorpe, and the Rolling Stones' *Exile on Main Street*, with photos by Robert Frank. Those influences were not so bad, however, some of my printing decisions were: I used contrasting matte paper thinking its graphic look was more "artistic."

I won a production grant! It was popular for photojournalists to take photos of punk kids and disenfranchised youth, but I guess my work seemed different since I was supposed to be a "tribal member," producing some kind of self-representation. My pics, in other words, were not anthropological voyeuristic snitching but, perhaps, the real exhibitionistic thing. The famous Mexican photographer Graciela Iturbide wanted to meet me. Were these my fifteen minutes? All of a sudden I had to really learn how to make photographs in order to have a solo show. The problem was that my only "real" punk friend was Paco and, in fact, he just considered himself his own avant-garde experiment. By that time I had already figured out that the kids with the leather jackets and thin sunglasses in Mexico – the ones that took pills and did outrageous things at parties in Mexico City – were not into the socialist libertarian ideals that led me to them, but rather, into singing with bad English accents and diverging into new wave, gothic, new romantic, and other new trends. Meanwhile, poor kids in the outskirts of Mexico City, in a neighborhood called Santa Fe, robbed a butcher shop to give steaks to the people. They called themselves the 'Sex Panchitos.' Their lumpenproletariat sense of punk aesthetics involved sniffling glue, doing a stiff spastic dance, and communicating in an incomprehensible slang that functioned more like ambient sound than dialogue. The genie had escaped its frivolous middle class bottle to become a serious infection: I had to find (or make) the scene.

The equipment came first. With the money from the production grant I went to New York to buy a Contax camera with a couple of beautiful Zeiss lenses. I stayed in the apartment of my Puerto Rican friends' grandma in the Bronx. I saw PIL live. Afrika Bambaataa opened the show by scratching and rapping to an audience that mostly booed, not realizing the future that Jonny Lydon was already envisioning. Preppy girls ripped their clothes in the middle of the concert to fit in better with the crowd. The concert ended when Lydon pushed into the audience one of the bouncers who was trying to keep kids from diving off the stage. Then, I went to Toronto to visit Paco and take more photos. He was studying in the Ontario College of Art, making pornographic silk screens printed on fur; his apartment was an installation and his clothes pieces of sculpture. Alejandra was bored. Her English was bad and the novelty of the snow wore out after a few too many cold days. The two of them were like fish out of the water in Mexico, but these waters were far too icy. They ended up arguing at the subway station for a long time, while I sat on the floor as old ladies tried to help me, or ask me what was wrong with them. I shot photographs of everything I saw, and most often it was not clear who was the boy or the girl. The Zeiss 28mm was so crisp and sharp that I could see the thread of the jackets when I enlarged the negatives. Toronto seemed like London or New York and therefore like the "real" thing. But it was neither.

Mireya was a quiet preppy girl in high school; she was tall and cute and somehow ended up in Toronto with her divorced mother. She came to Mexico on vacations but seemed lonely when I met here there. I suggested that she hook up with Paco, explaining that, despite his looks, he was a nice guy who also had brothers and a wife who were fun. She met them and started going to all the clubs. By the time I saw her in Toronto she had turned into a skinhead and appeared drunk as she gave the finger to my camera.

* * *

Back in Mexico, I went out one Sunday with my family to have lunch. When we returned, the door of the house was open and the windows of the bathroom broken. Things were all over the floor. Since there were not many valuable things in my house, I went running upstairs fearing the worst. The camera was gone. The fast 28mm wide-angle and the even faster 50mm Zeiss lenses were both missing, reminding me of how taxes are often paid in the third world. With a sense of anger and a borrowed Nikon, I started going to parties and looking for gigs.

Juán Carlos Lafontaine and his brother Mario lived in the middle class southern suburb of Villa Coapa. Their Catholic mom kept the house impeccably clean; the decoration was elegant in its kitsch. Juan Carlos dressed in black like a priest, had an architectonic postmodern hairdo painted cold black, wore sunglasses, and played the synths. Mario dressed in colorful drag with funky wigs, pop necklaces, and glasses. He was a fabulous soul singer. Both were uniquely chubby and wore make up. Together, they were the unlikely, legendary duet, 'Maria Bonita.' Their roundness made them also known as "las toronjas" (the grapefruit). Juan Carlos would pull his brother onto the stage with chains as Mario crawled, claiming that he was so fat he could not walk. The

Botero painting-like scene and the bizarre performance included sexual-
ized, perverted versions of well-known lullabies and children's songs by
Cri Cri, in Spanish. If there's no possibility to commercialize your music,
get radio play, or breakout of a scene that is destined to be underground,
then you might as well be as provocative as you want.

By the time I met them, the band was splitting due to irreconcilable
aesthetic differences. Juan Carlos was into gothic and electronic music
and Mario into soul and high energy. Both were promising stars of an
advertising industry that could take advantage of their talents, information, and sensibilities in a palatable and superficial way. They were excellent draftsmen, in a pop manga way, and earned good money making
trendy ads for soda and car companies. They spent it on equipment,
fashion, toys, books and records. They were incredibly sensitive to style.
For Juán Carlos, politics were fashion. Industrial and gothic music made
him interested in black uniforms and constructivism: a confusion of fascist and socialist visuals. My idealist positions became relevant to him, in
relation to the image of his new band, since their industrial sounds called
for a "socialist" look. He imagined me in suspenders, knickerbockers,
a long-sleeve undershirt with buttons, steel-toed boots, a shaved head,
and old circular frame glasses. Despite my still limited musical skills, if I
could be that *and* hold a bass, then I had a band. Alejandra and Rosalba
were friends of my sister and a bit intellectual: Rosalba studied English
literature, and Alejandra architecture. For Juán Carlos, that meant elegant dark dresses and sculptural hairdos with shaved designs that would
hopefully imply celestial voices. So, with his 3 human models (or props?)
and the addition of Carlos García (a keyboard player with some experience) the band, 'Das Happy,' was ready to appear on television. Was it?
It seems it was, because it did.

Juán Carlos did not speak English but was convinced it was not
necessary. He thought that his accessories, his precise clothes, and his
hairdo could immediately communicate with Siouxsie (yes, the one from
Siouxsie and the Banshees) if only she saw him on the street. He imagined England as a place filled with people like him: a place where he
could be understood. There was no way to explain that it was also a
conservative place, with old ladies drinking tea, ruled by the Tories and
Margaret Thatcher.

* * *

The center of the underground scene became the 'Disco Bar 9,' a gay
bar in the relatively eccentric Zona Rosa neighborhood. On Thursdays,

they had cultural activities and events sponsored by a magazine called *La PusModerna*. Before 11PM, some cheap ethylic substance mixed with Coke was served free so that people would get loaded early to ease the acceptability of culture and lust. Most bands played there at some point, and performances also ranged from boxing matches to avant-garde experiments. Bodies slammed, covered in sweat around the "pomo" decoration. I was hired by the magazine to document the scene and in a little room I made some portraits. I still wonder how this place was so exceptionally tolerated. North of the city, the only real punk bar opened up: it was called Tutti Frutti and was owned by a tall Belgium hardcore guy named Danny and his girlfriend, Brisa. He had a big hairdo that made him look like a palm tree. He liked The Cramps. The place had a cool jukebox and was decorated with toy cars on the wall. We had to drive far to get there and after a wild night it was even harder to drive back.

Eventually the punk thing mutated more than it faded out. Some trends even seemed to make sense locally. Ska, for example, blended with a Pachuco revival: the guys from 'Maldita Vecindad' sported some kind of a contemporary version of zoot suits at their gigs. I was painting more at the time when I figured out that the whole subculture was just becoming culture, and that we were somewhere else. What happened with these people?

* * *

LIFE IS SHORT

For some it was. I remember a girl being arrested after smashing a glass bottle into the face of an important military man's daughter. Pepe Guadalajara, the singer of a band called 'Los Casuals' had to go to New York to be able to score some smack and self destroy. Thirty years later it would not be necessary, since globalization has made the product not only available but locally produced for export.

AND THEN YOU DIE.

Beautiful Colombina was a goddess. With her thick lips and dark skin she looked like a voluptuous actress from a 1940s Mexican black and white movie, and dressed the part. Dancing late at night in the club, I pretended to eat the Rohypnol she gave me, thinking that I didn't need the aid of a catalyzer to let myself be abused by her. When we got to her apartment and her friend Luis Carlos wanted to join us, I figured out the reason for the pill. Last I heard, she was going out with a drug dealer in Cancun who shot her to death.

Others survived for the better: Guillermo Santamarina "Tin Larín" was, until recently, the curator of the Museum of Contemporary Art of the National University in Mexico. Even after helping a lot of artists he still buys records, dresses sharp, and tries hard to reject an establishment where he reluctantly belongs. Paco "El Vox" left Canada and went to Spain with his family. He played in a psychedelic band produced by Malcolm McLaren, called 'On,' that was never really distributed. Eventually, he became "Professor Angel Dust" in Barcelona and organized legendary parties in a club called La Paloma. He recorded and produced some kind of Latin hip hop and dance music with other well known acts like La Mala Rodriguez. I did a cover design and a video for him.

Paco's story seems to have a sad ending but hopefully it is not *the* ending. He was invited to DJ in Panama and on the way back home – with his beautiful African wife, Kene Wang Nowka, and his little baby daughter – they were caught trying to sneak four kilograms of blow through the airport. Considering that nowadays you cannot even get past security with a tube of toothpaste, this had to be one of the stupidest things one could attempt. To no avail, Paco tried to tell the Central American law that they were framed; he said they were threatened by some mugs who followed them with guns and told them that the security guards were bribed, and would let them pass. But they were arrested and their daughter was taken away. They were given eight years. At least now, time passes a little faster with cell phones and access to the Internet. Paco recently released a track that featured his wife singing over the phone; it is some kind of tragic Caribbean funeral march that he produced with a computer. The monitor of his laptop is now the window from his cell.

Juán Carlos Lafontaine is now Mateo Lafontaine and 'Decada2' exists somewhere in the pixels of MySpace. Through the web, he looks younger and more handsome than twenty years ago. The most successful ones, though, were certainly not the eccentrics and the radicals that I felt compelled to photograph. Saúl Hernandez dropped out of high school to be a rock star, which seemed like foolish career suicide since there were no rock radio stations, or even places to perform. He used to play corny progressive rock that most of us heard with contempt; he told a story of giving Robert Fripp a demo tape of his band and he was then convinced that *King Crimson* had copied him. Somehow his band, 'Caifanes' (which later became 'Jaguares') became an improbable hit that made rock music in Spanish a popular reality. In fact, Robert Fripp even opened for them in Los Angeles.

The most unlikely case of fame came from an annoying kid from the Communist party who used to rat on the stoners and gays in high school: two groups whose actions were considered serious offenses according to the orthodox morals of the Principals this kid befriended. His name was Gabriel but we used to call him "El Pájaro" (the bird) because he liked "El Pajarito" Cortés Sánchez, a famous player from Club América, his favorite soccer team. His father was a muralist painter that worked with Siqueiros and had the same last names of Orozco and Rivera, but without any relation to those famous muralists. Gabriel was a soccer jock with artistic pretensions and wanted to do a social realist mural in the school. Later, he dated the daughter of a local corrupt politician and it seemed he would become an official cultural bureaucrat or artist. What no one would have ever imagined is that, after being ignored by the local galleries and the emerging art scene, Gabriel would move to New York to reinvent himself in the total opposite direction. All of a sudden he had solo show in the Museum of Modern Art in New York. His ambiguous, post-conceptual gestures became an inoffensive and acceptable antithesis of the Mexican School, and easy to export: the empty signifiers that passed for indecipherable concepts became hot commodities in the times of NAFTA. The commercial, modern and international qualities of his work made it ideal to officially represent the culture of the conservative neoliberal government that replaced the old ruling party of the institutionalized revolution.

* * *

And You May Find Yourself Living In A Shotgun Shack
And You May Find Yourself In Another Part Of The World
And You May Find Yourself Behind The Wheel Of A Large Automobile
And You May Find Yourself In A Beautiful House, With A Beautiful Wife
And You May Ask Yourself: Well...How Did I Get Here?

And as for me, I came to the land of *Love and Rockets*. I have not found my rocket yet, but I did find love. Echo Park in Los Angeles is my Hoppers. Maggie, Hopey, and my cousin, Speedy Ortiz, are fictional characters from a comic strip but they seem as real and as close to my friends and family as anything I ever saw in a representation. They would reveal to me that in a city without a center, there cannot be a periphery. The sectarian divisions of my youth that separated musical and artistic genres collapsed in Los Angeles where, since the beginning, The Plugz were recording anarchist versions of "La Bamba." Heavy metal and punk also mix and, together with hip hop, can form an unlikely artsy/radical/political vehicle like Rage Against the Machine. Here in LA, the sounds of my father's band are still remembered and are not a source of shame anymore as they blend with the twang of the Fender Telecaster, the blast of the sax, and the ageless tempo of rockabilly. Los Lobos music sounds better with time, like a good wine.

* * *

There were no conditions for the punk scene in Mexico to be anything but underground and, because of that, it often produced extreme things: it simply could not "sell out." The problem today is not selling out but to not be bought in the first place. According to the liner notes of the record *Cruising With Ruben and the Jets*, Ruben Sano declared in 1955: "The present day Pachuco refuses to die!"

The present-day punk also refuses to die!

Style is not created or destroyed, it just transforms.

BRIAN TUCKER

PUNK PLACES:
THE ROLE OF SPACE IN SUBCULTURAL LIFE

WALKING UP TO it, the house blended into the neighborhood, which was a collection of slightly worn rental properties, early 20th century row houses, and a few private residences. White paint chipping off the wood siding, an old Pontiac, taken up permanent residence in the yard surrounded by weeds, and several current and former gardening projects behind the car greeted anyone approaching. Bikes were seemingly strewn everywhere, attached to every conceivable spot one could conceivably lock up to. The porch had seen better days; its screens fraying in various stages of disrepair and it was filled with five gallon containers that were used to ferry food to and from Saturday Food Not Bombs lunches, as well as various bike parts, recycling bins, and gardening tools.

There were usually eight or so permanent residents who had rooms of their own and a collection of traveling punks, activists, and couch surfers who would come and go. If a gathering or convention were in town, people would be crashing everywhere; one might step over several people going from one room to another. Weekday mornings there would be small children playing and running through the house, several people living there provided babysitting for friends. Friday nights punks would come over and cook for Food Not Bombs the next day, the living room would be filled with people chopping vegetables, the two kitchens both brimming with people cooking vegan food, chatting, and drinking beer.

The walls were littered with art projects of housemates and the kids we babysat, flyers for shows in town, and an assortment of maps, postcards, and notes from visitors. In the downstairs kitchen there was a chore sign up sheet, which would at times provoke house meetings that could go late into the night. There were two ancient videogame consoles in the living room. Which, incidentally, was the only room in the house that hadn't been converted into a bedroom, the procurement of these was a mystery; there were rumors, but all we could get out of the interested parties was that they were 're-appropriated.'

My bedroom, which I couldn't afford on my own and therefore had to sublet my bed to another housemate in favor of the couch, doubled as the house library. It had originally been a dining room that opened into the kitchen and the living room, so there were flattened cardboard boxes duct-taped to the doorway to section it off from the living room, and a throw rug hanging off the doorway to the kitchen. In our happier moments, we'd claim that privacy was bourgeois; at other times we'd just grumble as people drifted in and out. Two piles of clothes sat under the loft, one mine and the other my roommate's, both of us having neglected to ever buy a dresser.

The basement was full of science experiments; there were several home-brewing aficionados living in the house who had taken it over after we decided we'd no longer be having punk shows down there. In a house where getting the dishes washed would provoke a four hour-long meeting regarding the politics of housework; none of us really wanted to hash out who would have to clean up afterwards. Anyway, we were the activist house in town and there were two other punk houses that focused primarily around holding punk shows.

At the time, our house was the headquarters for Food Not Bombs, Columbus Copwatch, and a splinter faction of Anti-Racist Action. Several book clubs and sundry other organizations held meetings in our living room as well. Columbus, while having a fairly sizable punk scene at the time for a city its size, couldn't support its own meeting place or punk-run music venue, so most radical activism or DIY activities took place in someone's home. House decisions were made using consensus based procedures in weekly house meetings. The house itself served to dissolve distinctions between public and private life; it was a home, a meeting place, and a site of politics. It was a means by which we could, at least in limited ways, live our politics and experience the possibilities of alternative ways of organizing ourselves.

If one takes seriously a notion that practices at least inform, if not constitute, political subjects, it follows that one must take the politics of place and spaces seriously; if politics are embodied and immanent, then where these practices take place potentially facilitates, colors, or discourages actions. Wendy Brown, calling for feminist political spaces, writes, "Our spaces, while requiring some definition and protection, cannot be clean, sharply bounded, disembodied, or permanent: to engage post-modern modes of power and honor specifically feminist knowledges, they must be heterogeneous, roving, relatively non-institutionalized, and democratic to the point of exhaustion."[1] This conception of political spaces need not be exclusively feminist, it may facilitate the development of democratic citizens more broadly. In *Participation and Democratic Theory*, Carol Pateman links the expansion of sites of participatory democratic practices to the creation of a more engaged and empowered citizenry.[2] Margaret Kohn, writing in *Radical Space*, claims, "Political spaces facilitate change by creating a distinctive place to develop new identities and social, symbolic, and experiential dimensions of space. Transformative politics comes from separating, juxtaposing, and recombining these dimensions."[3]

The desire to create places, whether they are bounded in physical space by walls or formed by the collections of people whose temporary association creates a provisional sense of place (within an already coded space), is an under-theorized aspect of subcultural studies. Sartorial resistance to hegemony has a dual function; it is both an expression of dissent and the creation of *sites* of resistance that bring together resistant subjects in a given location in time and space. According to Yi-Fu Tuan, "Space is transformed into place as it acquires definition and meaning."[4] Punks, whether at shows, in their homes, or through inhabiting other spaces, create places for themselves within liberal or capitalist spaces. A punk show transforms a rented room at the local YMCA or VFW hall into a punk place: a site of conviviality, of contestation and of the dissemination of ideas. And just as familiarity turns a collection of homes and businesses into a neighborhood, the sight of punks hanging out, the sounds of bands playing, and even the layout of merch tables one sees upon entering the show, also function to transform space into punk place. Punk places create, transform, and strengthen punks as political subjects; they are the spaces in which, it is hoped, one also feels comfortable and safe to express one's self.

THINKING SPATIALLY

But what exactly are we studying when we consider space? David Harvey offers three categories of space and space-time: Absolute (which describes relatively static things existing in the world), Relative (which describes the movement of a thing through space and time), and Relational (in which time and space become inseparable).[5] These three categories are utilized primarily to describe material phenomena and offer little in the way of explaining less tangible phenomena like feelings or experiences. But when mapped onto the "tripartite division of experienced, conceptualized and lived space," his definitions allow for more precision when describing space.[6] For example, one could describe a show taking place at a VFW hall (the intersection of absolute and material space), the experience or feeling one gets by inhabiting that space (absolute spaces and spaces of representation), touring networks that brought a band to the show (relative and material), the feeling one gets traveling to or from the show (relative and lived), as well as the memories of past shows as they color the present (relational and lived). This approach enables one to think about spaces and the ways in which one experiences them dialectically, with each combination leading to many different possible outcomes.

I want to emphasize this dialectical relationship between punk behaviors, places and practices to disrupt trends in cultural studies that are over-committed to textual readings of subcultures (and their spaces). As Henri Lefebvre warns, reading space textually excludes the actual experience of inhabiting the world; it reduces "space itself to the status of a message, and the inhabiting of it to the status of a reading. This is to evade both history and practice."[7] However, the textual analysis of punk is not to be dismissed entirely, for it provides tools useful for discerning the ways in which visual signifiers define or limit spaces, as well as a means for identifying the sorts of discourses deployed in the creation of a given space. Lefebvre's conceptualization of social space offers a useful framework for analysis:

> (Social) space is not a thing among other things, nor a
> product among other products: rather, it subsumes things
> produced, and encompasses their interrelationships in their
> coexistence and simultaneity – their (relative) order and/or
> (relative) disorder. It is the outcome of a sequence and set
> of operations, and thus cannot be reduced to the rank of
> a simple object...Itself the outcome of past actions, social
> space is what permits fresh actions to occur, while suggest-
> ing others and prohibiting yet others.[8]

The advantage to treating space as more than a 'thing' is that it leaves open the possibility of transformation; changes in social attitudes, politics, economics and technology all have the potential to change the ways in which space is produced, defined and inhabited. This approach also allows one to posit that space is constitutive of political subjects; the practices of subjects are at least partially contingent upon the spaces in which they take occur. If those practices are in some way subject-making, place has a role to play in its facilitation of actions.

It is also worth considering two changes in the ways we experience space and place in contemporary America, inasmuch as they shape the resistant nature of punk subculture in its relationships with spatiality. First are the ways in which information technologies have changed both the ways we experience and the ways we act in space. Joshua Meyrowitz, combining the insights of McLuhan and Goffman in *No Sense of Place*, contends that electronic media like radio and television have radically diminished the role of physical space in modern life. Second, Margaret Kohn argues that the increasing privatization of public places, from the commons to the shopping mall, have diminished democratic possibilities in the U.S. Punk can be considered a reaction to both phenomena, in a way making a rather conservative move toward a reconstruction of place and the public sphere.

In "Art in the Age of Mechanical Reproduction," Walter Benjamin posits a connection between the effect of art and the means by which it is produced; new technologies enabled the mass production of works of art which served to change the ways in which it is experienced. Joshua Meyrowitz takes this argument a step further, arguing that the ways in which we experience the world are in part contingent upon communications technologies. Print, radio, television, and the Internet have progressively shrunk the world and changed the ways we live in it. The world is at our fingertips from inside the home, which dissolves hard and fast divisions between the public and private spheres. Since we need not exit the private sphere to access the public, the need to move physically into a public sphere is diminished. Meyrowitz writes, "electric media affect social behavior-not through the power of their messages buy by reorganizing the social settings in which people interact and by weakening the once strong relationship between physical place and social 'place.'"[9] Electronic media collapses distances in absolute/material space, leading to changes in the ways we experience those places and distances in relational/lived spaces. This collapse of real and represented space and time is accelerated with each advance and technology; absolute space is rendered smaller and smaller until it is accessible in representational forms in its entirety within the home. One need never leave the home to experience the world, or at least to experience it as simulacrum, "Places visited for the first time now look familiar if they (or places like them) have already been seen on television. And places that were once very different are now more similar because nearly every place has a television set, radio, and telephone."[10] In some ways, this could be seen as a victory of the

Enlightenment, our abstracted selves now have access to the entirety of the world without ever having to leave the private sphere. Experience becomes divorced from material reality, or at least altered by it in such a way as to negate the necessity for physical interaction with it.

In *Brave New Neighborhoods*, Margaret Kohn similarly argues that public spaces that once fostered democratic subjects are being replaced by private spaces fostering private subjects, not through any act of the state but by the logic of capital:

> The technology of the automobile, the expansion of the federal highway system, and the growth of residential suburbs has changed the way Americans live. Today the only place that many Americans encounter strangers is in the shopping mall. The most important public place is now private.[11]

Access to these new privatized public spaces is often contingent upon one's ability to pay, or at least to appear as one able or willing to pay, to enter, "The private sector may be able to provide social spaces but it is unable to provide public spaces, for example, places where all citizens can come together...As long as entrepreneurs sell collective goods at market prices there will be market segmentation based on ability to pay."[12] Privatized spaces segregate along class (and other) lines, providing not just goods for sale but also a sense of place in which one's comfort is predicated upon the absence of the Other. The privatization of public spaces stunts the growth of a polity and shifts the goal of public life from critical engagement with one's neighbors to comfort provided by insularity:

> Public space strengthens a democratic polity by providing a forum for dissenting views. But public space has another equally significant, albeit more illusive, effect. It influences the way that we are constituted as subjects and the way we identify with others. The privatization of public space narrows our sensibility by diminishing the opportunities to encounter difference.[13]

Emboldened by the collapse of space facilitated by electronic media, it seems that citizens are more and more willing to accept mediated representations of the Other than to leave their insulated world and meet such people face to face.

Punk, to a certain extent, is a reaction to the changes in space and place that Meyrowitz and Kohn write about. As a youth subculture,

historically, it lacked the capital to utilize effectively a great deal of electronic mass media, aside from the occasional pirate radio station or public access TV show.[14] The emphasis was face-to-face punk communities
also privileged geographical difference insofar as the lack of a homogenizing technology facilitated different scenes in different locations; it
was a source of pride, or at least a point of interest, that different scenes
produced different bands, zines and fashions, each with particular histories, politics and styles.[15] The DC sound is different from mid-western
emo, which is different from New York Hardcore, and so on. The ritual
of going to a punk show also underscores the myriad reasons why place
matters and how physical spaces reassert themselves within subcultural
experience. Narratives of attending shows often focus in some way on
a sense of place, and most notably, how it is cultivated through specific
spatial rites of passage that might be invisible to outsiders. For example,
punks located in the suburbs or rural areas and must often travel to a city
for shows, and the journey itself becomes a crucial part of 'the show':

> Once we got to Philly, we switched trains to head to the
> Northeast, getting off at the Margaret/Orthodox stop in
> Frankford. We had no idea where we were going, blindly
> following all the other punks into some uncharted territory
> far from home. It wasn't until the mid-90's that I figured
> out where the hell this place really was.[16]

One could also point to the experience of entering a show space for
the first time and seeing "the turmoil of 'da pit'"[17] In these and other
ways, punk is an attempt to re-establish a sense of place, to create both a
feeling of home and a space for contestation and self-expression.

Indeed, what struck me about my first show was not the music, but
this sense of place. I could listen to records at home but the show provided a space for me to meet the sorts of people I wasn't about to encounter in the rural/suburban town where I was then living. In between
sets, kids huddled around merch tables, buying zines and records from
the bands themselves. The front stage/back stage distinction was virtually non-existent since we were in a YMCA, and at most DIY shows,
there wasn't a stage at all; the band and the crowd shared the same space.
At larger shows or fests, which often necessitate the rental of an actual
concert venue, bands often still opt to play on the floor with the audience.[18] In this way, the punk show is a phenomenon quite different from
other performative arts; the music itself was often not the most important thing going on, though it was certainly the catalyst for bringing

people together. One might be just as attracted to the ad hoc market place of merch tables (depending on the size of the show), and at fests there might be classes on DIY home brewing, self-defense, political organizing, or anarchist decision-making structures.

These spaces, however, are still in a way 'private.' Although anyone is allowed to enter, punk is a largely white, male, straight, and middle class subculture; those belonging to a different social group often do not feel particularly welcome. Further, since these spaces are also based around punk music, and therefore still follow the logic of market segmentation, people with little interest in loud music would probably not ever consider attending. But punk is not attempting to reconstruct the public sphere, rather, it creates spaces where at least some people can experience something that they feel resembles a community: a sense of place.

HETEROTOPIAS

It is my contention that punk places can be seen as heterotopias of resistance that function as sites of subject-constituting knowledges and practices; not as firm structures outside dominant power, but as ad hoc shelters in which members of a subculture can experience some semblance of freedom. The heterotopia, according to Michel Foucault is "a sort of place that lies outside all places and yet is actually localizable... it has the power of juxtaposing in a single real place different spaces and locations that are incompatible with each other."[19] Foucault's rather ambiguous notion of heterotopia eludes normative claims involved in conceptualizing liberatory spaces; he uses cemeteries, gardens, motel rooms, brothels, and colonies as examples. The heterotopia is divorced from any one partisan goal, left or right, but he sees it as, "the greatest reserve of imagination for our civilization...where it is lacking, dreams dry up, adventure is replaced by espionage, and privateers by the police."[20] Margaret Kohn builds on Foucault's idea in defining a heterotopia of resistance as a place that exists as, "a real countersite that inverts and contests existing economic or social hierarchies. Its function is social transformation rather than escapism, containment, or denial."[21] Like the autonomous socialist spaces Kohn describes in Italy, punk places contain possibilities unexpressed or impossible in current modes of living. This conception of heterotopia allows one to reconcile the ways in which spaces can at once be resistant and in some ways and at the same time remain sites of power, exclusion, and normalization. Power never disappears; the gaps we take shelter in might shield us from certain discourses but not others. It is in this way that the concept of heterotopia seems most compelling; it allows greater precision in describing spaces and their relative value as sites of resistance. It also points out those small moments, which may not seem ostensibly political, when politics are connected to everyday practices.[22]

Heterotopias of resistance connect politics with the everyday practices and real spaces, and they also provide the back stages and shelters that dissident knowledges and discourses require.[23] In addition, they allow not only for the communication of such knowledges, but their development as well. "Paying close attention to political acts that are disguised or offstage," Kohn argues, "helps us to map a realm of possible dissent… practical forms of resistance as well as the values that might, if conditions permitted, sustain more dramatic forms of rebellion."[24] Punk is, in its own way, a site of dissident knowledges and practices that stand in resistance to the culture industry and dominant order. The culture industry, deploying modern marketing techniques and demographic studies, attempts to be everything to everyone, a move not only toward aesthetic homogenization but also toward a disciplining of bodies and knowledges to create desirable subjects. Punk places facilitate what Foucault calls popular knowledges, those particular, local, disqualified knowledges (whether progressive or reactionary) that may stand in opposition to dominant generalizable discourses and claims on universal truths.[25]

A PUNK PLACE: 924 GILMAN

Punk places tend not to last long; punks come and go and typically wreck the place. There are a few that have weathered the storm for more than a few years, including the Dischord house (home of Dischord records), ABC No Rio (a venue in New York City), and 924 Gilman St. (a collectively run venue in Berkeley, California). For those of us punks in the Midwest, trying desperately to create and maintain scenes and spaces, 924 Gilman was a model, an inspiration, and a glimmer of hope. It was not only a punk space that managed to survive, but to survive by following its own rules.

Started in 1986 by *Maximumrocknroll* creator and editor Tim Yohannon, 924 Gilman has survived several battles with local businesses, the city government, various skinheads and malcontents, a hostile social and political climate, and gentrification. It has remained constant through changes in style, in politics, in its volunteer staff and attendees, and it also survived the pop-punk boom in the early 90's that took place within its walls; it was once home to popular bands like Green Day and Rancid. It was often a site of internecine conflict within the scene, fights about what counted as punk, fights about politics, inclusion, and exclusion.

Its association with *MRR* also meant that punks across the country, and the world, would often read about the most mundane details of day-to day-operations, petty arguments between staff members, and plenty of gossip.

American punk and hardcore was in the doldrums in 1986, the year 924 Gilman opened. Citing an increasingly routinized, apolitical scene, Yohannon argued for a reinjection of the political into punk:

> When I leave a show, I want my brain and imagination to
> be as exercised as my body. That would be really radical.
> Lyrics and good intentions aren't enough. It's time for a
> whole new front, a humorous, biting, multidimensional,
> and imaginative way to confront our society – right there at
> the show. If gigs are boring and staid, redefine them and it'll
> rejuvenate punk. It's the dimension we've all been wanting
> – not a whole new form of music, but a whole new way of
> delivering it.[26]

Yohannon eventually gave up control over Gilman, leading to a procession of different owners, but much has stayed the same. The space would not book racist, misogynist, or homophobic bands or tolerate such behaviors from those attending, though it should be noted that this rule often had the effect of depoliticizing the space and hampering those who felt that such injunctions did little to address less visible forms of discrimination within the scene. If someone could not afford to pay the door price for the show, they were allowed in at a reduced rate if they agreed to work in some capacity during or after the show. Perhaps most importantly, Gilman St. rules and practices were decided by democratically-run meetings at which any member could attend and participate.[27] Taking part in meetings served as training in participatory democratic decision-making – something that is increasingly hard to find in a market-driven liberal order – and they were also immortalized in punk culture itself. The Mr. T Experience is among thousands of punks who have paid tribute to 924 Gilman St:

> If you've got nothing better to do
> there's a meeting every Sunday afternoon
> you can make a speech
> you can rant you can rave you can preach
> at Gilman Street it's democracy
> it's just one big family

it's a bunch of geeks
it's a load of freaks
it's a club it's a place it's a thing
it's Gilman Street.[28]

CONCLUSION

Popular culture within liberal democracies plays a significant role in constituting political subjects, though it functions slightly differently from other sites of power relations. Because it constantly desires the new and the novel to be incorporated and commodified into mainstream culture, it also expands and creates more gaps and shelters within its domain. It is this, in part, that allows for subcultural spaces to emerge, and for some of these houses, garages, warehouses, rented VFWs and parking lots to actually become places and, occasionally, heterotopias of resistance.

Punk places provide a shelter from the more homogenizing aspects of capital. They are sites within the dominant order that simultaneously function as glimpses of different ways of living. They operate in such a way as to unify, at times, disparate activities into modes and practices of resistance. 924 Gilman is just one example of a punk place that emphasizes both the ways that culture is *done* (not just spoken or represented), and also the ways in which people might live out possibilities unavailable to them in dominant culture.

NOTES

1   Wendy Brown, *States of Injury* (Princeton NJ: Princeton University Press, 1995), p. 50.

2   Carol Pateman, *Participation and Democratic Theory* (New York: Cambridge University Press).

3   Margaret Kohn, *Radical Space: Building the House of the People* (Ithaca, NY: Cornell University Press, 2003), p. 4.

4   Yi-Fu Tuan, *Space and Place* (Minneapolis, MN: University of Minnesota Press, 1977), p. 136.

5   David Harvey, "Space as a Key Word," *Spaces of Global Capitalism: Towards a Theory of Uneven Geographical Development* (New York: Verso, 2006), p. 121-125.

6   Ibid., p. 133.

7   Henri Lefebvre, *The Production of Space* (Malden, MA: Blackwell, 1991), p. 7.

8   Ibid., p. 73.

9   Joshua Meyrowitz, *No Sense of Place* (New York: Oxford University Press, 1985), p. ix.

10   Ibid., p. 125.

11   Kohn, *Brave New Neighborhoods: The Privatization of Public Space* (New York: Routledge, 2004), p. 70.

12   Ibid., p. 196.

13   Ibid., p. 201.

14   This has changed since the late 90's, the Internet has begun to act as a homogenizing force in the punk scene and has changed the need for physical places to a limited extent; the centrality of the punk show to the punk scene having somewhat mitigated a total change in the scene. It is yet unclear what the long term effects the internet will have on the scene, though it is at least in part blamed for the increasing difficulties of punk print publications.

15   Alan O'Connor, "Local Scenes and Dangerous Crossroads: Punk and Theories of Cultural Hybridity," *Popular Music*, Vol. 21, No. 2 (2002): 225-236.

16   Bull Gervasi, "Land of Hope and Glory," in ed. Chris Duncan, *My First Time: A Collection of First Punk Show Stories* (Oakland, CA: AK Press, 2007), p. 80.

17   Joseph A. Gervasi, "Clenched Fists, Open Eyes: My First Punk Show," in ed. Chris Duncan, *My First Time: A Collection of First Punk Show Stories* (Oakland, CA: AK Press, 2007), p. 55.

18   "Fest," short for festival, is typically a weekend-long series of shows at one location featuring anywhere from fifteen to thirty bands. For a large fest, punks often travel cross-country.

19   Foucault, "Of Other Spaces: Utopias and Heterotopias," in ed. Neil Leach, *Rethinking Architecture: A Reader in Cultural Theory* (New York: Routledge, 1997), pp. 352 and 354.

20   Ibid.

21   Ibid.

22   In her description of Italian houses of the people, Kohn writes: "Part of the political effectiveness of the house of the people was precisely to make the most basic elements of social life, such as drinking a glass of wine in company, into an act of identification with socialism, at least in the broader sense of a popular movement for economic change and political inclusion of the working classes." Ibid., p. 94.

23   James C. Scott, *Domination and the Arts of Resistance* (New Haven CT: Yale University Press, 1990).

24   Ibid., p. 20.

25 Michel Foucault, "Two Lectures," in ed. Colin Gordon, *Power/Knowledge: Selected Interviews and Other Writings 1972-1977* (New York: Pantheon, 1980), p. 82.

26 Tim Yohannon, "Column, Dec. 1986," in ed. Brian Edge, *924 Gilman: The Story So Far* (San Francisco: Maximumrocknroll, 2004), p. 7.

27 Edge, *924 Gilman*, pp. 375-377.

28 Mr. T Experience, "At Gilman St.," *Big Black Bugs Bleed Blue Blood* (Rough Trade, 1989), EP.

AFTERWORD

I STILL TELL this story: *punk rock saved my life.* In fact, I can easily trace my intellectual, political genealogies through this punk story, since it was my first issue of *Maximumrocknroll* (found in an "alternative" boutique called The Black Cat in downtown San Diego) that introduced me to the semi-covert wars of the Cold War United States, wars engaged on behalf of "freedom," by way of columnist Jane Guskin of the Gilman Street project Yeastie Girlz. A decade later, and during my own tenure as a shitworker at *Maximumrocknroll*, I began to write about the gift of freedom as a medium and metaphor for the workings of liberal empire. While in graduate school, I graded undergraduate essays while green-taping records for the immense Maximum archive, and carried Michel Foucault and dissertation chapters in my beat-up bag to punk shows.[1] Now, I start classes with the cacophonous music of Trash Kit and The Younger Lovers, to get us dancing (literally maybe, figuratively yes) to a fierce and joyful beat. As with so many of the contributors to this collection, punk absolutely shapes who I am as an academic in forms and feelings both notable, and still unfathomable.

At the same time, I also observe a wary distance from academic studies of punk – *Sex Pistols, so what?* As Zack Furness catalogs so thoroughly in his introductory essay, the queries are often so narrow and so conjectural as to tell me nothing about the scene I know to be a discordant cluster of promises, forms of actions, feelings, events, and missing persons. I am also suspicious of claims that academic study "legitimizes" punk, somehow. Punk doesn't need legitimacy, since legitimacy can so often mean disciplining an object, and its normalization; as an academic object of study, legitimacy implies passage through hierarchical fields of inquiry via evaluation, classification, and other administrative-bureaucratic measures (high art versus "low" art).[2] Moreover, there *are* punk historians, punk archivists, and punk theorists who operate *without* the academy to trace threads of continuity, compile thorough records, and question

agreed-upon stories about race, gender, and sexuality. These are two reasons I have been reluctant in my own work to take punk as an object
of study: I do not want to participate in its assimilation into something
like capital (an "exotic" object traded for exchange in the academy), or a
canon (not least because punk is such a sprawl), and I reject the idea that
punk is not itself a scene for the rigorous production of knowledge. This
is not to say that I don't believe good scholarship can be produced, or
that non-punks can't be its producers (punks can be crap scholars too),
but that I am all too aware that punk is an unwieldy object of study.

And so, as academic (and popular) studies of punk proliferate now,
I rarely recognize myself in such studies, even when these studies invoke
my name as an object of study. In the last decade, we have been witness
to appeals and attempts to remember, record, and even to revive riot
grrrl circulating throughout punk and academic cultures. The zines I
wrote, or edited, appear often in these studies, and it is often a surprise
to me what unfolds from these critical labors about these zines, about
me. I understand this, in some measure – as scholars, we often consider
(and perhaps suspend) our objects in the times and places we find them,
emerging from an assemblage of moving parts (histories, economies, discourses). And in doing so, we treat with our objects and the circuits these
travel apart from authors, or intents. So I know well that the things we
make – zines, musics, fliers, events, our bodies in becoming – can and do
follow wayward lines of flight, and encounter others in times and places
we cannot predict nor should we preempt.

At the same time, it is disorienting to read studies that hope to understand "our" true feelings through modes of difference or depth – especially because of my own suspicion of the long-established belief that
true feelings (including the more politically efficacious ones, such as resistance) await release in internal spaces. I know too well from poststruc-
turalism and postcolonial feminist studies that the figure of the resistant
outsider (the native, the woodcutter, the person of color, the teenaged
girl, the punk) becomes the occasion, the "raw" material, for another's
speech and expertise. And, as Rey Chow has so memorably observed,
the scholar who studies the outsider, and who wishes for this other to be
"authentic," resistant, and disruptive, is too often a desire for the non-
duped, sliding into the desire to *be* the non-duped, "which is a not-too-
innocent desire to seize control" – and so, I began to be more seriously
interested in what these studies about punk, and riot grrrl, did beyond
what they claimed to do.[3]

I became interested in the terms of time, or timing, just as Beth
Stinson and Fiona I.B. Ngô, editors of a special issue of *Women &*

Performance called "Punk Anteriors," wrote in their initial call for papers, "Revisions to the phenomenon of punk have been circulating since its inception. This issue seeks to capture the performance of those revisions, conducting a genealogical mapping of the punk movement, scenes, music, ethics, and aesthetics utilizing queer and feminist punk analytics. While some valuable feminist critiques of punk have surfaced – mainly to lionize the riot grrrl movement – many uneasy questions around race, nation, and sexuality remain unarticulated in feminist and gender performance scholarship." This call for papers was indeed timely, especially with riot grrrl becoming the subject of so much retrospection (as of this writing, there are easily a score of scholarly and popular monographs, documentaries, and exhibitions completed or in progress). This retrospective turn, with its subsequent institutionalization of some stories about riot grrrl and not others, had been troubling me: What does it mean (for instance) to define punk feminisms through riot grrrl without a memory of *other* punk feminisms? What falls out when women of color feminisms are observed to be a frequent citation in grrrl zines (bell hooks being perhaps the most popular), but not an ongoing contestation within the movement? That riot grrrl was about girl love, girl community, girl empowerment, is not a bad story, or a wrong story, but there *is* another, more difficult story. We know that one origin lies with musician Jean Smith who, inspired by the 1991 Mount Pleasant race riots in Washington DC, wrote to Bratmobile band member Allison Wolfe, "We need to start a girl riot." But the Mount Pleasant riots erupted around immigration, race and police brutality, and to imagine a "girl riot" in response suggests that gender or sexuality are apart, rather than indivisible, from these concerns.

These questions about history making pushed me to at last turn to this past as an object of study, and to refine an argument I'd first published in *Punk Planet* over a decade ago, that sought to intervene in riot grrrl feminisms to center race as a crucial analytic, rather than a obligatory descriptor (for instance, riot grrrl is often observed to be a white and middle class phenomenon, which I argue about punk in general is both true and false). Eventually, I wrote an essay for this special issue to argue that how the critiques of women of color from within riot grrrl or punk are narrated is important to how we remember feminisms, and how we produce feminist futures. In doing so, I locate riot grrrl within a broader critique of the historiography of feminist movement, first to dispute the narrativization of women of color feminisms as an interruption in our reckoning with the "big picture" of feminisms, such as riot grrrl; and then to question the progressive teleologies of origin, episode and succession that would limit the "problem" of feminisms to its critics (the woman of color as feminist killjoy, as Sara Ahmed put it), or to the past ("we have learned our lessons now and hereafter").[4] The problem lies in a form of periodization, which also goes for punk stories – that is, how certain critical inquiries (whether riot grrrl, queercore, or racial critique) are captured as belonging to a particular historical moment, as uttered in the sentiment, *"Theirs was an important intervention, and we learned our lessons,"* though we continue to live with such things as racial liberalism or masculinist dispositions having not ended. In challenging modes of history making, then, the question of punk anteriors insists that the narrativization and institutionalization of the past – or some pasts above others – absolutely informs the sensations of the present and possible future.

As with time, we might also consider anew the question of space (as Brian Tucker does for other ends in this collection). For instance, the narrativization of punk as a white phenomenon is both true and false. It is absolutely true that punk traffics in a racial hegemony built in part on intimacy with but also distance from the racial, colonial other. Punk music, punk looks, can trace their origins through the blackness of rock 'n' roll and young street toughs, even as this provenance is ignored, or disavowed; the clubs that fostered nascent scenes were often located in neighborhoods populated by people of color, and operated by them as well – consider Mabuhay Gardens (San Francisco), Raul's (Austin), Madame Wong's and the Hong Kong Club (Los Angeles) – though these cramped quarters often led to racial tensions and sometimes riots.[5] As Daniel Traber notes in this collection, certain forms of transgression reified otherness as unproblematic scenes of authenticity, but such transgressions enhanced the one who desired to be, as it were, non-duped. This has often meant that some punk quarters refuse to admit an ongoing possessive investment in whiteness, whether in claiming racist cool, or antiracist cred. I am not romantic about punk for these reasons, and the compilation zines I made called ...*Race Riot* are a testament and an archive of just these troubling revelations. As Michelle Christine Gonzales wryly notes in the 2000 documentary *Mas Alla de los Gritos/Beyond the Screams*: "People in the punk scene are notorious for saying 'racism sucks,' but when it comes down to having friends of color, it's cool until they open their big mouths. There are desirable people of color and there are undesirable people of color, and if you're too brown or too down, then you're going to piss somebody off or make somebody uncomfortable." At the same time, as non-academic *and* academic archivists and historians such as Iraya Robles, Osa Atoe (*Shotgun Seamstress*), Martin

Sorrendeguy (director of *Mas Alla*), James Spooner (*Afropunk*), Jeremías Aponte, Michelle Habell-Pallan, Beth Stinson and Fiona I.B. Ngô aptly demonstrate, punks of color are a vital but also a discomforting presence. These and other critics reclaim the too-often unobserved significance of punks of color including Poly Styrene, Alice Bag, Pat Smear, the Brat's Teresa Covarrubias, Conflict's Karen Maeda (United States), the Nasty Facts' Cheri Boyze, the Go-Go's Margot Olaverria, *Search & Destroy's* V. Vale, and *Maximumrocknroll's* Tim Yohannon, in shaping but also straining the bounds of punk possibility. As artists and archivists, they also otherwise pursue what might be called a multisubculturalism (a coinage I attribute to San Francisco-based queer punk art band Sta-Prest), traversing punk, hip hop and other scenes to trace their entangled and often troubled genealogies. Such vexing intimacies trouble the usual story of punk as a white riot, both disrupting their reverberant absence from an archive, but also disavowing their appropriation into that archive as an uncomplicated presence.

It also seems to me that the "truth" of punk as a white riot (to summon The Clash) actually creates the dominion it purports to describe, especially where a denial of coevalness, in Johannes Fabian's well-known phrasing, erases those histories and articulations concurrent with, or indeed preceding, the perceived movements of punk from the West to "the rest." The development of Western modernity and liberal capitalism over time, and their expansion across space, as postcolonial critics observe, underwrites the premise of empire as the universalizing story of human historical consciousness. Too often, punk studies replicate this historicist consciousness, through which punk unfolds from an imperial center *alongside* modernity and capitalism – such that anthropological accounts, or news reportage, describe punks in the so-called Third World through a sense of their belated arrival, their distance from "our" here and now.[6] This description of the anachronistic punk reproduces, insidiously, an imperial ontology. Of course, as Vincanne Adams and Stacy Leigh Pigg write, "It is crucial to remember that locality is socially and historically produced in and through a dynamic of interaction. The local is not a space where indigenous sensibilities reside in a simple sense; global processes undo and remake the particularism of the local as it stands in contrast to the seeming transcendence of the global."[7] But there is no reason to presume that a global force must and will result in homogenization, as Rubén Ortiz-Torres shows us in his essay, and his haunting photographs. Elsewhere, Golnar Nikpour observes that the emergence of late '70s punk is inextricable from the dramatic connectivities wrought by two centuries of empire and modern capital. She offers that twinned processes of global urbanization and proletarianization heralded the capitalist *cosmopolis* in both colony and metropole. "This could explain why in 1976-78 we see punk scenes not only in London and New York but also in Istanbul, Sao Paolo, Tokyo, Mexico City, Stockholm, and Warsaw. If there was a punk scene in Istanbul before there was a punk scene in say, suburban Iowa (and there was, as far as I know), then the movement of ideas is not from 'West' to 'rest' but rather a product of a particular historical moment in the global city, a moment that is rife with tensions not only between colony and metropole, but also town and country."[8] Such provocations as those offered by Ortiz-Torres or Nikpour are indispensable, illumining for us some of the troubles with not just "punk studies," but with those disciplines from which such studies hope to capture their elusive objects. That is, rather than presume a priori that punk is a white riot, or an import that comes intact from an imperial center, we might instead pursue – or indeed acknowledge that scholars in these other places *but also punks themselves* are already theorizing these questions – more empirical (for the social scientists among us) and nuanced inquiries about multiple racial, global projects that crisscross each other in webs of connectivity and exchange.

For these reasons, and for others still unfolding, the stories we tell about punk *do* matter. And as Furness also observes so well, these stories about punk are *never just about punk*. Such stories are about feminist historiography, and about imperial fictions that circulate as truths, as well. The archive is a political and cultural meaning making machine for the passage of objects into what Foucault calls knowledge's field of control and power's sphere of intervention, and for "minor" objects in particular, we know well how troublesome such a passage might be. It is as such that the figure of the punk as on the outside, but nonetheless elevated in academic studies to a second-order of signification through a series of appropriations into an existing interior – that is to say, the story we already "know" – might troublingly replicate the spatial arrangement of the globe wherein progress and punk spreads out from an imperial center, or that "tame" or contain the rupture or revolution to a moment in an otherwise continuous history. Without arguing that "punkademics" are the future – and here I absolutely include non-institutional historians, archivists, and theorists in the designation – at least it might to said that it is through some of their alternative or anterior genealogies of queer and feminist theories and movements, postcolonial and anti-imperial critiques, and mappings of intimacies and antagonisms between people of color and punks, that we can imagine punk otherwise.

NOTES

1   Donate to support the record archive and the ongoing publication of *Maximumrocknroll*. See details at http://www.maximumrocknroll.com.

2   It can be noted, as Fiona I.B. Ngô does, that the disciplining of "punk studies" might also offer forms of personal legitimacy and academic capital for (former) punks. Personal correspondence, December 29th, 2011.

3   Rey Chow, 1993, *Writing Diaspora: Tactics of Intervention in Contemporary Cultural Studies* (Bloomington: Indiana University Press), 53.

4   Sara Ahmed, 2010, *The Promise of Happiness* (Durham: Duke University Press), 68; Mimi Thi Nguyen, Summer 2012 (forthcoming), "Riot Grrrl, Race, Revival," in a special issue "Punk Anteriors" of *Women and Performance* edited by Beth Stinson and Fiona I.B. Ngô.

5   I thank Iraya Robles, Jeremías Aponte, James Spooner, and Fiona I.B. Ngô for conversations about these concerns.

6   Here I thank Golnar Nikpour, Mariam Bastani, and Jeremías Aponte for their insights.

7   Stacy Leigh Pigg and Vincanne Adams, 2005, "Introduction: The Moral Object of Sex," in *Sex in Development: Science, Sexuality, and Morality in Global Perspective*, edited by Vincanne Adams and Stacy Leigh Pigg (Durham: Duke University Press), 11.

8   Golnar Nikpour, personal correspondence, 27 December 2011. See also Nikpour's review of *White Riot: Punk and the Politics of Race*, edited by Stephen Duncombe and Maxwell Tremblay, in *Maximumrocknroll* #345, February 2012.

AUTHOR BIOS

MILO J. AUKERMAN is a biochemist at DuPont, where he specializes in crop genetics research focused on the genus *Arabidopsis*. He is also the lead singer for the Descendents, in which he specializes in songs about coffee, love and rejection. Dr. Aukerman has appeared on dozens of records since the early 1980s and co-authored numerous articles in scientific journals. He is the only contributor to *Punkademics* who has a limited edition, collectible bobblehead toy designed in his likeness.

MARIA ELENA BUSZEK, PH.D. is a scholar, critic, curator, and Associate Professor of Art History at the University of Colorado Denver, where she teaches courses on Modern and contemporary art. Her recent publications include the books *Pin-Up Grrrls: Feminism, Sexuality, Popular Culture* and *Extra/ordinary: Craft and Contemporary Art*; contributions to the anthologies *It's Time for Action (There's No Option): About Feminism; Blaze: Discourse on Art, Women, and Feminism;* and *Contemporary Artists*; catalogue essays for numerous national and international exhibitions; and articles and criticism in such journals as *Art in America, Photography Quarterly,* and *TDR: The Journal of Performance Studies.* She has also been a regular contributor to the popular feminist zine *BUST* since 1999. Dr. Buszek's first concert was Huey Lewis and The News. Her second was the Descendents. From 1988-1994 she worked at record stores in Omaha, Nebraska, as well as at Omaha's much-loved, sadly-departed pirate radio station, KRCK.

ZACK FURNESS saw his first punk show – Split Lip and Planet Earth – in the cafeteria of an Indianapolis high school when he was 14. In addition to moshing for the first time, seeing a fistfight between two skinhead girls, and having someone in a band actually talk to him outside the show (unthinkable with his then musical heroes of Metallica and Danzig), he also received a high speed tutorial on SHARP vs. Nazi skins, something called 'straight edge,' and a group of folks called 'vegans' who were described to him (by someone only slightly less young and naïve) as "people who don't drink milk or eat cheese." Zack didn't know what that meant, but he knew that Split Lip was pissed off. And the music was amazing. Since that time, he played in various punk bands over a 14-year span, got a PhD, and now works as Assistant Professor of Cultural Studies at Columbia College Chicago. He is the author of *One Less Car: Bicycling and the Politics of Automobility* (Temple University Press, 2010), the co-editor of a forthcoming collection of critical/cultural essays on the NFL (Temple University Press), and a member of the *Bad Subjects* Production Team. His writing has also appeared in several books, journals, and magazines such as *Punk Planet* and *Bitch*. Most importantly, he is a teacher.

ALASTAIR 'GORDS' GORDON likes all things DiY punk rock and always knew he was out of step with the world. He became a 'punkademic' via an early, total rejection of formal schooling and its traditional teaching methods. His 'extracurricular' education germinated through listening to Discharge, Crass, and anarcho-punk records, peer discussion and a love of reading anarchist theory from an early age. This interest was eventually channelled into playing in stupidly insignificant punk rock bands in the mid-80s. Eventually, the limitations of the musical world and a government 'push' to get countercultural malingerers off unemployment benefit statistics led to a (free) University education. Gords currently vents anger at the world singing, touring and recording with the band Geriatric Unit, and playing bass in Endless Grinning Skulls. To date he has played on more than a few punk records: you win no prize if you find them all. Gords' passion as a 'punkademic' is informed by a healthy desire to seed dissent towards all forms of neoliberal capitalism. His scholarly passion is for ethnography and critical theory and he is currently working up a sweat writing his 'Dr. Punk' thesis for publication. He is currently a Senior Lecturer in Media and Communication and member of the Media Discourse Group at De Montfort University, Leicester.

ROSS HAENFLER is an Associate Professor of Sociology at the University of Mississippi. He is the author of *Straight Edge: Clean Living Youth, Hardcore Punk, and Social Change* and *Goths, Gamers, and Grrrls: Deviance and Youth Subcultures*, and co-author of *The Better World Handbook: Small Changes That Make a Big Difference*, an action-oriented guide to creating a more just and sustainable world. He appeared in the documentary *Edge: Perspectives on a Drug Free Culture* and the National

Geographic channel's *Inside Straight Edge*. An award-winning teacher, Ross' courses include social movements, youth subcultures, men and masculinities, and political sociology. Pictures from his youth reveal too many Metallica t-shirts, a series of mullets, and a bleach splattered denim jacket with an Iron Maiden "Killers" back patch. Ross lives in Oxford, MS with his partner, Jennifer, and daughter, River.

CURRY MALOTT is Assistant Professor of Professional and Secondary Education at West Chester University. An unabashed Marxist, Curry is interested in advancing theoretical and practical applications of critical pedagogy just about everywhere. He is the author and editor of numerous books, including *Critical Pedagogy in the 21st Century: A New Generation of Scholars* (IAP, forthcoming), co-edited with Bradley Porfilio; *Policy and Research in Education: A Critical Pedagogy for Educational Leadership* (2010, Peter Lang); *Teaching Native America Across the Curriculum: A Critical Inquiry* (2009, Peter Lang) with Chairwoman Lisa Waukau and Lauren Waukau-Villagomez; *A Call to Action: An Introduction to Education, Philosophy, and Native North America* (2008, Peter Lang); and *Punk Rockers' Revolution: A Pedagogy of Race, Class, and Gender* (2004, Peter Lang) with Milagros Peña. Curry is the main organizer of the 2011 *Critical Theories In the Twenty First Century* conference at West Chester University of Pennsylvania (http://Ct21st.org).

DYLAN AT MINER was raised in rural Michigan and spends his time traversing the contested and colonial borders of North America. An artist, activist, and historian, his writing has appeared in numerous journals, books, edited volumes, and encyclopedias. A middle-aged hardcore kid, Dylan is not ashamed that the first two zines he published were named *Skagboy* and *Fukboy*, respectively. Although now a long hair, he still has a large tattoo of the word REGRET on his head thanks to the life-changing Unbroken album. Still freegan, straight edge, and anarchist, he teaches at Michigan State University.

RYAN MOORE is Associate Professor of Sociology at Florida Atlantic University and the author of *Sells Like Teen Spirit: Music, Youth Culture, and Social Crisis* (NYU Press, 2010). He has also written for *The Chronicle of Higher Education*, including the essay "Is Punk the New Jazz?" Before securing his current position, he was as a vagabond instructor in academia's reserve labor army, teaching thousands of undergraduates at UC San Diego, the University of Kansas, and Colgate University. As a graduate student he was involved with the successful campaign to unionize academic student employees at the University of California, and he currently serves as Second Vice President of the FAU chapter of the United Faculty of Florida.

TAVIA NYONG'O teaches performance studies, critical race studies, and queer studies at New York University. He is working on a book about the intersections of punk and queer in the 1970s.

MIMI THI NGUYEN is Assistant Professor of Gender and Women's Studies and Asian American Studies at the University of Illinois, Urbana-Champaign. Her first book, called *The Gift of Freedom: War, Debt, and Other Refugee Passages*, focuses on the promise of "giving" freedom concurrent and contingent with waging war and its afterlife (Duke University Press, 2012). She is also co-editor with Fiona I.B. Ngo and Mariam Lam of a special issue of *positions: east asia cultures critique* on Southeast Asians in diaspora (2012), and co-editor with Thuy Linh Nguyen Tu of *Alien Encounters: Pop Culture in Asian America* (Duke University Press, 2007). She further publishes on queer subcultures, punk feminisms, and the politics of beauty. Nguyen has also published zines since 1991, including the compilation zine *...Race Riot*. She is a former *Punk Planet* columnist and a *Maximumrocknroll* shitworker, and co-author of the research blog on dress and beauty threadbared.

ALAN O'CONNOR was one of the founders of Who's Emma, a volunteer-run punk space in Toronto in the 1990s. He is currently Director of the PhD Program in Cultural Studies at Trent University, in Canada. His new book is on the underground music and theatre scenes in a small Ontario city.

WALEED RASHIDI's first album purchase was in the first grade: a five-dollar LP titled "Chipmunk Punk." A Los Angeles-area native, he is an adjunct Communications instructor at California State University Fullerton and Citrus College. He has interviewed several hundred music artists as a freelance journalist for a variety of regional and national publications. Rashidi has also performed in numerous rock, jazz and punk bands over the past couple of decades, racking up endless interstate miles via DIY van tours, playing in dozens of states. And he still spins his "Chipmunk Punk" LP on rare occasions.

HELEN L. REDDINGTON was an accidental musician, being co-opted to play bass in Brighton's notorious Joby and the Hooligans in 1977 before leaving to form The Chefs, who recorded three sessions for BBC's Radio One (two for John Peel) and later, Helen and the Horns, a four-piece featuring Helen on Vocals/Guitar and sax, trumpet and trombone, both under the pseudonym Helen McCookerybook. An accidental career as an academic followed, with a lecturing post on the University of Westminster's pioneering Commercial Music course; this is where she completed her doctorate, which developed into her book *The Lost Women of Rock Music: Female Musicians of the Punk Era* (revised/reprinted in paperback by Equinox, October 2011). Compilation, *The Best of the Chefs*, appeared in November 2011 on the label Damaged Goods.

STEVPHEN SHUKAITIS is Lecturer at the University of Essex, author of *Imaginal Machines: Autonomy & Self-Organization in the Revolutions of Everyday Life* (Autonomedia, 2009), and co-editor (with David Graeber and Erika Biddle) of *Constituent Imagination: Militant Investigation/Collective Theorization* (AK Press, 2007).

MICHAEL SICILIANO is both a good-for-nothing punk and a bit of an academic. From 2001-2007 he was an active member at the cooperatively run DIY show space called the Mr. Roboto Project in Pittsburgh, PA. He has played in punk and hardcore bands for over a decade, most recently playing bass in the Chicago band, Birth. He completed an MA in the Social Sciences in 2010 at the University of Chicago and is currently a PhD student in Sociology at UCLA.

RUBÉN ORTIZ-TORRES was born in Mexico City in 1964. Educated within the utopian models of republican Spanish anarchism, he soon confronted the tragedies and cultural clashes of the post-colonial third world. After giving up the dream of playing baseball in the major leagues he decided to study art. He went first to the oldest and one of the most academic art schools of the Americas (the Academy of San Carlos in Mexico City) and later to one of the newest and more experimental (CalArts in Valencia, CA). After enduring Mexico City's earthquake and pollution he moved to LA with a Fulbright grant, only to survive riots, fires, floods, more earthquakes, and Proposition 187. During all this he has been able to produce artwork in the form of paintings, photographs, objects, installations, videos and films. He is part of the permanent Faculty of the University of California in San Diego and his work is featured in the collections of The Museum of Modern Art in New York, the Los Angeles County Museum of Art, the Museo Nacional Centro de Arte Reina Sofía, in Madrid Spain, and others.

ESTRELLA TORREZ's work centers on language politics and migrant farm worker education. Having worked in the fields, Estrella attended migrant summer programs as a child and has worked as a migrant educator, including research for the Office of Migrant Education. This Midwest Xicana has taken an active role in multiple Latina/o and American Indian organizations, ranging from working within grassroots organizations to establishing graduate mentorship programs at the university level. She has a BS in Elementary Education from Western Michigan and an MA in Early Childhood Multicultural Education and Bilingual Education from New Mexico, and she recently completed her doctoral dissertation in Educational Thought and Sociocultural Studies with a concentration in Bilingual Education, also from New Mexico. Presently, Estrella is an Assistant Professor at Michigan State University's Residential College in the Arts and Humanities, as well as core faculty in the Chicano/Latino Studies Program, the Center for Gender in Global Context and the Center for Latin American and Caribbean Studies.

DANIEL S. TRABER is Associate Professor of American Literature and Popular Culture at Texas A&M University at Galveston. He is the author of *Whiteness, Otherness, and the Individualism Paradox from Huck to Punk* (Palgrave Macmillan, 2007) and currently finishing a manuscript on culturcide and non-identity that will include his article on punk preppies published in *The Journal of Popular Culture*.

BRIAN TUCKER is a working on his PhD in Political Science at University of Massachusetts, Amherst.

MINOR COMPOSITIONS

Lightning Source UK Ltd.
Milton Keynes UK
UKHW010607050519

342118UK00001B/47/P